An Elias B(

The Shift

A Time of Change

Book One

Compiled by

David Tate

Contact Publishing

-.-. --- -. -. - .- -.-. -

www.contact-publishing.co.uk

A Contact Publishing Ltd. book © 2004 David Tate

2nd edition United Kingdom

The Elias transcripts © Mary Ennis.
Editor's Note: Except where noted, the information contained in this book is a compilation of material
from the Elias transcripts. The names of individuals asking Elias questions have been replaced with a "Q."
Session numbers are noted at the end of each excerpt:

Sessions #2 – 63 took place in 1995
Sessions #64 – 143 took place in 1996
Sessions #144 – 253 took place in 1997
Sessions #254 – 349 took place in 1998
Sessions #350 – 532 took place in 1999
Sessions #533 – 749 took place in 2000
Sessions #750 – 975 took place in 2001
Sessions #976 – 1230 took place in 2002
Sessions #1231 – 1488 took place in 2003
Session #1489 –   took place in 2004

Edited and compiled by David Tate

British Library Cataloguing in Publication Data
A CIP catalogue record of this book is available from the British Library

ISBN 0-9547020-1-8

Cover Design by Rick Jones

Contact Publishing
Suite 346
176 Finchley Road
London NW3 6BT
www.contact-publishing.co.uk

Dedication

In loving memory of a dear friend, Vicki Pendley,
without whom this book would not have been possible.

Acknowledgements

Many expressions of heartfelt thanks to my friends Mary Ennis, Vicki Pendley, Cathy McCallum and Ron Churchman.

And, of course, not forgetting those who regularly attended the Elias sessions in Castaic, California, with whom I shared many fun and entertaining times:

Gail Becker – Joanne Helfrich – Paul Helfrich – Nicky Wilson – Jene Fielder – Bobby Houle – Tom Boyd – Jeremy Key – Mike Wilson – Drew Sokol – Bob Becker – Jim Pickerell – Norm Farb – Rita Farb – Paul Tews – Sue Hooyenga – Debi (Oona) – Stella Moran – Margo Reed – Howard Reed – Laura Carlson – Lynda Symans – Ben House – Anne Kontoyannis and of course Elias!

Contents

Preface

My name is David. I had my very first conversation with Elias on July 3, 1997 (session #189). Little did I know that the conversation that day would lead me on a journey of self-discovery – a journey unlike any I could have possibly imagined.

We all are searching for the "truth." Some of us have found it in religion, others in science. It doesn't really matter how or where you find your truth, but when you do, it's like discovering a language that speaks to you in such a way that it is as if you have found "home." What I was hearing in Elias' words was my very own language that somehow, and for whatever reason, I had forgotten. I found my truth, my home. My next challenge however, was to remember all that I had forgotten. Within that process, I am now coming face to face with who I really am.

My intention is not to glamorise my experience, not to say that it hasn't been wondrous, but when you're truly ready to connect with self, the bigger picture, the experience can be likened to riding a giant roller coaster. I'm still on that journey, as are many of my friends I have met along the way, but it's a journey that I know leads me back home.

From as far back as I can recall, I had always felt that there was something not quite right with the picture of my reality. Like us all, we're born into a world where from the moment of birth we are bombarded with the belief systems of our parents and all of society's, the belief systems which hold together the very reality in which we all struggle to function and operate. However, I began to question those inherited beliefs that were presented to me as truths that were set in stone, unchangeable and invincible. It was in my questioning that I had set in motion the starting point of a journey, a journey that would take me on a ride of my very own treasure hunt. Hidden along the way I discovered puzzle pieces that seemed to fit into places within my life's picture, whereas before there hadn't appeared to be any place for them. My reality, my canvas of life, I was discovering, was in fact not complete at all and the biggest and final puzzle piece that I had yet to find was to be found within the information of the Elias material.

Born in the United States, I had in fact spent most of my life raised in the heart of London, England, where upon leaving school, I entered into the colourful world of show business. I danced and sang my way through life for several fun filled years, sharing many a stage with those of a more celebrity status. Then one day I found myself, along with the rest of my team of fellow dancers, performing in front of Her Majesty the Queen in a Royal Command Performance at the London Palladium. My life, it appeared, was perfect.

It was soon after this time that I began to notice a feeling of dissatisfaction steadily growing within me. I was fast falling into a spiralling abyss of dissatisfaction, disillusionment, and a host of other disturbing and illogical fears and insecurities. Worst still, I did not know why or from where these feelings were coming. After several years of struggling to live with them, I decided to leave England for awhile and head for the United States where maybe, as they say, a change would be as good as a rest. With no major plan in tow I travelled across the United States, never really staying too long in any given town or city until I arrived in California. Maybe it had to do with the scenic mountains and miles of sandy beaches, and the row after row of exotic palm trees with the everlasting days that more or less promised continuous sunshine and bright blue skies. For a while I felt I was in paradise, but, only for a while.

It wasn't long thereafter that those feelings that had haunted me daily would return. Not being one to take medication or seek medical help, I turned to what I had often found helpful in the past. And, I was in the perfect place: California, the epicentre of the western world of 'spiritual Dom' home to many a guru and spiritual practitioner.

After months and months of feeding myself with enough spiritual mantra and 'Lapsong Souchong' teas, I eventually had to admit nothing was working. I was now in a place of 'Terrified.' It was soon thereafter, thank God (or who knows what I would have done to break free of this inner turmoil) I met a couple of women who would lead me to my first encounter with Elias. From that moment on I would begin to discover more about myself than I had ever before thought possible. This isn't to say that my struggle with my inner demons abruptly ended that day, but the information Elias presented to me would indeed, if not immediately, begin the process of eliminating them.

I first met Mary, the woman who channels Elias, while working as a waiter in a small family restaurant in Valencia, California. I had only ever heard or read about the phenomenon of channelling from those who had themselves experienced it first-hand. From what I understood at the time, it is when an individual goes into some type of transcendental state which then allows the personality or spirit of a dead person to speak through them. I was therefore a little nervous but also somewhat excited to find myself about to experience this spiritual phenomenon first-hand myself.

When I first arrived at the given address, I was greeted at the door by Vicky, a friendly and attractive young woman in her late thirties and a very close friend of Mary's. Vicky was also the chief transcriber of the Elias material. I found a comfortable spot on a rather large L-shaped divan and then Mary arrived shortly thereafter and introduced herself. Like Vicky, Mary was also in her late thirties.

Once we all became acquainted, Mary then announced that if I was ready that she was ready to introduce me to Elias. Sitting cross-legged on the floor just a few feet away from me, Mary began her process of allowing Elias to come through. Closing her eyes and taking in small yet deep breaths, Mary's body began to rock gently back and forth. I watched intently, never once taking my eyes off of her in the hope that I would actually be able to see the moment when the spirit or energy of Elias would enter Mary's body. With those thoughts in my mind, a smile began to appear on Mary's face, an expression as if she, or was it now he, Elias, knew what I had been thinking. Her eyes slowly opened and adjusted to fix her/his focus on me. It was in that moment that I knew that I was no longer in the presence of Mary. I could actually sense the presence of another personality. For the next two hours I was to witness a phenomenon that only experiencing it would have otherwise led me to cast doubt and suspicion.

My first encounter with Elias inspired me to continue to seek information about myself, as well as through the sessions that others had with him. I found that the information Elias delivered to many people was also helpful and applicable to me. It was primarily for this reason that I decided to compile this book from thousands of transcripts. I hope you too find it helpful for you.

If you believe in God, in Karma, reincarnation, higher levels, lower levels, Buddhism, any religion, science, or no religion at all; or if you are at a place in your life where you are experiencing some kind of emotional turmoil, or struggling to understand life PERIOD, then I dare say that this book will in some way be beneficial to you. Allow me to introduce to you Elias and to share with you the knowledge that he has offered over the years and presently continues to do so.

Many may recognise the similarities of that which Elias speaks, to that of other spiritual and self help material. However, the information in this book could best be described as 'Missing Links', new 'Puzzle' pieces that have come together to add new light to ALL of which we presently have knowledge. This material adds a totally new dimension to the ever-growing picture that forms our reality. Our reality, according to Elias, is in a present state of a major change, an action that Elias refers to as a 'Shift in Consciousness.'

Prologue

On April 29, 1995, Elias first introduced himself by way of what he terms an *energy exchange* with a woman named Mary Ennis. This exchange is similar to what many call channelling, although Elias says that these two actions are different. Basically, channelling involves an interaction with one's own *essence*, or soul, while an energy exchange involves a mergence and exchange with another essence.

In the early sessions, he sometimes used terms that were more in line with mass belief systems, but as we became more familiar with his language he later clarified them or used new terminology altogether.

Elias first introduced himself as:

I am an energy personality essence. I occupy an area of consciousness which shall be known to you henceforth as Regional Area 4.

In this realm, I occupy a position of teaching.

I speak to you in response to you all in your questioning of this shift in consciousness, which is occurring upon your planet within this time framework in this present now, in which you are all involved.

You hold wonderings. You look to your present now and you hold questionings of validity of purpose, of missions, (grinning) of action.

Within this present now, you are experiencing what I have termed to be a shift in consciousness. You are moving out of your religious era and moving into a new reality which you are creating. (#270)

You do not need to be creating floods, famines, earthquakes, holocausts to be gaining your attention and initiating movement into what you view to be a new era. You may easily move into your new awareness without all of your fireworks! (#145)

Elias delivers the information in a session format that involves question and answer-type dialogs with individuals and groups in a forum setting. As of this writing, there have been over 1,000 sessions covering dozens of topics that have been transcribed to over 10,000 pages. Elias uses his own specific terminology, which is carefully chosen so as not to reinforce mass belief systems. A Glossary of Terms is included in Appendix 2 at the end of this book to help the reader become familiar with Elias' concepts. Also, *The Sapling Story* referenced by Elias appears in Appendix 1.

To date, the information offered by Elias covers every topic imaginable. I have attempted in this first book, therefore, to offer the reader a condensed version of some of the topics that Elias has spoken about – questions asked and answers given – that pertain to experiences in our everyday lives. Topics that inspire us to ask, "Who am I? What about God? What is our purpose? Why is there so much suffering?" and much more.

Elias has introduced many ideas and concepts since he first began speaking to us. Some of these are perennial – they have been around for millennia – and some are quite innovative, or what Elias calls "boat-rocking." Some may be acceptable to you, others may be more challenging.

The information that Elias delivers shines a brilliant light onto these age-old questions that have previously been answered by others we call "teachers of enlightenment." Elias, therefore, offers us more of what we already know.

For now, within the action of this shift in consciousness, the veils that have been separating us from the full knowledge of ourselves are beginning to thin, allowing us to remember all that we truly are.

Another door is about to be opened. Are you ready to walk through?

Introduction

The Shift

Presently, in our world today, an event is taking place that is quite unlike any we have previously experienced. To many, this event might be compared to that which seers and prophets have long been predicting – a new age, a golden age that will arise out of much conflict and devastation. However, according to Elias, we are creating this event, and therefore have the choice to create it with ease and harmony. Elias calls it the *shift in consciousness* – a global change affecting every one of us.

Elias says we are creating this shift in consciousness because we, as a species, have become bored. We have exhausted our creativity in our present state and now wish to explore new areas of consciousness. We have spent the last two millennia creating a reality based upon religious beliefs, which have been purposeful and have served us well. But now we desire to move in different directions, and we are beginning to "remember" our deeper connections to the vastness of our own consciousness.

Elias has provided information specifically designed to avoid trauma during the shift in consciousness. According to Elias, this shift started at the beginning of the 20th century, will continue until approximately 2075, and is specific to this particular dimensional reality.

ELIAS on the shift

You are engaging a global shift in consciousness. This age is shifting the expression of consciousness. Throughout your history in this physical dimension, you have collectively chosen to be expressing a male energy, for you associate all of your manifestations in relation to gender in this physical dimension, for sexuality is one of the two base elements of the design of this physical dimension. In this, you have generated all of your history to this point in an expression of male energy. You are shifting that energy expression to a female energy expression.

Now, this is not an expression of shifting a balance of societies necessarily or altering the construct, so to speak, of your male and female genders. It is merely shifting the expression of energy from that of the intellectual to the intuitional.

In this, as you shift this energy, you are also redefining terms, for you are shifting from an outward expression to an inward expression, placing value and turning your attentions to the individual and allowing the expression of the individual to be directing themselves, rather than the previous expression of projecting attention outwardly and allowing other individuals to be directing of the masses.

In this, as you turn this attention, you widen your awareness, for the emphasis is expressed upon self and the expression of the feminine, the intuition. In this action, there is a necessity to redefine terminology, and as you redefine terminology you actually redefine your physical reality. You alter your perceptions, which perception is the mechanism that generates all of the physical manifestations within your physical dimension. Therefore as you alter your perception, you alter your actual physical world and your physical reality.

In this, you also are generating a new action that you have not incorporated previously in this physical dimension, and that is the action of acceptance of beliefs — not eliminating beliefs, for they are an integral design of the blueprint of this physical dimension — but the action of acceptance of these belief systems and therefore neutralizing their affectingness in limiting your choices, and therefore also allowing yourselves individually and collectively to generate a tremendous expression of freedom.

Now, this freedom actually is altering your physical reality, and as you insert this shift in consciousness fully into your physical reality in objective terms — which you are now engaging in this century — you shall be altering the construct of your societies, your governments, your movement in relation to what you now view as work and play.

In this, as I have expressed previously, in a manner of speaking you laid your groundwork in your previous century. In your 20th century, you moved in the expression of the subjective movement of this shift in consciousness. Now in this century, you are beginning the objective insertion of it; the actual alteration of your reality in physical terms.

This also generates conflict and many expressions of trauma for many individuals throughout your world. For the action of addressing to belief systems and acceptance of them is quite unfamiliar, and this action generates tremendous expressions of trauma within individuals and en masse. This is the reason that there is also an acceleration of information which is being offered through essences, such as myself and many other expressions of energy throughout your world, in lending energy in helpfulness that you shall not generate tremendous trauma, for it is unnecessary. Therefore, as you offer yourselves more information as you widen your awarenesses, you allow yourselves less trauma, and this is the point of my engagement with all of you in offering information to you.

In this, you already are beginning to view tremendous changes and alterations and also tremendous upheaval, and you also view many, many, many individuals choosing to disengage in this time framework for they choose not to be physically interactive in this shifting objectively, for there is a subjective recognition of the challenge which is expressed in this shift.

Now, these individuals continue to lend energy to the accomplishment of this shift but are choosing to express that nonphysically rather than experiencing the objective physical affectingness of this shift. But those individuals that choose to continue within their physical expressions and manifestations as this shift accelerates are beginning, and shall continue to do so, to generate much more of an excitement in relation to the discovery of these new freedoms that you are each and all offering to yourselves.

You are also all widening your awarenesses to the point now that you recognize that you present yourselves with tremendous challenges and that the energy expressions are quite real and quite strong, and you participate in expressing these energy surges collectively within your physical dimension to assist the movement of this shift. But even these energy surges may be quite challenging in your objective physical reality, for they are also quite unfamiliar and they are being expressed quite strongly. (#1052)

Chapter 1

YOUR PURPOSE IS EXPERIENCE

"Experience is your best teacher. This will offer you information to build upon. I may explain the concepts to you many times, as I have! Now you may experience, and you will teach yourselves."

(#55)

Chapter 1

YOUR PURPOSE IS EXPERIENCE

ELIAS: Upset and "upendedness" shall be the order of the day, with the incorporation of the information that shall be being delivered to you; for even within your new creation of your new religion of "metaphysics," you are taught or led to believe that this focus, or your lifetime, is a striving for a "better reality." There is an ultimate discounting of this reality that you create, and of your focus and your creativity.

You are told that you narrow yourselves; that you do not see all that you may see. I express these concepts to you also, but simultaneously I express to you that what you create is not insufficient, and it is no less reality than any other area of consciousness. You are told that this focus that you experience is an illusion. "This is your dream state, and your dreaming state is reality." This is another discounting of your creation of your self.

I shall not offer you information to be discounting of any of your creations. This is your reality. This is a reality. This is a manifestation of reality, and it is a perfect manifestation of reality. It is not flawed or errored. You are not flawed, and do not create errors. You do not make mistakes, for there are no mistakes. Therefore, many shall experience upendedness with this information. You have asked to challenge your established belief systems, and so you shall.

Your focus involves ultimate precision; an immaculate preciseness; an ultimate creativity. You create a selectivity intentionally. If you were not wishing to be selective, you would not choose to engage physical focus. There are, as has been expressed, essences choosing not to engage physical focus of any type, so to speak. There are essences choosing to be engaging other physical focuses quite foreign to what you view to be your physical focus, but you present have chosen. You have not been "thrust into!" You have chosen, purposefully, this physical focus, this manifestation, and you create it perfectly for your own purposes, which is your experience.

Day one, chapter one, Elias: Your purpose is experience. (#126)

Chapter 2

THE SHIFT

"You hold wonderings. You look to your present now and you hold questionings of validity of purpose, of missions, of action. Within this present now, you are experiencing what I have termed to be a shift in consciousness. You are moving out of your religious era and moving into a new reality which you are creating."

(#270)

Chapter 2

THE SHIFT

An Overview

ELIAS: What be this air that hangs so very strangely upon this time period presently that moves you all in a new, strange direction that is unclear? "What is my purpose? What is my direction? Where are we moving? What does our future hold? " These are questions that have been presented to this essence and that all of the individuals presently upon your planet are inquiring of, for these are strange times … changing times, but interesting times!

You engage presently what I have designated in my terminology as a shift in consciousness, which is occurring presently and escalating and is affecting of all of you individually and also en masse. Odd and peculiar events occur within your present time framework, and this moves more intensely as you move forward within your linear time. In this, waves occur in consciousness.

Let me express to you that there is no separation within consciousness, and although you view yourselves to be separate individuals, and within this reality objectively you are, you are also not. You are all interconnected within consciousness, and you hold no separation. You all hold affectingness to each other en masse and individually, and in this you share many experiences.

Presently, within this now, a wave is occurring within conscious-ness which is directly involving this shift in consciousness. Many individuals are beginning now to be experiencing elements of trauma and confusion.

Now; let me also express to you that as I have expressed many times previously, the reason that I speak with all of you is to be offering information in regard to this shift in consciousness, and in that to be affecting in lessening the trauma that shall be associated and IS associated with this shift. And now, it begins.

I have been speaking for a time period with many individuals as to this shift in consciousness, but I have also been offering information to all of these individuals of self, that they may better understand their individual selves and interactions and therein hold a greater understanding of the action of this shift in consciousness.

This shift is global. You have agreed within essence to be creating a new type of reality within your particular dimension, which is this, and in this physical manifestation you have exhausted your wonderment with your experiences that you have created previously, and now move into a new area of experience.

What is your purpose within this dimension? Your purpose is to be manifesting for the experience of physical focus within a dimension that is focused upon the sexual and emotional aspects of physical experience. Experience is your purpose. (Grinning) You have no mission. You have no method. You have no process. You are not in school. You are not upon a lower plane, and there are no masters that are above you that are guiding you along your path, for you have no path! You merely hold experience.

You are essence. You each before me presently are an individual focus of your essence. You are a focus of attention of your essence, and your essence holds countless focuses of attention.

This be important for your information, for within the action of this shift these focuses shall bleed through to you, for there is no separation and for you are loosening the veils in consciousness that you have held throughout millennium in this particular physically manifest dimension.

Presently, as I have stated, another wave within consciousness is occurring. Waves in consciousness occur continuously. Some of these waves hold more of an intensity than others. Now; let me explain briefly a wave in consciousness. You create waves in consciousness continuously. You label these waves objectively through your belief systems. Let us use an example that I have presented many times to individuals, for it serves the purpose well:

You create seasons of actions. You create seasons of waves that you respond to. Within your physical seasons of your year, you also create a wave season; a cold season, a flu season. This is a creation of a wave that you participate within en masse. You all individually create this, and in agreement en masse you manifest this. Individually you create your own individual expression or participation within this wave, or you choose not to participate within the wave. You always hold the choice to participate or to not participate, but the wave of energy in consciousness holds such an intensity that many individuals DO participate within these waves.

This is not what you would term to be an objective choice. You do not think, "I recognize a wave in consciousness is occurring. We have created this. I shall participate. I shall become ill." No. You do not express to yourself, "I shall become ill, for this shall be contributing to the commerce of our society." Or, "I shall be participating in the exchange of consuming pharmaceuticals and engaging truths that our economy shall benefit."

No, you do not. You merely participate. Subjectively you DO choose for your own reasons, and those reasons shall be beneficial to you, for you do not choose any experience within your focus that is not beneficial. It may not hold pleasantness; it may not hold joyfulness. It may hold uncomfortableness or distress, but it is beneficial. Beneficial is not positive or negative. In actuality, there is no positive or negative! There merely is choices of experience.

In this, you create presently another wave; not in the area of physical affectingness as your seasons of illness, but you create an intensity of a wave presently within consciousness en masse which is designed by you to be addressing to belief systems. This particular wave you have created within a huge swell which is affecting not only of you individually, but greatly en masse — within your societies, within your governments, within your countries, within your world — but these you may view quite easily. You may look to turmoil within many areas of expression objectively outside of you, so to speak … although there is no outside of you! (Grinning)

In this, you may look to other individuals experiencing conflict. You may look to societies, you may look to communities, you may look to business you may look to all elements and view upset. This may be in what you term in your belief systems positive or negative — either. It holds an intensity, and it is obviously viewable all about you.

But although you may allow yourselves the enlightenment of expressing to yourselves and other individuals that you understand and see that this is an action of this shift in consciousness moving throughout your communities … for you are so very enlightened and knowing! But as you experience these elements within your individual experiences, you question and you express, "Why am I experiencing this intensity? Why do I experience this conflict? Why do I experience this confusion? Why am I creating what I am creating?" Or, "Why is someone else creating what they are creating for me?" (Intently) No other individual creates for you. You create your reality individually. Every aspect, every element of it, you create. You draw yourselves to other individuals' creations, but you are creating of this also, for you are drawing yourselves to their creations. Therefore, you are participating and you are within agreement.

Within this present now, this wave which is occurring, and has not crested presently yet but continues to build and accelerate, is affecting of individuals in different manners. If you are experiencing conflict within relationship, if you are experiencing conflict within business, if you are experiencing conflict or confusion within self, within understanding, within belief systems, this is connected to this wave, and you have created a choice to be participating within this present wave in consciousness, and this also is directly related to this shift in consciousness.

The base element of this shift in consciousness is to be identifying, recognizing, and addressing to the belief systems that you hold and to be accepting of these belief systems — not eliminating, not altering, not changing, but to be accepting of these belief systems, which therefore renders these belief systems neutralized, which shall be creating of this new establishment in consciousness; for if you are not affected by those belief systems that you hold, you allow yourselves the opportunity to open to your awareness and you allow yourselves to view more of your reality.

I have stated many times, this shift in consciousness is limited to this dimension. This is YOUR choice within this dimension upon this planet in this reality, and in this you may be allowing yourselves to drop these veils within your singularly focused attention and allow yourselves to be interactive and viewing of so very much more of your reality that you create within essence. This offers you the opportunity to view and participate within the action of transition, which until recently, so to speak, in relative terms, individuals have chosen merely to engage the action of transition after disengaging physical focus.

Disengagement of physical focus, as you are most probably aware, is that moment that you choose, which you DO choose, to be disengaging of this manifestation, or what you commonly address to be death. I do not choose to engage the word death, for there is no death. There is merely emergence, which is birth. Therefore, at the moment of disengagement, you are birthed, not "deathed."

But within this action of being birthed and an emergence, you enter into an action which is termed to be a transition. This transition is to be shedding completely of the objective awareness and the belief systems held within the objective awareness, that you may re-emerge — not newly emerge, but re-emerge — yourselves into non — physical focus and move into whatever direction you choose to move within, for you are within a continual state of becoming, and that is what you are. Therefore, if you inquire, "What am I?" or "Who am I?", you are essence and you are within a continual state of becoming. This is consciousness. This is essence. This is you.

As to this wave and its affectingness and your participation within it, you may also be choosing to be participating within this wave but not within conflict, and in this you may be creating of tremendous excitement or elation, heightened senses, a time period of heightened awareness, but you also shall be addressing to belief systems, for this is the action of this particular wave. This be the reason that more individuals are presently experiencing confusion and conflict, for they are addressing to their belief systems.

All of the creations that you engage that you view to be negative or confusing are those that are addressing to your belief systems. All of those experiences within this time framework that you choose to engage of heightened senses and elation or excitement are the acknowledgment to yourselves that you have been addressing to belief systems, and this is your validation that you are accomplishing moving through elements of your belief systems. Therefore, there may be different expressions, but the action is the same. It is merely dependent upon your position and how you have addressed to your belief systems … or not addressed to your belief systems!

In this, let me be clear in expressing to you, these waves have been moving more frequently within what you would term to be a recent short time period. Within your recent few years this action has been accelerating, and now you move into an immense wave addressing to that very core of the action of this shift in consciousness, and that is the addressing of belief systems, and in that, the most affecting belief systems are those of duplicity and acceptance.

You all hold the belief system of duplicity. There is no individual upon this planet within this dimension that does not hold the belief system of duplicity, but in moving into the areas of acceptance, you also move into the area of accepting of duplicity automatically, in part, and therefore begin the neutralization of this belief system, which holds the greatest stronghold with you. You believe that you are good and bad simultaneously, and this is duplicity, and you believe that all other individuals are good and bad simultaneously. This is duplicity. And no individual is good and bad, for there is no good and bad! It is merely choices of experience.

There is no element within your dimension — there is no element within essence — that is good or bad. You merely hold belief systems that express this to you that you believe, and you create your reality in accordance with this, and this perpetuates the lack of acceptance within self and within other individuals, and this creates conflict and the perpetuation, and over and over and cycling and circling and continuing. And this be the action of your shift, to be altering of this reality and recognizing the reality that there is no right and wrong, there is no good and bad, and there is no necessity for judgment.

And also let me express to you that each time you view yourselves or another individual to be right, you are creating a judgment. You do not merely create judgment in expressing wrongness, for each time that you express rightness, you also express wrongness automatically, for some element must be wrong if there is an element that is right! This is how you have created your reality and your belief systems, and it IS your reality and it is a very STRONG reality, and it holds to you very strongly and YOU hold to IT very strongly, and you resist the letting go of these belief systems, for they are familiar. And this is what you have created for millennium and this is what you recognize and this is comfortable, and although you express you are not comfortable, you continue to create uncomfortableness, for it is familiar, and in that it is comfortable.

(Humorously) What is uncomfortable is the unfamiliar — strange beings visiting you, strange qualities within your experiences, and the "wooo" (grinning) of all of the unknown elements that exist within your reality! You are leery of plunging yourselves directly into the middle of your Bermuda Triangle within your own home, but this triangle holds wondrous elements and within it you hold wondrous creativity! And this is what you magnate to presently, although you hold to your energy and you hold to yourselves in fearfulness, for it is unfamiliar and frightening, but it is wondrous also! And therefore, the knowing within you that you are so accomplished at NOT listening to any longer re-emerges within you and allows you the wonderment of your own remembrance; your remembrance of self, of essence, of what you are, and the amazement of your own unbounded creativity, which it is!

· Each of you holds wondrous gloriousness! There are no limitations to your accomplishments. There are no limitations to your energy. There are no limitations to your connectedness EXCEPT within the area of the holding to your belief systems, and as you hold to them you also create your own limitations and you do not allow yourselves to view the wondrousness of what you have created within this dimension.

This particular dimension is exceedingly diverse, and you have offered yourselves within this particular dimension the opportunity to explore immense creativity and creations. Look about you at what you have created already! And now you move into the area of not expressing outwardly in the creation of your planet, of your world, of your inventions, of your expressions, but now you move into the MORE expansive area of creativity, in expressing what you are and who you are and what you may access. You hold presently the ability to access ALL of your focuses of essence. The veil is very thin. You have created this! You may access other areas of consciousness, not within "chanting trances" (grinning) but within your objective waking state, that which you manipulate so very well and have accomplished so very well within.

Within your objective expression, you may expand now. It is not limited to creating outside of you, but may manifest in what you may view to be outside of you as projected by within you, as accessed from within you. But in this, your key is to be addressing to these belief systems, and the most powerful of these, as I have stated, is that belief system of duplicity, which blocks you tremendously en masse and individually.

Acceptance is the lack of judgment in any area, which may be sounding quite simplistic to you all, but I shall be wagering to express to you that your accomplishment objectively of this action shall not be quite so easy, (laughter) for you shall find yourselves within situations every of your days expressing a lack of acceptance, either to yourselves or to another individual. But be assured, this also is not negative! This is your OPPORTUNITY to engage this action. This is your opportunity to express to yourself, "This be not bad; this be not good. This be my opportunity to create my choice." For as you allow yourselves the hold of your belief systems, you also limit your choices and you express that you do not hold choices. You are bound; you MUST be. You must not be! I express to you, extremely not! You merely believe that you are locked, but you are not, and each opportunity that you present yourself within, within each wave, offers you the viewing of new choices.

You need only relax momentarily and stop momentarily and view your own action; NOT view another individual's action, but view YOUR action and view YOUR belief systems, for it matters not the expression of another individual. This be not your responsibility. You hold enough responsibility for self, which is tremendous! Therefore, why shall you assume false responsibility for another individual? This shall be overwhelming! In your terms physically, you do not possess enough time to be assuming responsibility for any other individual upon your planet, for your time framework is consumed merely with your own responsibility. But you assume responsibility for other individuals, for this distracts you from the responsibility of self and allows you to not address to self, and also allows you to continue in your familiarity of your belief systems of duplicity and your belief systems in acceptance and the lack of that therein.

Acceptance is the word; acceptance of self in recognition that you are not bad, that you are not good, that your expressions are not bad, they are not good. They merely are.

Q: I'd like to understand the difference between the action of choosing and the action of judgment.

ELIAS: Choice is choice. It does not involve a judgment or the lack of judgment. It is merely an action, a choice, a decision that you hold to move in one direction or another direction, to be creating of one probability or another probability. A judgment is a projection of a belief system. Choice may be influenced by belief systems, but it in itself is not a belief system. Judgment is. Judgment is always an element, a bird of the cage, an element of the belief system. Choice is merely an action which is not a belief system in itself. (#284)

Chapter 3

A SHIFTY QUESTION

*"The action of this shift is to realize and actualize
a more comprehensive expansion of your abilities
and your creativity within this dimension;
a realization of self and a remembrance of essence."*

(#251)

Chapter 3

A SHIFTY QUESTION

Q: What is the purpose of the shift in consciousness?

ELIAS: You have chosen, within this dimension, a new experience in creativity. You have chosen, within what you term to be your history, certain actions and experiences for long time periods, in your terms. These have been purposeful for those experiences. You presently move away from your religious era, which has continued for quite some physical time period, into a new awareness in consciousness, to allow you an expanded creativity and allow you to utilize your abilities of essence within physical focus. You are expanding your reality to encompass more of essence and more of your own creative abilities. (#203)

The purpose of the shift is to be widening your awareness, and in this allowing you greater creativity and a greater knowledge of your own abilities that you may be accomplishing within. This allows you less limitations and more accessibility to exploration of your reality within this dimension. It is also the action of this shift to be accepting those belief systems which you hold, that they may not be quite so limiting of your abilities and your creativity, and allowing you a freer expression of essence and less separation from essence. (#252)

Within the action of your shift, you shall understand more of your self. You shall understand and be in greater communication with your essence. You shall understand how you create your reality. You are already moving into this area. You are already investigating the availability of consciousness.

Within the action of your shift, what you presently view to be barriers shall not be viewed as barriers. Those actions that you express dismay towards presently shall be effortless within your shift. Your dream time shall be recognized as reality. The interaction and the understanding of this time element that you engage within another area of consciousness shall be much more efficiently utilized. Your mobility shall be much greater.

Your understanding of your self, of your physical expression or body, of your own consciousness, of the connection and intertwining of all consciousness that is manifest with you shall all be clearer. This shall enable you to move more efficiently, more effortlessly, through your focus. It shall also enhance your creativity, allowing you the ability to use more of the creative qualities that you already possess, but use little of.

Within non — physical areas of consciousness, you are utilizing this creativity; and for the experience that you have chosen to this point, your limitations have served you well. You have chosen the direction that you have created. You have chosen this specifically for the experience physically.

Now that you have experienced a time frame of this physical manifestation throughout all of your focuses, not only this particular one, you have recognized that you are now ready to move into a more highly creative area of consciousness incorporated with physical focus. Just as little children move through stages acclimating themselves to their environment, their circumstances, and learning interaction with individuals, you throughout your history have also chosen to be learning to acclimate yourselves to physical manifestation. Be remembering, you possess all knowledge already. You have chosen to forget.

You have chosen a highly specialized focus. The creativity within the manipulation of energy that you exert to create physical focus and its highly efficient workings is truly miraculous, in what you term to be miraculous. (#132)

Now; within the present engagement of action of movement of this shift, you are widening your awareness to be affecting within changing of probabilities established within your religious element. These are very strong belief systems. You have created very strong expectations globally, of events that you have chosen within probabilities to occur. Within the action of this shift, you may be altering of these actions within a recognition that it is unnecessary to be creating of devastation for your attention. You do not need to be creating floods, famines, earthquakes, holocausts to be gaining your attention and initiating movement into what you view to be a new era. You may easily move into your new awareness without all of your fireworks!

I have expressed to you previously, your religious element, your era, shall not disappear without struggle. Although you have chosen and agreed collectively to move into a new awareness and you have chosen the probability of this shift, many are reluctant to be moving. YOU are reluctant to be moving! As your own consciousness widens and you experience new elements within your daily experience, you pull back. You hold reluctance yourselves! You are not jumping into this shift with both feet! You hold to your belief systems quite strongly. You find it difficult to be accepting of belief systems. You continue with your religious era and with its manifestations.

Each individual offers themselves information that will speak to them to be accomplishing in the movement of this shift, but within the beginning throes of this shift the movement is not easy, just as within the movement of a revolution there is turmoil and conflict. You engage within a global shift of consciousness, which is a much greater mass event than a revolution of a country. It is a greater action than your world war. It is tremendous.

Therefore, there shall be conflict. You would not be speaking with this essence were you not approaching this shift. (#145)

Collectively, many, many, many of you, within consciousness, as manifestations of this physical dimension, have asked for helpfulness, have asked for information, and I, as one essence in conjunction with many other essences, have responded and continue to respond.

But I am not merely the only essence that shall be responsive. There are myriads of essences that are continuously responding to energy and inquiries that you project, and I may express to you that within this time framework, this action occurs more frequently, for you collectively have chosen to be creating an action which we term to be a shift in consciousness. This is evidenced throughout your globe presently, and becomes more so, day by day.

In this, many of the actions of this shift in consciousness are confusing objectively, and many are creating of expressions of conflict.

Many of the movements of this shift in consciousness create beyond conflict and manifest in trauma, and therefore, you have expressed individually and collectively that you wish to be receiving information that may be lessening of your conflict or your trauma as you continue movement within this shift in consciousness, and you have requested helpfulness.

The expression of helpfulness is not merely offered in interaction of communication or information, but in actual offerings of energy that essences express and project through layers of consciousness to you within this physical dimension to be helpful in your movement.

· This is your choice that you have engaged this action of this shift in consciousness, and in this time framework now, as you have moved linearly into your new millennium, you also are engaging the actual insertion of this shift in consciousness into your objective reality, your official reality. Therefore, many more manifestations materialize, for in actuality, you become more aware, and this is the point. This is what you have chosen. This is your design.

This is what you are moving into quite purposefully: widening your awareness, opening your periphery within consciousness, and allowing yourself objectively — not merely in concept or theory and not merely subjectively, but objectively, within your waking state — to be aware of much more of you as essence, of consciousness in its entirety, and of your ability to be creating and manipulating in energy within all of consciousness.

You have created limitations within your physical reality for an extensive time framework quite purposefully, and this is not bad or wrong. But you are choosing a new experience now, and in this new experience, you choose to offer yourselves more freedom, and in the expression of freedom, you choose to be incorporating more of reality in this physical dimension.

Now; I have stated that this action also incorporates trauma, and you are experiencing and witnessing trauma within your world. How shall you move to be eliminating these expressions of trauma and conflict? By familiarizing yourself with you, by familiarizing yourself with your beliefs, and allowing yourself to move into the expression of acceptance — acceptance and trust of self, acceptance of your beliefs; not elimination of self or of beliefs, but acceptance of those beliefs and of self.

This is the movement WITHIN your beliefs, the knowing that you hold beliefs that are basic to the design of this particular physical dimension, and not creating judgments upon those beliefs but allowing yourself the recognition of them, and in that action, eliminating the automatic response that you create in relation to them.

To this point, you have held belief systems in this reality and you have automatically responded to them, which eliminates many of your choices. It narrows your field upon which you may play. It also creates obstacles within your movement.

In this, as you become aware of the belief systems that you hold, you also recognize the automatic dictation that these beliefs express to your perception, and as you become more aware of this dictating by your beliefs in automatic action, you may allow yourself to choose, and choose other expressions, and not limit yourself to those that are familiar to you in the automatic responses. (#704)

Belief systems are unique to physical focuses. They are an element of physical focuses. Your individual physical focus here upon this planet, within this time/space and within this dimension, is not the only physical focus and not the only physical manifestation that holds belief systems. There are many dimensions which are physically manifest. All physical manifestations hold belief systems.

In widening your awareness and accepting of belief systems, you nullify their power. You allow yourself more probabilities, for you allow yourself more knowledge and more choices. You do not feel bound to these belief systems. Within a strong belief system, you are held. Any belief system that you hold strongly holds you! It eliminates many of your choices, for you may only see even more selectively and narrowly within that belief system. You allow yourself no information beyond that belief system. Therefore, you are bound. As you accept the belief system, not with the intention of changing or eliminating the belief system, but acknowledging that it is reality and that it is accepted, it loses its power, therefore losing its hold, allowing you more choices (#133)

This shift in consciousness is limited to this particular dimension. It is not a shift in consciousness which encompasses other dimensions or other physical dimensions, but you shall hold the ability, as you hold presently if you are choosing to be engaging of this ability, to access other realities at will. Their awareness of your interaction shall not be objective to them, but you shall hold an objective awareness of your interaction. Example: You wish to engage another physical reality; extraterrestrials. You wish to view another physical reality which is manifest. You may, by merely stepping sideways, engage this action. It shall be as effortless as moving from one room to another. You wish to engage an individual that has disengaged physical focus. You shall hold the ability to be in active communication and interaction with another focus in non — physical communication. Your abilities for mobility through consciousness shall exceed any known element that you hold presently.

And how shall you accomplish this action of this shift? It has already begun. You are already participants.

You presently are embarking upon a new quest within consciousness. You stand now upon the eve before the dawn of the realization of your creativity. Let me offer to you that within your mythology, you express the story of Saint George slaying the dragon to create safe passage and ease for the masses, eliminating the threat of harmfulness. Within imagery, this is the symbol that you may present to yourselves in your action in compliance with this shift in consciousness. Much energy has been lent throughout your millennium to the prophecies and the predictions of trauma and of destruction, which you approach now your time framework marker, the dawn of these predictions. They are probabilities, but they are not actualized within this particular reality yet. Therefore, you hold the ability to actualize different probabilities. (#270)

Let me express to you: many, many predictions have been offered in conjunction with this shift in consciousness. Many predictions have been offered for much of your history and you view them to be coming to their culmination now, which in one aspect there is truthfulness in this, for you ARE moving into the end throes of this shift in consciousness and its accomplishment, but all of these predictions are probabilities. They are not set in stone, and you have the ability to be diverting of these predictions.

(Intently) This be another reason that I speak with individuals within physical focus, to be reminding them that you hold the ability to alter probabilities. It is your choice which probabilities you insert into your officially accepted reality.

In this, I offer information that masses of individuals may draw themselves to, and in this collectively direct their energy in the area of creating less trauma and diverting the probabilities of destruction and harmfulness that much energy has been lent to throughout your history.

Therefore, these predictions hold much energy and continue to hold much energy, and may materialize into your officially accepted reality IF they are continued to be lent energy. But you also hold the probability of diverting those predictions, those probabilities, and creating different actions.

It is unnecessary to be creating of destruction and doom and trauma. It is more efficient to be creating of ease, and the manner in which you create ease is to be listening to self and not accepting all of what is offered by what you perceive to be outside of self.

In like manner, I express to all individuals to not be following of this essence. I do not require disciples. I do not solicit followers. I am encouraging of every individual to be following of themselves, to be acknowledging of themselves, and to be recognizing that it is unnecessary for you to be continuing within your belief systems of authorities and other individuals that shall direct you.

YOU hold the ability to direct YOU! You do not need any other individual or essence to be directing your movement. You may direct your own movement, and create wondrous experiences in your own direction! (#293)

I do not offer this information to you, that you may become enlightened beings and hold the secrets of the universe! I offer this information to you, that you may offer to yourself no expression of trauma within the action of this shift. Therefore, that which offers you trauma or conflict I offer you the suggestion that you eliminate.

In this, what I am expressing to you is, if you are experiencing conflict, examine that which is creating of this conflict, and you may be choosing a different direction of attention, and you shall eliminate your conflict. THIS is the point.

Individuals confuse themselves, for they view this information and my interaction with you as their opportunity to become spiritual, enlightened beings.

Do not delude yourself in this area, for this is your own expression of objective confusion. You are already enlightened, spiritual beings! You do not need or require my helpfulness to be accomplishing of that! You are already expressing of that action.

What you have inquired of — as to my helpfulness — is merely an engagement to be lessening or avoiding or eliminating trauma that you may be creating in conjunction with this shift in consciousness, and this be the reason that I offer you information. And you, within your physical focus and your intellect, complicate the information which is offered to you. It is not as very complicated as you perceive it to be! (#370)

The awareness within your planet is growing. You stand upon the threshold of the dawn which shall insert different probabilities into your officially accepted reality, not those probabilities which have been prophesied. These probabilities are the remnants of the religious era, which has been in acting capacity for much of your time framework; a millennium. You have come to the point that this particular creation in consciousness in this reality no longer serves you. Therefore, it is also confining of your creativity, and you have chosen to be eliminating of this and moving into a new action of creativity.

In this movement, you hold a recognition of the unnecessary–ness (grinning) of trauma and destruction within the creation of a new era.

You have already felt your birth pains within this century. It is unnecessary to be creating of negativity, in your terms. (#270)

This shift in consciousness is already accomplished. You merely view that it is not accomplished yet, for your perception resides within a linear time framework. But in actuality, time is simultaneous. Therefore, it is already accomplished. You have all collectively, upon this planet within this dimension, agreed and chosen for this shift in consciousness to be accomplished. Therefore, it shall be! It is merely a question of whether you are choosing to be incorporating information and widening your awareness to not experience trauma, or to be experiencing trauma. This also is your choice. (#355)

The initial expression, or what you may term to be the beginning of this shift in consciousness, was initiated at the beginning of your previous century, that which you identify as your 20th century.

Now; in the movement into your new century, your new millennium, you are creating a different type of movement in conjunction with this shift in consciousness. But as you view your previous century, you may allow yourselves to recognize the difference in movement and awareness objectively that has been expressed throughout that particular century, which is expressed differently than the other time frameworks throughout your history.

This shift in consciousness extends to what I have approximated as three-quarter mark into this new century, and at the mark of your movement into your new millennium, you have moved the action of this shift in consciousness to be now inserting it into your actual physical objective realty.

Much of the movement that has occurred in your previous century has been subjective ... in a manner of speaking, for the objective IS expressed in harmony to the subjective movement. But the awareness of the action of this shift in consciousness in your previous century has been expressed subjectively, and imagery has been expressed objectively in reflection of that subjective movement. Now you move into an objective expression of it, in which individuals throughout your globe begin an objective recognition that they are participating in this movement. The identification of beliefs is becoming objectively known in awareness throughout your globe.

In this, as I have stated previously, all individuals are participating within this shift in consciousness, but to this point, all individuals may not have recognized objectively an identification of that movement. As you move further into this new millennium, this becomes evidenced more and more clearly, throughout all cultures, throughout your globe, in which there is an objective recognition of what you are participating in, and of your movement ... in redefining your reality. (#737)

Q: Has a shift of this magnitude taken place in our physical reality already...

ELIAS: No.

Q: ...prior to this? This is the first one?

ELIAS: Of this magnitude, yes.

Q: What others have occurred?

ELIAS: You have created several Source Events previously. This is also a Source Event.

Now; a Source Event is a movement that is chosen collectively by all of the essences participating in the reality. Source Events are of such a magnitude that none of them are entirely fully inserted into your physical reality, for your physical reality is not expansive enough to accommodate an entirety of a Source Event, as is the situation with this Source Event also. But this particular Source Event is what you would term to be your largest Source Event to this time framework throughout your history, for it is altering many expressions of your reality and it is affecting of the entirety of your planet, your world.

You have incorporated other Source Events — religion, scientific — but this is incorporated globally. There is no small tribe in any corner of your world that is not affected. There is not one individual throughout your world in its entirety that is not affected by this particular Source Event.

Q: Is there a Source Event of this magnitude in the future?

ELIAS: This would be your choice, for what is the future? An illusion. As I have stated recently, the future is always followed by the present. Therefore, what is the future (confused laughter), if the present is after the future? (Elias chuckles, very amused)

The future is a projection, my friend. You never arrive at the future, you merely project to the speculation of the future, and once discontinuing your projection to the future, you return to the present which follows the future. (Scattered applause and laughter)

Q: What would happen then if it were possible to stop projecting to the future?

ELIAS: Ah! You would discover your liberty, for you would be present in the present! And THAT is your point of power. (#1368)

Chapter 4

WHY ARE WE HERE?

"The reason you are manifest within this dimension – your purpose, your mission, your reason – is to experience. You are not manifest within this dimension in a school. You are not manifest in this dimension to be accomplishing of great deeds, although you may be choosing to be experiencing this. You are manifest within this dimension, and any physical dimension, merely to experience the purity and qualities of physical action."

(#270)

Chapter 4

WHY ARE WE HERE?

ELIAS: Why are you here? Why have you manifest within this physical dimension? Is the purpose of this action clearer to myself than it may be to you within this present moment? I may express, quite! Yes, it is quite clear to me why you have manifest within this physical dimension, and I view that it is quite unclear to you why you have manifest in this physical dimension.

In simplicity, you have manifest in this physical dimension merely to explore and experience.

You are not engaging a mission. You are not placed here by any higher power. You are not subject to this physical dimension as identifiable by a lower or learning plane, for you are not learning. You are not teaching; you are not learning. You are experiencing.

And I may acknowledge you in your identification of terminology, for you are, quite accurately, a traveler. You are a traveler through this physical dimension, choosing to be exploring all of the wonders of how you may create a reality in whichever manner you are choosing, and all of the myriads of experiences that you may explore in relation to the design of this physical dimension.

This physical dimension is designed by you collectively to be experimenting and exploring through the channels, so to speak, of emotion and sexuality, and coupling those with a design of filtration of how you perceive all of your reality, which is defined as your incorporation of belief systems.

Within this particular physical dimension, the basic elements of this reality are belief systems, are the design of sexuality, and the exploration of emotional qualities and expressions.

Now; beyond this, it is the incorporation of your belief systems that influence you in the thought process that you have been placed in this physical reality, and that you may be called upon in some manner to be accomplishing some mission, some higher purpose.

In actuality, you already are your highest purpose. Therefore, there is no action to accomplish in becoming greater or better or higher than you already are.

You become confused in this physical reality, for you have created expressions of separation.

You are an identification of consciousness. You are all of consciousness. You are identifiable, as consciousness individually, as an essence. That essence is the identification of personality, a quality which defines you uniquely as an expression of consciousness, but simultaneously, you are all of consciousness.

In this, you occupy every aspect of consciousness. Whether you identify a particular area of consciousness as physical or nonphysical, you are it.

You are not here IN a place. You are here AS the place.

All that you view around you, all that exists within what you know objectively as your universe, IS YOU. It is not outside of you. It is not that you are placed within it as a small entity occupying this space, but that you ARE that space, and more. What you identify presently as you, in this moment, in this physical manifestation, is a focus of attention. That focus of attention creates a singularity in its concentration, and therefore appears to be separated from all else, within what you know. But in actuality, it is merely the designation of that focus of attention that creates that illusion of separateness.

Now; I may also express to you, there are other essences that are not physically focused, or that may be physically focused, but not in this particular physical dimension.

There are many, many, many physical dimensions which are occupied by many, many, many types of manifestations. There are many areas of consciousness that are non — physically focused.

What I am expressing in that identification is that the attentions are not focused in a manner in which they interact physically or in conjunction with physical matter.

This particular attention IS focused within a physical dimension. You create physical matter. You have created a physical body and form which you identify as you, but you are much greater than merely the expression of that one physical form.

You have chosen to be creating that physical form and participating in this physical reality to experience, to explore. (#704)

Let me express to you, you are not participating in a race; you are not manifest in this physical dimension to learn or to teach or to be taught. You are essences of consciousness — you already know.

You have manifest in this physical dimension to explore and experience this particular physical design of consciousness. You are travelers. No other individual within your physical dimension possesses more knowledge or more spirituality or more awareness than you. Therefore, what shall you learn from another individual? I am not a teacher, nor is any other individual within your physical dimension, for this implies that another individual holds more knowledge than do you or that you are less than any other individual, and you are not. (#937)

You have manifest in this physical dimension to incorporate a different expression of experience. The familiar is to be experiencing that folding in within consciousness in nonphysical expressions. This is the nature of consciousness and it is quite familiar. What you have chosen is the challenge of that experience and movement in relation to the physical, the expression of generating physical imagery, physical manifestations from nonphysical, something from nothing.

For in terms of corporeal expression, consciousness is not physical; it is not a thing. And you are consciousness, not a thing but a movement, a flow, an energy. In this, the wondrousness of what your purpose is is to be generating all that you are generating from no thing. You are not a thing, and view what you create! You have generated not merely yourself in physical form but an entire universe surrounding yourself, and this is all an expression of you. It is your exploration of YOU and what you are. This is your purpose, to be exploring all that you hold in capability of generating. And look what you have already generated — the entirety of the universe, for it is all an expression of you, in wondrousness of you.

Therefore, what is your purpose but to appreciate what you are and what you generate, for all that you view in all of your reality is an expression of you. All that you view within all of your universe from the tiniest speck of sand to the most distant star is all an aspect of you and what you generate. Therefore your purpose is to recognize this and to appreciate you. (#997)

Chapter 5

WHO AM I AND WHAT IS ESSENCE?

*"Within reality, there is no separation. All is consciousness.
There is no differentiation of one entity as opposed to another
entity, although within consciousness there are personality tones.
These are not images or entities that you may create small
images for. They are tones within the whole of consciousness,
which is the direction of consciousness, which creates you."*

(#185)

Chapter 5

WHO AM I AND WHAT IS ESSENCE?

ELIAS: When you think of yourself, who do you think of? Do you think of yourself as your body? No. But, you also do not think of yourself in terms of your essence. You think of what you have termed your soul, or your mind, or your self, or your psyche. All are terms for your physically focused consciousness, that part of your essence which you have divorced for the purpose of experience.

You only think of yourself as this you. You may believe in an immortal and ever creating soul, but somehow you even disconnect with that until you believe yourself to be...dead! (Laughter) Then, somehow, your immortal creating soul becomes you, miraculously! (Laughter, and then, very dramatically...) This shadowy cloud that is you, in your soul, "flies away" and becomes part of the universal consciousness, which we do not understand what this is. But, in returning to the "real world", in your waking alive state, you do not view yourselves as your soul. You view yourselves as...yourselves!

This physical focus, although only a part, is not an only. It is equal in importance and focus, as any or all other parts of your essence, just as each of you belongs to an essence, but is also part of the Creating Universal One and Whole. Energy is not separated. There is no division in any form. It may take on form if it chooses, but energy is energy. It is not something that can be divided. You cannot cut it into pieces. You cannot separate it, ever. It is not separable. This is how you are all connected. This is how we are all connected. Energy is everything universally, in every dimension. It only manifests in different forms or frequencies, but there is no difference, and it cannot be divided. It is not an entity. It is nothing you may hold. Therefore, you cannot separate it. (#11)

I shall express to you that you are a manifestation, a focus of essence. You manifest within this particular dimension as a focus of essence which holds its attention in one area, which is you. You are also all of essence. Essence is much greater than the one manifestation within a physical focus, although each physical focus holds all of essence within it. (#285)

Essence is a term that is used for your benefit, for your understanding of identification of a tone of consciousness which holds a certain direction, a certain intent for its creation of manifestation. All consciousness holds intent within its own valuefulfillment. Essence is that tone which chooses manifestation within personality for certain experiences. This is you. (#147)

Essence is what we will term a portion of this encompassing whole, although not a portion! (Smiling) Within your limitations of language, it is impossible to express to you the lack of division and separation; this being why I express to you to conceptualize these concepts that I offer to you, for within your thought patterns within physical focus, it is not possible for you to completely eliminate all separation and be understanding of these concepts. When I express to you that essence incorporates all systems, that all systems are open and available to you, this is what is incorporated by consciousness. You possess this. Every element of consciousness possesses all elements of the whole.

Each element chooses to manifest according to its desire and function. A flower manifests to the fullest of its ability. The units of con-sciousness that make up this flower are the same as that which you possess also. The flower's intent and function is to be a flower. Your intent and function is to incorporate intellect and

---

[1] The Clarity Exercise session #122a_092296

intuition, to be directing of your universe as you have created it. Therefore, make no mistake; you direct all of your physical manifestation, in every area. We have discussed this many times within previous sessions. You create your individual reality, and collectively, you create the reality en masse. Therefore, you are the creators of all that you perceive ... and far beyond. (#79)

You are essence. Therefore, you are much larger and greater than you view yourselves to be within one particular focus. This now which you identify, and the you that you know and that you are familiar with, is one focus of essence.

Now; as we discuss an individual focus, be not misunderstanding that you may think to yourself that you are merely a piece or a part of an essence, for you are not. You are the entirety of essence. Your attention presently is focused in one direction. This is not to say that this is all of you. It is merely the direction of your attention that you are focusing upon, and you may view your physical manifestation presently, now, and offer yourselves an example of this type of action.

You perceive one physical body form. This you identify as you. Within this one physical body form, many actions are occurring simultaneously. You hold five outer senses which are continuously, nonstopping, processing input of stimulation and information of your environment and of yourself, but you are not holding your attention within the action of your outer senses. Therefore, you are not noticing all that is being processed and all that is being created within the action of the function of your outer senses.

Within your physical body form, there are infinite actions that are occurring simultaneously, and you are not focusing your attention upon any of the actions that are occurring continuously within your physical body form.

Outside of your physical body, many actions are occurring. You are participating in interaction with other individuals. You have created an environment in which you are participating within and you have created a world which is affecting of you, and you are affecting of it. But within a particular moment, you may not be holding your attention in the area of noticing any of these elements that are all occurring simultaneously. You may hold your attention quite singularly, and merely be aware of one action.

Presently within this very moment, now, you are aware of the interaction that you are listening to with myself. You are not holding your attention in the area of any other action that is occurring within this dwelling.

This is not to say that actions are not occurring. They are, and you are also participating in these actions by your mere existence within this room.

The point of this explanation is to offer you slightly more of an understanding of how very many actions occur. It is your perception which identifies what you view, and within your perception, you view where you are directing your attention.

As essence, you are directing your attention — one of your attentions — to this particular focus, and you are participating in this focus. You do not allow yourselves the awareness of all of the other focuses which are occurring simultaneously. (#488)

You are experiencing many other types of experiences in other physical dimensions. You are not merely this singular form that you view. You think, within your thought process, of your reality as being limited to merely what you view physically within THIS one focus of attention. This is not the all of your reality. This is not the all of you! Each of you are wondrous creations, are wondrous creatures that inhabit countless dimensions simultaneously.

All of your focuses are occurring now, simultaneously, within this dimension and within all other dimensions, and within THIS very creative dimension, you have created the perception of linear time. What an excellent creation! VERY creative, for in this you have created sub — dimensions within your dimension, for this dimension is a physical dimension, and within this dimension you have created the sub — dimensions of time aspects. Therefore, you have past and you have future. All of these time elements are also occurring now, presently, simultaneously. You view expansiveness of yourself in holding other focuses — past focuses, future focuses. They are all occurring now. You merely hold the perception that you hold past focuses or future focuses.

I have offered an analogy previously that I shall offer to you that may express a visual, that you may be understanding more of the vastness of yourselves, although this analogy is also quite limited.

In this, I express you to view yourselves as being a room. Your physical self is a room, and within this room there are hundreds of televisions, and each of these televisions holds one channel, one picture, one play, one scenario, and each of them are different, but they are all contained within this one room.

Each of the screens are a focus of you. They are all a creation of you, an aspect of you, and they are all contained within you. You are one of these television screens. You are one focus of attention of essence, just as within your physical body you may focus your attention upon several different areas of your physical form simultaneously. You may be aware of your vision, of your hearing, of your finger tapping, of stimulation of side of your body, of a throbbing toe, all simultaneously. In like manner, your essence is aware and interactive with all of these focuses of attention simultaneously, and viewing all of these television screens at once.

Time within its linear form is merely a perception that you have created for your experience within this particular dimension, that you may be experiencing fully in a much slower manner, that you may savor each of your experiences that you create within physical focus. You have created quite an amazing dimension within this particular reality! (#324)

You are much more multi-dimensional than you view yourselves to be. You look to yourselves; you view one physical form, one solid body. You are much more than this one form, for each and every experience and age that you have created within this physical focus exists simultaneous with you presently, and continues. You merely focus your attention very singularly. Therefore, you view one body, one singular thought process, one you. But you are much more than one you, for each moment does not disappear. It is continuous. Just as you have not begun and shall not end, each moment has not begun and shall not end, for this is the nature of consciousness. It is only your perception within this dimension that creates the camouflage of a progression of successive moments. In actuality, all moments are now, and there is no other but now. There is no future; there is no past. All is present. (#307)

Simultaneously, what you would identify as a past life is you, but is not you, for it holds its individual qualities and choices and free will, and it is its own director of its composition, in like manner to you. You are all affecting of each other, for you all are one essence.

Within you, you hold all of the qualities and attributes of all of the other focuses of essence, but they are not expressed within your individual reality, for this is the point of a focus.

A focus is a direction of attention. Therefore, in like manner to yourselves within this particular focus — or what you term to be a lifetime — you may concentrate your attention in one area, and this shall block much of the activity that occurs simultaneously within your reality. But within your perception, you shall view where you hold your attention.

You may physically be occupying a very busy city, and you may be standing upon a very busy corner within your very busy city, and you may be focusing your individual attention, in the midst of all of the activity and action that is occurring about you, upon reading a book, and you shall block all of the stimulus and all of the information and all of the recognition of all of the activity that surrounds you, for your attention is focused upon the book.

Even your physical senses shall block information. Your physical hearing, your sight, your smell, your touch, your taste, shall block all input, for you focus your attention very intently in one direction, and in that action, you are creating a very similar action to the action of essence and focuses.

Each focus holds a direct stream of attention in one area. Therefore, your perception is that you hold one body, that you occupy one time framework, that you occupy one physical location, that you move physically from one location to another, that you move within a time framework. These are all of the elements that you create in focusing your attention singularly in one specific direction. This is a focus. This is what you are creating within your attention presently.

You express to me a greeting and the identification of your name, You express to me, this is you. This is your identification of yourself, and you view yourself to be one singular entity, one male individual. I express to you that this is merely a perception of attention.

In this, your attention focuses a projection into a specific area of physical reality which creates physical matter in conjunction with linear time, and in this creation, your attention moves you throughout this focus and allows you to experience and notice all that you create and all that you encounter and draw to yourself in conjunction with your creations, but it is very singularly focused. Simultaneously, in this one focus's attention, there are myriads of other focuses of attention.

What I am expressing to you is that you ARE essence.

Although I express to you that you are a focus of essence, for the attention of essence is focused in this particular reality, you are no less essence than you are yourself reading your book. You are no less you, merely that you focus your attention reading your book within the midst of your very busy city.

The city continues to be within existence, and it continues to be within YOUR existence, and you continue to be within that reality, but you are not participating in your attention. You are physically participating, but your attention is not participating in all of that reality.

You ARE essence, and your attention is focused in many different areas, and it is occurring all simultaneously. (#486)

Make no mistake; you are reality. You create reality. The reality that you create is your focus. This is the reality that holds your attention. Therefore, within this individual focus, it is of supreme importance; for it is what you identify as you. Understand this clearly; for within our discussions of probabilities, probable selves, alternate focuses, and counterparts, you shall lean automatically to discounting the supreme importance of yourself.

You each hold a belief system, aligned with mass belief systems, of the duplicity of self, and also of the lack of importance of an individual focus. You may view, within your thoughts, that you are an important individual. You may express to each other that you believe you are worthy and important. In actuality, you prove out daily that you do not believe what you express. You wish to believe, but you hold belief systems, aligned with mass belief systems, which discount the individual. Therefore, it is quite easy for you, and also quite automatic for you, to be discounting of the importance of yourself when faced with what you view to be your "greater" self. The word greater does not necessarily denote "better." It is more expansive, for you are more expansive than you realize.

You have been offered an exercise to be focusing upon this attention, to be focusing upon your clarity within this focus[1], in allowing yourselves the ability to hold greater clarity within your awareness of other focuses. I have expressed to you, many times, that you are affecting of all of your focuses, and also, they are affecting of you; for you are them, although they are themselves, but they are also you.

Consciousness is much greater in the terms of expansiveness than you presently, not ever, but presently, possibly understand. There are infinite aspects of consciousness. There are infinite connections; but as you focus singularly, you do not recognize the expansiveness of consciousness, or your own being. I express to you this evening to be allowing yourselves to widen the belief system that you are "less," for you are not. (#126)

Q: You have and many others have said that this particular dimension is very intricately designed, and I feel that I can kind of sense the intricacy of this design. Could you just correlate one, or state a comparative analysis between one dimension and another dimension, how intricate this particular design is? Why is this more intricate than other dimensions? I just want an example. (Pause)

ELIAS: (Slowly and deliberately) I may not necessarily offer you a comparison, but I may express to you that this particular dimension incorporates tremendous diversity. You allow yourselves within this dimension to explore consciousness in similar manner to the natural exploration of consciousness...

Q: By essence?

ELIAS: Yes, but within a physical expression, incorporating an objective awareness. Although there are some physical dimensions that do also incorporate an objective awareness, this particular dimension in its design expresses more of an attention upon the objective expressions and the exploration of what you may create through your abilities in an objective manner.

Consciousness is not a thing. Therefore the expression of generating things is a tremendous exploration. For as essence [and] being not a thing, to generate things from no thing is a challenge, and within this physical dimension the expression of generating physical matter, physical expressions, physical things, is immensely diverse — therefore the tremendous intricacy of this particular dimension.

As I have stated, there are other physical dimensions, and there are other physical dimensions that incorporate objective expressions and awareness.

Now; within those other physical objective dimensions there may be an incorporation of some diversity, but the detail may be less. For each physical dimension is created purposefully to explore consciousness as itself in different directions or, in your terms, for a different point. This particular physical dimension incorporates extreme diversity and attention to detail...

Q: It's been tweaked quite a bit, is that right?

ELIAS: In a manner of speaking, yes — in such detail that you generate this vastness of a universe which in actuality, as I have stated many times previously, is a projection of each individual.

This is a tremendous expression of diversity which is allowed within this particular physical dimension. The attention to detail is so very immense, to the point of incorporating vibrational qualities of color to the smallest speck and to the most immense spectrum. You do not merely incorporate the ability in this physical dimension to generate physical manifestations in relation to the tiniest grain of sand or the vastness of your creation and projection of the universe...

Q: Galaxies.

ELIAS: Correct — but you also offer yourselves tremendous movement of self, of yourselves as consciousness. You allow yourselves the expression of outward projection and folding inward.

Q: In a sense, we can do things that we cannot do as essence. Focuses can do things in a way that is different than what we can do as essence. Is that a true statement?

ELIAS: It is a different expression, yes; but you ARE essence.

Q: I realize; but essence being, we focus here and then we can do those things, yes?

ELIAS: Correct.

Q: Right, right, right. It is beautiful. It is beautiful; it's wonderful.

ELIAS: You are correct. It is an amazing expression of consciousness to generate an intensity of expression of energy and manipulate that energy in a manner that produces a physical display in such wonder from no physical. (#989)

Q: I have a question. I'm a scientist. This is a parallel to the enigma that science has in regard to the fact that according to science, we are a happenstance and a probability that occurred. We the scientists do not believe that everything is consciousness, but that somehow we were unique in the fact that somehow it evolved; consciousness evolved. Then you have talked about links and gestalts of links and various degrees of consciousness; that the can has consciousness and the dog has consciousness and we have consciousness; but yet we have a unique consciousness. We are an energy personality essence that has certain creative and reflective capabilities, and yet we are composed of the same thing that everything else is, of links. What is the magic in the gestalt of links that we are, and why is this kind of development of the links possible? Where does it break, from one being just a non-energy personality essence to one that is? (Pause) That's my serious side again! (Laughter, and Elias grins)

ELIAS: What distinguishes a personality essence is the arrangement of consciousness, but this is a distinguishment in expression and arrangement. It is correct that all manifestations do not possess essence in your terms, but there is no separation within consciousness. Therefore, there is no break point or division between essence and consciousness, for all springs from this consciousness. You refer to the object of a can. This object would not exist had you not created it. Therefore, it is an element of you. Therefore, it is also an element of essence. Within itself, it does not possess essence, but there is no differentiation within consciousness.

Q: It can relate to essence consciousness then?

ELIAS: In a manner of speaking; but this may be confusing to you, for you differentiate. You view consciousness as separated into two factions. One is essence, another is consciousness. There is no separation. There is no dividing factor.

Q: But there is certainly a differentiation!

ELIAS: There is no dividing factor. There are no sections. There is no separation.

Q: It's like simultaneous time, isn't it?

ELIAS: Quite!

Q: Fascinating!

ELIAS: Just as your physical form is a projection of essence, all physical manifestations are a projection from within essence. All of essence is consciousness. Your projections are arrangements of consciousness projected into physical form or matter; into physical elements containing atoms and molecules. Essence *is* consciousness.

Q: The arrangement of links ... does that imply that the links have many attributes and features alike, like faces to a crystal on them? Am I explaining that correctly? They have many different attributes or facets to their characteristics. They have many characteristics, so that they can be used in any reality or in anything. They are everything. Or is this strictly an arrangement that's important?

ELIAS: Links of consciousness hold the quality of versatility, and may rearrange themselves to accommodate any creation. They are ultimately multidimensional. They are also, as all of consciousness, simultaneous. Therefore, they are everywhere at once.

Q: It would not be possible to use one of the inner senses, the expansion and contraction of the tissue capsule, to be able to see a link, would it?

ELIAS: No, for it is not a "thing."

Q: Or to sense it?

ELIAS: Yes, you may sense the action of a link of consciousness, although you will hold no identification for this.

Q: It's just beautiful how everything can be created from these links. It's just fabulous! Oh, and the other question was this: As there are different realities, you wouldn't know if there are different cosmoses with different links, or would you?

ELIAS: Consciousness is consciousness. It may create itself in infinite different actions and manifestations. There are also, within the same space arrangement, infinite universes.

Q: But that is part of this cosmos, the infinite universes. Is there ever a plural to the word cosmos?

ELIAS: There is no end or limitation to consciousness. Therefore, what may be beyond no limitation? You must incorporate an ending or a boundary to incorporate another "thing." There are no boundaries. There is no limitation. It is infinite. (#167)

Q: Is there an infinite source where all energy comes from?

ELIAS: You! (Smiling) Which is quite infinite — unlimited!

Q: So there's no one, greater than all? There's no supreme energy source?

ELIAS: You — you are the supreme energy source and being.

Q: And the reason that I don't know that is so that I can experience this?

ELIAS: Yes, in a manner of speaking, for within this physical dimension you have created veils of separation, and you have forgotten…

Q: But why?

ELIAS: …intentionally to be creating the purity of the experience of exploration in the design of this physical dimension.

Q: Could you say that again?

ELIAS: You have purposefully created veils of separation to allow yourselves to be exploring this physical experience in the purity of it. (#850)

Q: I have a question, Elias, about oneness, how we're trying to become the one consciousness again and not separate from everything. Do you have any suggestions on bringing ourselves back to one?

ELIAS: Let me express to you that within the new rising belief systems — what we term to be the "enlightened era" (grinning) — individuals move in the direction of a new type of separation which is camouflaged with the identification of oneness or wholeness.

Within an actual sense of the term of eliminating the separation, or LESSENING the separation, I express to you that your most efficient movement is to be addressing initially to self, and in this addressing to self, allow yourself to recognize your own belief systems and your own actions of separation, for your own behaviors shall express to you each time you are separating yourself from other individuals and from all that you create within your physical focus.

Let me also express to you that as you manifest within physical focus, there shall always be an element of separation to an extent, for you are choosing to be manifest within a physical dimension. ALL of essence may not be expressed within ANY physical dimension. This is not to say that you do not possess all of essence, but all of essence may not be expressed through physical focus.

Therefore, in a manner of speaking, within physical dimensions, regardless of which physical dimension you are speaking of, there shall always be an element of separation, but as you move more fully into the action of this shift in consciousness, this aspect of separation lessens more and more, and you allow yourselves more and more of a remembrance of essence and therefore more of an incorporation of essence into your physical focus.

In this, as I have been expressing, the greatest movement of this shift is to be accepting of belief systems. I may not be emphasizing this to you enough! As you begin to allow yourselves to move in this direction [of] acceptance of self, trust of self, and addressing to the belief systems that you hold — NOT eliminating these belief systems but addressing to them and accepting them — this shall be the most affecting action that you may incorporate, in your moving in the direction of less separation and incorporating more of an interconnectedness objectively with all that is created within your physical focus.

Let me express to you, I am aware that you view these concepts to be quite elementary and that you view this to be quite simplified. In actuality, these concepts may be your most difficult actions to be accomplishing.

You may move easily in the direction of expressing to yourself and to other individuals, "I am one with my planet. I am one with nature. I am interactive with all other individuals. I am one with all that is within my physical focus, within my universe." These are words easily said. The reality of these words that are so very easily said is not so very easily accomplished, for you have created millenniums of separation. You have created much time framework with many belief systems that reinforce all of your separations.

As you walk upon your physical earth, you may feel a bond to this planet, but you do not view yourself to BE it. You do not feel its rhythms within your physical form as an element of yourself ... not as ITSELF, but as YOURSELF. This is truly a lack of separation!

As you interact with another individual, you do not interact with another individual as yourself. You interact with another individual as separate from yourself, outside and apart, for you view yourselves in physical forms.

You hold a physical form, a physical body. You are a female. You are a certain height, a certain weight, a certain color. You move in certain manners. You grow in certain intervals. You view a tree to be certain height, a certain color, a stationary creation. You view another individual as outside of you, different, separate and apart. You do not view the energy that is intermingled with you all. You view a collective awareness, or what you may term to be a collective consciousness, as some elusive element outside of yourselves. It is not within you. It is some element outside of you that you reach to attain, as if you may grasp this elusive, floating, cosmic element. It is within you! You ARE, in actuality, ALL intertwined and interconnected.

This be the reason that I express to you, as you move in the direction of the influences of many of your belief systems: as you hold a judgment upon any other individual, you ARE placing this judgment upon yourself. For every action that you move in the direction of creating, that you view to be outside of yourself, is merely a mirror objective image of what you create within yourselves. For in actuality, there is no separation. There is only the separation of your objective awareness, your perception within your physical focus. But in actuality, your energies are all intermingled and are not separated. (#320)

... You have created a physical reality which incorporates in its design the expression of separation, which has created an efficient design within this reality in the manner in which you have chosen to be experiencing it.

But you are changing your reality. You ARE incorporating this shift in consciousness quite purposefully. Therefore, you are altering your perception of your physical reality, which in actuality alters the reality itself.

In this alteration of your reality, one of the most important and strongest expressions that you are moving into in altering your perception is dropping this veil of separation, continuing to be manifest with this physical dimension to be experiencing physical manipulation of consciousness, but dropping the veil of separation in the manner in which you have associated with your reality previously.

But this aspect of dropping the veil of separation also creates a TREMENDOUS alteration of your reality, for your association automatically moves in the defining of yourself and any other aspect, any other manifestation, within your dimension as separate entities.

You associate that you are you, a creature is a creature, another individual is another individual, a mountain is a mountain, an ocean is an ocean, a tree is a tree, and all of these are separate entities, and all of these create their own reality, and all of these create their own choices. In relation to consciousness, this is correct; in relation to the links of consciousness, this is correct. In relation to YOU as all of consciousness, this is incorrect, for you as all of consciousness are allowing yourself to focus attention into a physical manifestation.

You are not a separate entity. You are a projection of attention, and in like manner, all that this focus of attention views and interacts with is a creation of that focus of attention. Your physical self that you recognize as an individual, a physical body, is a projection of your attention, and every other aspect of your entire universe is also.

Therefore, you are you, and all that is within your reality is a projection of you also, for it is all created through your perception — other individuals, your creatures, your world, your universe — and each individual is a focus of attention, and each individual is also creating the same action. Therefore, within this one physical dimension, within this one physical reality, there are billions of physical realities being created, all simultaneously, and that is expressed merely in this one moment in this one time framework. There are NUMBERLESS realities being created in this moment in relation to simultaneous time, without the veil of separation of time frameworks.

You view your universe to be one entity and that you are an entity placed within it, and that all other aspects of your reality are other entities placed within your physical universe as separate from yourself.

Q: And placed in it outside of me.

ELIAS: Correct!

Q: The truth is, I've placed them there.

ELIAS: You have created ALL of it. You may look to the billions of individuals that occupy your planet, and each of them is creating what you are creating: their own individual projection of the entirety of their universe. For you are ALL consciousness, and in actuality, there is no separation of consciousness.

In simplistic terms — without moving your thought process into overwhelmingness (Elias smiles) — you move your attention to you, and allow yourself to concentrate your attention upon you and what you are creating, for this is the design of this physical dimension, allowing aspects of consciousness, focuses of attention, to create an entire universe through their perception, and to move and manipulate energy in that physical universe.

Your physical universe may appear similar to [your friend's] but it is not entirely the same, for it is created by you and through your perception. You may, in a manner of speaking, share experiences with [your other friend]. You may choose to be creating similarities of your universes, and within your identifications you may create similar expressions of your creatures, of your environment, but they are not identical, for you create YOUR creatures, she creates her creatures.

Q: And many times they're the same creature, or if we...

ELIAS: You associate that it is the same creature, for this is the design of separation.

This is the mechanics of separation. In actuality, you are creating your perception, which is the projection of your reality.

Therefore, all that exists within your reality is a projection of you, and all that is presented within your reality offers you communication. For the design of this physical dimension, incorporating separation, is that you shall present yourself with numberless reflections of you, for you are the only aspect of your reality that you have forgotten and that you do not know.

Therefore, you present yourself with reflections of yourself continuously. You create reflections of yourself in the magnificence of the design of your physical environment. You create reflections of yourself in challenges and struggles that your creatures may engage. You create reflections of yourself in the majesty of what you identify as your wildlife and its self-sufficiency. You create reflections of yourself in conflicts and confusions with other individuals. You create reflections of yourself in every aspect of your reality, to offer to you communication as to what you are and what you are creating. All of this offers you information, and you efficiently move beyond all of these types of communications through reflections to yourself and offer yourself precise communications within yourself.

You are quite intricate. You create inner senses, you create outer senses. You create impulses, you create impressions, you create emotion, you create physical expressions within your physical body, all of which serve as a communication to you, to precisely identify what you are creating and choosing within each moment of your reality.

Now; the element of separation and lack of acceptance, which are the two movements which you incorporate in this shift, are those that allow you to be redefining how you have been associating with your reality, and allow you a clearer recognition and interpretation of what you are actually creating.

Q: That's the exploration part of interpreting the communication and interpreting the reflection, and not viewing the reflection as something wrong, gone awry. So everything can be viewed as a positive, so to speak, reflection?

ELIAS: In a manner of speaking. As you move more into a genuine expression of acceptance and recognition of a lack of separation, it moves beyond an association of positive, and moves into the neutral. (#766)

Chapter 6

WHAT ABOUT GOD?

"God is not a cosmic entity, sitting and passing judgment upon you from some distant area of consciousness! god is YOU. Your ideas, your concepts of god are all your own projections, mirror images of what you know yourselves to be, and you project this knowing outwardly in an objective manner and create the perception of an element outside of you which you term to be god, and as you battle with self, you also battle with god, for they are synonymous."

(#327)

Chapter 6

WHAT ABOUT GOD?

ELIAS: This evening, we shall engage in a discussion of consciousness. This will also involve subject matter with reference to the Creating Universal One and Whole, for this is consciousness. Think of your present belief systems, which greatly incorporate your scientific technology, and ask yourselves with your rational, logical intellect, how you may arrive at conclusions of an impersonal universe, and elements possessing consciousness, extending from non-conscious matter.

Within your present belief systems, you accept that a cosmic explosion occurred and created your universe, this being completely random and possessing no consciousness. Your world began as gasses, rock, elements not possessing life, to your estimation; and from this, through your belief systems of evolution, you believe that miraculously, somehow, consciousness was incorporated into matter accidentally. If you inquire to me, I will express to you, this possesses no logic. Matter did not appear "cosmically" within this explosion and then create consciousness. Consciousness was; is.

I will express to you that in your terms of viewing in time elements, for you are focused within time, we shall use terminology of "before," which is also now, (smiling) but we shall be indulging of terminology that you may relate to. Therefore, before the organization and orchestration of your universe, as you view it, was consciousness. Before essence, as you interpret it, was the whole. You may use any term you are wishing for this action. I do not use the term "being" purposely, for your term of God or All That Is or The Creating Universal

One and Whole, whatever you choose to call it, is not a being. It is all consciousness. It is an action. It incorporates all. (#79)

As to your relationship with The Creating Universal One And Whole, your word for this essence is insufficient. Your word is god; a very small word for a very small concept! The Universal Whole is all things and part of all things. In relation to creating, you are part of it and it is part of you, but it is greater than its parts. You are creating forces. There is no higher essence than your own. (#6)

God is a focus point. It is a point for you to identify with, in not understanding your separation of your essence. All essences in all manifestations understand, intuitively, that there is more than what is manifest. In this, you must imaginatively create an explanation. Some believe a star to be god. Some create many gods, through natural elements around them. In actuality, these identifications are more correct than your religious focuses with singular gods, for you, in essence, are god. Therefore, everything that is created, all of nature, all elements, all universes, are incorporated in you.

It is, realistically speaking, quite difficult for you, in physical focus, to incorporate this concept. In actuality, this is not only a concept, for this is truth. You may think that you believe that you are god, but even in expressing this verbally, you will find a "twinge" inside of you, for you have been taught that this is quite presumptuous of an individual, to profess to be god! You must be a "lunatic" to be thinking you are god! How amusing [that] we have so many "lunatics" running around, and that these "lunatics" have created so many worlds!

I have expressed to you that the Creating Universal One and Whole is you, but is also more than you, just as you are you in your body, but you are more than you. It has always been!

I am quite aware that all of your established religions profess this same truth, although you do not truly think of this, for you are always thinking in matters of time, of a beginning and an end, and in a forward motion. You cannot help this, for this is what you physically experience. You may conceptually think in other directions, but you do not actually incorporate this in your reality. (#20)

You have been familiarized with the term All That Is. This also is correct in terminology, as to consciousness. There is no singularity of consciousness that may be separated out to be designated as god. Therefore, god did not create your planet, or you. You created you, and you also created your planet and your universe. If you wish to place the terminology of god upon any separate entity, you may apply this term to yourselves, for you are!

All cultures throughout your globe hold the belief system of an "other;" a supreme being; a god. This is an interpretation, which has been modified throughout the centuries, of what became [of] the concept of essence;

for as you moved into physical focus, focused, as you chose the type of experiment within physical focus that you desired to continue, you moved away from memory. In moving away from your memory, you chose to be forgetful of essence, but within you, you continue to hold knowings; small urgings. These are what create your questions, for there are elements within you that you know, but you cannot remember.

Therefore, you ask questions; and when you ask questions, you offer yourselves answers; and within these answers, within your time periods, you take truths, such as essence, that you have forgotten, and translate them into gods. (#138)

In times past within your history, man viewed his connection to consciousness through his manifestation and concepts of gods, or other beings unlike himself. These have taken many forms. Within the culture of your Egyptians, many gods were created in forms other than man. Many gods were created in forms of both man and what you view to be beast, representing the connection of all consciousness. Many cultures have created their images of gods within other images. Your images of totems are a connection, in the same regard as man/beast images expressing man/tree or foliage connection.

Each of these expressions are physical manifestations, only to be representing the lack of separation between man and nature; for there is no separation between man and nature. There are no two elements. In actuality, you need no word "nature," for there is no separate element from yourselves. These gods, or images of gods, served as symbols, but they also held their own reality; for they were realistic focused experimentation within consciousness. (#118)

I shall explain to you that within your history of much time ago, in what you may view to be ancient time periods, your belief systems magnated to objectifying ideas of god within your understanding of self.

It is a projection of your knowing of essence and consciousness. Therefore, within your ancient time periods you will view the belief systems and acknowledgments of many gods, for you held still a recognition partially of the many facets of your essence. Therefore, your interpretation of your god was multiple. As you moved through your history, you also developed intentionally more and more objective focus. As you created a singularity of attention within the focus, you also altered the belief systems, continuing within the projection of your image. Religious belief systems presently express to you that you are created within the image of god. In reality, god is created in the image of you, for it is an inner recognition of a conceptualization of essence.

As you become more singularly focused, so also does your god. As you continue to recognize different aspects of self, you also incorporate this into your belief systems. Many, many religious beliefs throughout your planet — not only your Christianity — incorporate more than one aspect to one godhead, in recognition that you hold aspects of subjective and objective reality within the one you. Therefore, you translate this into a god. This is not wrong, and it is not invalid. It is also not non — reality, for all that you create within your belief systems within this dimension and this attention IS reality.

Therefore, as I have expressed to you all previously, in acceptance of belief systems there is a recognition that it matters not what you hold objectively within your belief systems. One is no greater or lesser or better or worse than another, and as you recognize that you are all one and that there is no separation ...

there is no difference in your belief system of your god as that of another individual that may view a god within a rock or another individual that may view no god or an individual that views god as themselves, for within actuality, you are! (#185)

You view god, within most of your religions within your globe, to be of male orientation, for this symbolizes, to you, power. As I have expressed to you previously, you view your gods as expressions within your own image. God has not created you in his image, for there is no "he"! You have created *him*, within your image, also creating your religious elements to be surrounding of this image of this all-powerful god. (#100)

You incorporate all the same as this action of god. You are the same; but it is more. It is more than the sum of all of the dimensions, of all of the universes, of all of the parts; but without you, it would not be either. Therefore, no separation, for you also are intimately a part. You incorporate your own individuality, your own intent, your own desires and focus; but you also incorporate all of it, and it possess, so to speak, all of you. No one element, to the most minute unit of consciousness, is any less than another. Therefore, there is no contradiction in expressing to you that you each, within your individuality, are the center of the universe; for this is true.

God is an experience. It is a movement; an action; all encompassing. All consciousness springs from it. (#79)

Chapter 7

WHAT IS TRUTH?

"Truths are absolutes. Truths are those elements which are not confined to one focus, or to one dimension, or to one reality. Truths are those elements of consciousness that are filtered through all of consciousness." (#137)

Chapter 7

WHAT IS TRUTH?

ELIAS: There are truths within consciousness, but as I have stated previously many times, these are not viewed by yourselves within physical focus as holding tremendous meaning, for your belief systems dictate to you what you think of as truths in many different areas.

Color is a truth. Tone is a truth. Energy is a truth. Consciousness and essence are truths. Reality is a truth. These are all constants within all that is. Any aspect, any element that is a constant which occupies every area of consciousness may be defined as a truth. Not all that you view within your belief systems and within your reality within this dimension are truths, for they are relative merely to this dimension and this reality.

You look to many elements in this particular dimension as being constants and as being truths, for you define this reality as "universal," meaning that this universe encompasses all of reality, which it does not. There are many universes within universes within many different dimensions which are all occurring simultaneously, and as I have expressed, all of your space arrangements, all of your dimensions are within each other.

All dimensions, all universes occupy the same space arrangements. They are configured differently, but they are all superimposed upon each other. They are merely veiled from each other. (#288)

You do not accept many realities that are truth, for you do not understand. As I have stated previously, truth within your focus is inconsequential. Your belief systems are consequential! You do not rule your lives by truth, although you think you do!

But I shall venture to express that I know not any individual that rules their life and their focus by color vibration!

I know not any individual physically focused that directs the entirety of their life within the truth of tone! These are truths. They are, within physical focus, inconsequential. Your belief systems are your gauge. Your belief systems, once again, are not bad, are not wrong. They ARE. (#147)

You shall become aware that I speak of truths seldom, for truths are constants and absolutes throughout all of consciousness, which within any particular dimension, they are not recognized. They are distorted and not completely understood, and the importance placed on them is little.

You search for truths within your beliefs and you look to philosophical areas or religious areas. Truths within consciousness are those elements of consciousness that are within ALL dimensions and that hold an element of significance within ALL areas of consciousness, physical and non-physical. Their translation may be different, but they are constants. (#275)

Q: I don't really view that there is a right and wrong as far as everyone else is concerned. I have my own views, but I understand that they're different for everybody, so that's not a hard concept for me. But the concept of there being a truth, it's kind of contradictory to me.

ELIAS: You do not understand, for within this physical focus the truths within the mass belief systems are inconsequential.

The mass belief systems attach the idea of truth to belief systems. These are not truths. Truths are unchanging and are relative to all areas of consciousness, not merely this dimension. Therefore, the constants that are in actuality truths are not recognized by the masses within physical focuses, not only this particular physical focus and dimension but within any physical manifestation.

Truths are not regarded in actuality with much value. Truths are those elements of which we have spoken previously – of consciousness and energy and tone and color and dimension and essence – but individuals within physical focuses attach the term truth to beliefs that they hold to be true and right.

What you view within physical focus is quite changing. Your facts are not truths, for they also are changing. Your own truths within belief systems are changing within your own time periods, within different societies.

Therefore, recognize that what the masses identify as truths are not. They are belief systems that they hold to be true, for they are elements of their reality. They are real, but they are not truths. They are inconstants. Truths shall be valued outside of the context of physical focus, where you hold no moral belief systems and no scientific belief systems. All ideas, thoughts, expressions, manifestations, are reality. This is not the same as truth, although truth is reality also, but they are not synonymous.

It is most amusing to be listening with individuals within our forum exploring their ideas of truths and wishing for examples of truths to be offered to them, for they shall not value those truths which are offered! They do not understand that these are constants within consciousness, not changing regardless of any area or focus of consciousness and manifestation and reality. They are wishing to be told that truths hold moral value, which they do not, for your moral value within your dimension holds no meaning within another dimension.

Within your own dimension within different societies, your moral truths hold no meaning for other societies. Therefore, they are inconstant. How may they be truths? They are not absolute. (#172)

Q: I know that through all of the sessions you have mentioned certain truths, and I would just like to hear sort of a run-down of the truths that have come up in our sessions, as opposed to belief systems. I'm aware of some, but I know I've missed some as well. You could give me some that you haven't talked about too, if you want!

ELIAS: Some truths. (Pause) Truths are constants that may not be eliminated or annihilated. Energy is a truth. Color is a truth. Vibration is a truth. Reality is a truth. You creating your reality is a truth. Consciousness and its different areas of awareness are truths. You are a truth. Belief systems incorporate a much wider area, for they incorporate much imagination, but even within this you incorporate truth, for all thought becomes imagination and all thought is energy, which is truth, which is also reality. Therefore, all imagination is a reality, which is also a truth! (Smiling)

Q: I guess I didn't want to be that confused! (Laughter)

ELIAS: Belief systems are those inventions that you create to explain what you do not understand. Truths are unchanging. Reality is a truth, but your viewing of reality is a belief system.

Q: I knew that!

ELIAS: (Humorously) I was already sure that you did! I am sure this was not much helpfulness to you, but if you are wishing to be spending a few eons with me, I may explain to you truths. Amazing, how one small word within your language incorporates such vast amounts of knowledge!

I will say to you that all of the truths are within you and accessible to you, and that you may find these truths yourselves. Do not take what another essence expresses to you unquestioningly as truth. You possess the truths already. Do not be misled by belief systems, which are incorporated by others to be misleading. I do not ask that you believe me. I instruct that you believe YOU! This will lead you to your truths, and you will not let you down, so to speak. (#45)

Q: Is love just something that we perceive? Is love a real thing? It's a feeling so it must be real, but with love we have all of these associations of love being good, and yet there is no good or bad. Can you define or explain or give us some understanding of the word and the feeling, and what love is? Is love a truth?

ELIAS: What you express within physical focus of love is an interpretation. Love is a reality. Love is a truth. This spans all dimensions, all areas of consciousness, all reality. Each dimension and physical focus holds its own individual interpretation of the action of love. Your interpretation of love within this dimension is a feeling. You also attach many, many, many belief systems to this concept. In actuality, love, being a truth, is dimensional; as color and tone. It holds many aspects of its own. You view this word as an emotion, a feeling, sometimes as an action. It is a dimensional quality of consciousness; a truth in itself. It holds its own integrity, as we have spoken earlier.

Within this dimension, you hold many interpretations and definitions of love. Within this dimension, you may experience an aspect of the reality of the action of this truth, although it is not frequently experienced; for in experiencing the true action of this reality and truth you must allow yourself, within your time framework, a momentary time devoid of belief systems and attachments, which may temporarily occur. This also is requiring of ultimate trustfulness. I express to you that you shall experience this only momentarily within physical focus, for this is the extent of the time framework that you shall hold the ability to hold the focus of the experience. Few individuals within physical focus experience this type of action.

You, within your definitions, would explain this action within emotional terms, and express elation within its true form. Few individuals experience this.

But as to your questioning of its validity and its reality, yes. This is a truth. This is a reality. It is unbounded by dimension or area of consciousness. It is only Interpreted and represented differently within different dimensions. Therefore, it is experienced differently; although as I have been explaining presently, if you are allowing yourself to be, within a moment, devoid of belief systems and open to the experience of the action of this truth, this also transcends dimensional elements; for each dimension shall experience the same action, achieving that particular moment in that event. Therefore, your interpretation of love is no matter, for within another dimension their interpretation of love may be quite different from your own, but their experience, given the proper allowance, shall be the same.

Q: So is hate a truth too?

ELIAS: No.

Q: So love is a truth of essence? Love is a truth that is part of essence? It exists as a part of essence?

ELIAS: It is a truth, period.

Q: Okay, and you defined it largely as an action.

ELIAS: Correct.

Q: As we see it as a feeling, that's somewhat of a mislabeling.

ELIAS: Not necessarily. This is your interpretation within this dimension within this physical creation, just as you interpret Source Events into physical actuality within mass events and individual events. These are realities also. They do not encompass the entirety of the Source Event, for it does not fit within the framework and confines of your physical reality; just as truths do not fit within the confines and framework of any physical reality, for they are boundless. All truths are dimensional, and action.

Q: So in that love is largely an action while it's also a truth, it's something that you choose because action implies choice.

Q2: Does it?

Q: To me it does! (Elias grins) Well, if we create our reality and that reality is making choices and all that we are is those choices, then doesn't love exist within our reality as a choice?

ELIAS: You are placing this within confines. The entirety of your reality is not based upon your choices merely. (Pause)

Q: Okay …

ELIAS: All of consciousness is action. (Longer pause)

Q: And? (Pause) That's all I get for now, huh? (Laughter)

ELIAS: (Smiling) You are limiting your thought process, boxing this concept into confines that you believe you may understand. Truths, in actuality, are beyond your complete understanding within an individual physical focus. Within essence, within the entirety of you, you hold the understanding; but within any given individual physical focus, the completeness of understanding of any truth is beyond your ability to comprehend.

All of consciousness is motion. All of consciousness is action. You are accustomed to viewing reality, as I have stated, as things. You individualize and objectify your reality, and you classify into things. This is how you perceive your reality. This works quite well within this given reality. This is not to say that it is the entirety of reality. It is not. Within consciousness, energy is not defined as things. Therefore, truths are not defined as things. It is difficult to convey to you, within the confines of your language, an adequate explanation.

I express to you that color is a truth. I am quite aware that within your thought processes, this registers as a thing. You may physically view what you think of as color, what you define as color. What you think of and what you define as color, within this dimension and physical focus, is an interpretation of a truth. It is, once again, a thing in itself, and it also is a symbol. You perceive the symbol. You view different colors that you attach words within your language to, such as red, pink, blue, green. You also attach vibrational qualities to these colors.

Within a greater reality, so to speak, color is an action and it is dimensional. Love is an action and it is dimensional. To your way of thinking, you may accept that color is dimensional, but you do not understand how it may be an action. To your way of thinking, you may accept that love is an action, but how may it be dimensional?

These seem to be inconsistencies, but outside of the singularity of physical attention, reality is quite expanded and unbounded. All of energy, all of consciousness, is motion. It is all a state of becoming. Therefore, so also are truths actions and states of becoming.

Q: Would it be fair to say that all emotions, like hate and joy and sorrow, are just objective interpretations or misinterpretations of the action that you just described as love?

ELIAS: Not misinterpretations; but yes, interpretations relative to your physical focus. I have expressed to you recently that there are existences, dimensions that do not incorporate emotion as do you. Their existence provides for value fulfillment equal to your own but within a different framework, for they have chosen a different experience. You have chosen a different experience. You have created many different dimensions for different physical expressions and experiences. Therefore, as you interpret emotion, this is relative to certain physical focuses. You are not the only physical focus that experiences and incorporates emotion, but all do not experience this creation. Therefore, when you express, "Is hate a truth?" No. This is an emotion which is relative to physical focus. This is a direct influence of belief systems. There is a difference between creations which have sprung from belief systems and truths which are interpreted through belief systems.

Q: So that makes love a fundamental, unlike all of our other emotions, a fundamental action of what I will say is the universe, but of consciousness. It is a fundamental aspect of being, as opposed to any of the other emotions that we feel. The conversation we had during break was almost a question of its importance relative to being. You're saying that love ... In the few weeks I've been here, you've used the word truth in relation to the things we've talked about very few times. If you're using love and describing that as a truth, then that says to me that its importance in terms of being is fundamental in all dimensions.

ELIAS: Correct.

Q: Well, that's pretty important!

ELIAS: Correct.

Q: I want to clarify a term. When you say love is dimensional and color is dimensional, does that mean multidimensional?

ELIAS: Correct.

Q: However, if I understand what you're saying when you say that love is a truth, that does not mean that our typical interpretations of love and descriptions of love are truth.

Q2: Right. Those are our interpretations, but it is a fundamental truth of being.

Q: Right, which we have very little understanding of, if I heard correctly. So the characteristics that we impose upon love are not necessarily accurate. They're not necessarily the picture. They are not the truth. The truth of love is something apart from the character that we give it.

ELIAS: This is not to diminish the reality of your interpretation!

Q: Okay, but the point being that lots of people equate love and hate as sort of equal counterparts to one another based on your definition, that would not be true because...

ELIAS: Correct.

Q: ... love is a truth and hate is an emotion filtered through belief systems. So love is not technically something that is filtered through belief systems, but our description of what we perceive to be love is filtered through belief systems, correct? So love is something truly apart from that, that we don't particularly understand very well and that we take an awful lot of liberties describing, and whether some of those liberties are valid or not is a separate discussion

ELIAS: You approach dangerous area! (Much laughter)

I take great issue with discounting of your creation, for you are quite accomplished and adept at discounting your creations and invalidating yourselves! Your creations are interpretations, but they are reality. They are not to be discounted. Your interpretation of a truth may be an interpretation in terms of consciousness non — physically focused within its entirety, but your interpretation of a truth within physical focus is reality. It also is not negative. It also is, IS, creative! (#152)

Q: I have a question for Michael tonight too. I almost forgot. Do you view yourself as a pragmatist?

ELIAS: (Laughing) I will express to Michael that in one respect, I will be saying affirmative; but there also is a key point, within pragmatism, to which I know differently; this being that you will find that your pragmatists view truth as relative. Truth, in this philosophy, is dependent upon experience. I express to you that there are truths that are unchanging. A pragmatist incorporates all of philosophy, and creates their own truth relative to their experience; but not beyond.

There are truths beyond physical experience; constants that are, within themselves, a priori, to which a pragmatist does not subscribe; but with the acceptance of reality, and also those things beyond physical reality, yes. I would agree to this. You may express to Michael that I am quite knowing that he incorporates the philosophy of pragmatism, as does also Ron, as do also many of you. Your truths, you believe, are based upon your experiences; and as they hold to be efficient, you hold them to be truthful. (Pause) I will express to you also that your view of efficiency is distorted.

Q: Can you explain that?

ELIAS: You view efficiency as what may be easiest. You believe this to be expedient. What you incorporate within physical focus may not always be your easiest path, so to speak, but it may be your most efficient for your intent. You may incorporate action which is needing of some effort initially, for you have trained yourselves within one direction. But within your action, your effortlessness comes.

Therefore, the pragmatist views the experiences as being true, if they are efficient, temporarily, but once another philosophy introduces itself and they are viewing this as efficient also, they are inclined to be discontinuing in one and moving to another, much as a leaf blowing through the wind. It incorporates effortlessness in allowing the wind to carry it, but it does not direct itself. In this same way, the pragmatist floats with what he views to be an efficient philosophy on a temporary basis.

I express to you that there are truths which are unchanging. Pragmatists do not believe in unchanging truths. All things to the pragmatist are changing, even truths. There is no truth within pragmatism! They are very aware of this fact, which they also incorporate quite well! Facts are very much within their focus. If a fact is presented, it is accepted.

Facts are changing. Truths are not. Throughout your history, many facts have changed! Within your present time, facts are changing! You will be learning, not from me but from those around you and from what you incorporate around you, that many elements of your reality are changing, but these are facts! Your scientists incorporate them as fact! You also incorporate them as fact. They are learning that their facts are not so "factual"! (Grinning)

Q: Is that because of the simultaneous time, and the changing of probabilities, would ultimately change the facts?

ELIAS: Correct. (Pause)

You do not incorporate a basic understanding of what and who you are. Therefore, how do you determine to understand what you have created within a universe? You do incorporate what you choose to call genius minds. All of you possess genius minds, but you look to these individuals as your geniuses, who connect slightly more, momentarily, with some information. They offer this information to you as great revelations of fact. They are, through their most powerful and magnificently gigantic scopes, viewing a pinpoint of reality!

You are all multidimensional creatures, and you study one dimension! Therefore, you base facts upon one dimension, and you express these as temporary truths. There are myriads of dimensions! Are you understanding of "time is meaningless?"

Q: I try!

ELIAS: No! Are you understanding that all space is here? No! Do you view other dimensions? No! Therefore, how can you base truths and facts upon one dimension? (Pause)

Your own outer senses, to which you trust in viewing a table or a wall, prove you to be perceiving, and prove themselves to be truthful to you; but you do not incorporate a trustfulness of these same senses when you are viewing another visualization of yourself! You are hallucinating, or your eyes are crossing, or you are being very creatively imagining! (Grinning at everybody) Your self is your truest reflection to you; but you reach, still, for objective facts. When your scientists learn to be reversing their focus to be examining subjective reality, they will more incorporate truthfulness than looking to the object outside! Just as your wider awarenesses go in, and in, and in! (#65)

Chapter 8

A DIVINE PLAN

*"There are no closed systems. There are no absolutes
that may not be altered within probabilities."*

(#185)

Chapter 8

A DIVINE PLAN

Q: Is there such a thing as a divine plan for every one of us on this earth at this time? Like individually, do we each have a divine plan already set for us?

ELIAS: Interesting question! Let me express to you that within the accepted belief systems within your dimension, you create many different words for different aspects of your reality. Essentially, many of these concepts are the same and hold the same meaning, but they also hold elements of distortion, for they are influenced by your belief systems.

In this particular question, you express an inquiry of a divine plan. In a manner of speaking, I may answer you with yes, for YOU are divine and you have created your own plan, in a manner of speaking.

Let me express to you that your plan, so to speak, is in actuality a line of probabilities that YOU create as you enter into physical focus. In this, as you choose to be entering into this dimension and physically manifesting, you create a line of probabilities that you potentially shall follow.

Now; let me also express to you that there are no absolutes. Therefore, you may be creating of any line of probabilities, and you may also be altering these probabilities at any given moment within your focus. You may also move outside of your own individual pool of probabilities and be incorporating other probabilities that you may view to be unlikely into your pool of probabilities.

These are situations that individuals move into within an individual focus, where you view the individual to be creating very unusual choices or circumstances within their focus. They may be moving in one specific type of direction throughout most of their focus, and suddenly they are altering the entirety of their focus and moving in a completely different direction. This would be a situation of pulling probabilities from outside of their individual pool of probabilities.

You each create a pool of probabilities as you enter into a physical focus. Probabilities are created within the moment. The pool of probabilities is a pool of potentiality. It is not a pool of actual events or choices that lie before you that you may choose from. It is an area of potentiality, and in this potentiality you may move in any direction of which you choose in creating your own probabilities.

Each probability is created within the moment. It does not lie before you. It is not as a tree with thousands of leaves, each representing a different probability, that you may pick one probability and actualize that one within your physical focus. The probabilities are actualized within each moment, but within the potentiality in the pool of probabilities and the immaculateness of your creations, all of the probabilities that you create within a focus fit together perfectly as an immaculate puzzle with no mistakes. Although you view that you are creating mistakes within your focus, you are not, for each choice that you are creating of, regardless of your own judgment of your choices, is perfectly chosen to be creating of a certain direction and moving you within your pool of probabilities to be creating of certain events and certain action and certain directedness in your focus, to move you in the directions of your specific intent within your individual focus.

THIS would be your divine path, for you are the god! And in this, YOU be the divine being creating of your own line, which is what you term in your terminology to be your path, and you are creating of all of the avenues that steer you along your path, so to speak.

I do not express this to be a path, for this is reinforcing of the held belief systems within physical focus that you are placed upon this planet by some cosmic power outside of yourselves, and you are destined to be following a path, and upon this path you are certainly upon a mission! (Grinning) No, you are not!

YOU have created this physical focus. You manipulate EVERY THING within this physical focus. Every creation upon this planet, every molecule of this universe, YOU have created and continue to create and are manipulating all of these elements as your theater, and you are all your own directors and this is your forum, your theater that you create your own play within. You have created this physical dimension to be experiencing. This, if you must be moving in the direction of holding a mission, would be your mission, to be experiencing.

This particular dimension focuses its attention upon physical creation for the experience of emotion and sexuality, and this is reflected in every aspect of your creations. Every element within your dimension holds an attachment of gender, and you project emotion into every aspect of your focus, for this is what you have designed this particular dimension to be experiencing. There are countless physical dimensions, this being merely one, and in this particular one, this is the direction that you have created. (#324)

In this, as you look to an individual focus, such as yourself, you choose within essence to be manifest as a focus of essence, a focus of attention, into one particular manifestation, one time framework, one location, one particular objective reality, and as you move through that one particular focus, you create lines of probabilities.

As I have expressed previously, as you choose to be manifest within physical reality, you enter that physical reality holding what may be termed as a pool of probabilities that you allow yourself to draw upon, and in this, there are many lines of probabilities that you allow yourself to choose from, in a manner of speaking.

This is quite figurative, for be remembering that all probabilities are created and actualized within the moment. They are not an element or a thing that is set before you or in front of you that you choose from. But in this, as you enter into a physical manifestation in one focus, you hold this pool of probabilities, and in this pool of probabilities, there are, as I have stated, many different lines of probabilities that you choose. (#481)

What you create within probabilities is a line. You purposefully create this line of probabilities in the same manner that you may engage your writing implement, your pencil, and as you draw a line upon your paper, the lead is creating of the line as you move the pencil. The line does not extend beyond before the pencil is moved to draw it. In this same manner you create probabilities, and in your creation of probabilities within each moment, you create those probabilities which are the most efficient for your attention.

You do not create mistakes. You BELIEVE you create mistakes, but you do not create mistakes within your creations of your lines of probabilities. You create each choice, each probability, in the manner that it shall gain your attention most efficiently.

Now; in this creation of these probabilities, not all of your probabilities that you create appear to you to be comfortable or appear to you to be good in your belief systems, but they are beneficial, for they attain your attention and they offer you information in the direction of your intent.

You may not hold an entire awareness objectively in understanding of what you are creating and how your probabilities fit together *immaculately* but they do fit together immaculately, and they are not mistakes. They are the most efficient choices and actions for each of your creations in each of your individual attentions. Therefore, you may place belief systems upon these actions. You may question.

But this also is the point of this shift in consciousness, that you may view objectively and understand and KNOW of your creations within your probabilities, within your line of probabilities, what you are creating and how you are creating of all of these choices, which also offers you more efficient choices within your belief systems. (#275)

Each line of probabilities that you choose to be actualizing in this particular physical dimension and objective reality creates a specific direction, and as you choose a specific direction, you also are NOT choosing to be inserting into this objective reality many other choices, but all choices are actualized. They are merely not all actualized in this one objective reality, for this is the manner in which you have created this particular physical reality.

Therefore, as you move through your individual focus and you create what you view as large or direction — altering choices within your focus, you also are creating, simultaneously, probable realities.

Now; these probable realities are directly related to the physical reality that you are experiencing, and they are actualizing the choices that you have chosen NOT to be inserting into your physical objective reality. Therefore, as an example, as you choose to be actualizing one probability of engaging an intimate relationship in partnership with another individual and you choose to be moving in a direction of probabilities with that individual, you each also are creating probable realities with probable selves that are creating many, many different choices that you have NOT chosen to insert into your objective physical reality.

This creates a type of parallel dimension in which you have created another you, which shall continue and shall be creating different choices from the choices that you view that you choose, but shall appear almost identical to you. Certain qualities of the probable self shall be different, but many of the manifestations of the probable self shall be the same as you.

In a manner of speaking, this is a type of action that you create within your physical focus which may be likened to the creation of clones. You create a clone of yourself and insert this into a probable reality, which becomes a probable dimension or parallel dimension to the dimension that you are experiencing, and from that point, that probable self holds its own individual identity and reality.

Now; realize that to that point, prior to that point, that probable self was not a probable self yet. It was an element of you, an aspect of you, an alternate self of you. At the moment that you choose an alteration in your direction within your physical reality, within your focus, you also create, figuratively speaking, a type of split, and in this split, you create the movement of a particular aspect of yourself, of this individual focus, which moves away from you — or what you recognize as you — and is inserted as almost a separate entity into a parallel reality.

Now; this parallel reality parallels your reality in the existence of its past, for its past shall immediately and simultaneously be created within that moment, for it has already experienced its past, for it is you. Its future and its present may deviate and may not necessarily continue in a parallel line, for at the moment of the choice or the figurative split, the probable self now holds its own reality and it creates its own choices, and it moves futurely within linear time framework into its own reality and shall hold its individual free will and personality and choices.

Therefore, this would be the distinction that is created between an actual parallel dimension, which is not a probable dimension, and a probable dimension holding probable reality and probable selves.

In this, the probable reality holds the ability to be moving away from a parallel line in its creations, and may be creating choices that in actuality are quite different from your choices, and in this, in like manner to yourself, it may also choose to be quite altering of its individual choices and personality expression, dependent upon its individual creations.

Q: Okay. Now, what attachment do I have to a probable self, if any?

ELIAS: I express to you that probable selves continue to be affecting within energy and interconnected with you in energy in similar manner to other focuses.

Other focuses hold their own personality and choices and individuality and identity, in a manner of speaking, and they exchange energy with you continuously and are in different manners affecting of you, as you are with them. In similar manner, you continue to be interconnected with probable selves and you continue to be sharing and exchanging energy with probable selves. Therefore, you continue to be affecting of each other.

For example, a probable self may be creating of a traumatic experience within their focus, and in this, as you are interconnected —for this is a probable self of yourself — you may feel, in a manner of speaking, an effect of this creation within the probable self's reality.

Example: Let us hypothetically express that you create a choice to engage in marriage in this reality, and in this, we shall temporarily skip over the probable self that would be created in that choice of direction. Subsequently, you move through your focus and you engage in the action of participating in facilitating entering focuses.

In physical terms, you engage children within your relationship. You become a father, in your very physical terms. You move through your focus, and you hold the reality of a family with three children. At a point in this reality, you choose to be engaging a fourth child.

Now; in that moment, you create a probable self which chooses not to be engaging a fourth child, but holds the three children in like manner to yourself, for its past parallels your past, for its past IS your past. Therefore, it already holds the experiences that you hold.

Now; in choosing different choices, as you move from that point, you engage the family of four children. The probable self engages the family of three children. You continue within your family of four children, and let us express that the probable self engages a situation in which one of the existing three children in that reality disengages; not one of your three children disengages, but one of those three children within the probable reality disengages.

The father, let us hypothetically express, becomes quite distraught and is experiencing trauma in this situation, and tremendous grief. This may be translated into your reality in a momentary expression of a feeling of concern for the same child within your reality, although no objective situation is occurring within your particular reality to be creating concern within you, but you feel momentarily a twinge of concern or grief or fear with respect to that particular child.

This is the translation of energy that exchanges between these probable realities.

Therefore, you may view that you continue to be affecting of each other, although you may not identify necessarily objectively the affectingness, for unlike another focus of yourself, which may continue to be quite influencing of you within an ongoing linear time framework, a probable self shall be momentarily affecting of you within an objective expression.

Another focus may be experiencing a situation of tremendous fearfulness in a scenario of drowning, and this may translate in energy within your focus of a tremendous ongoing fear of water, and this may continue for many years within your focus if you are not allowing yourself to be accessing that information and reconfiguring that energy.

But within the experience of a probable self, they may be experiencing the scenario of drowning, and you may momentarily lose your breath or you may experience a momentary anxiety or fearfulness in your movement into water, but you shall also dismiss this, for there is an immediate subjective identification that this is an experience and an exchange of energy which is occurring within a probable self, and it is unnecessary for you to be experiencing this also and continuing within that experience, for you ARE experiencing it already within the probable self.

Q: So basically, within a single focus, there are actually a myriad of individuals, each operating independently, creating their own realities in a multitude of dimensions. Is that correct?

ELIAS: Yes, you are correct, and within this objective physical reality that you recognize, that you identify you within, there are myriads of aspects of you which are participating also; not within parallel or probable dimensions or realities, but within THIS objective reality that you recognize.

Q: But they're not probables.

ELIAS: No. These are aspects of you. These are alternate selves, which is quite different. These are all the you's of you which are held presently within the now, within your recognized reality. They are all of the aspects of your individual focus, and they are not separated from you. They are continuously interactive and expressing and they are continuously experiencing.

You merely view yourself as one singular individual, but you are not. You are countless individuals simultaneously. You view yourself as one individual body. You are myriads of physical manifestation.

Q: Now, an aspect of myself, of my own probable self, with myself being a probable, which is naturally what I would be, then an aspect of myself would be my past selves as well as my future selves. Am I right?

ELIAS: Yes.

Q: Okay, and they all exist now, within their own nows, within an eternal now.

ELIAS: Yes. It is the picture of the painter creating the self portrait through the mirror, and the mirror, and the mirror, and the mirror, which extends endlessly. (Smiling)

Q: Sort of like a kaleidoscope.

ELIAS: Correct. (#481)

Q: If all these probabilities exist at once, then what is the true purpose of materializing them into physical reality?

ELIAS: Let us look to the creation of physical reality. It is as a game. Consciousness holds a tremendous attention in the area of exploration. It also holds a tremendous quality of playfulness and curiosity. Consciousness is curious to all that may be continuously explored and created. Therefore, you create physical realities, and in creating physical realities, you offer yourself a different type of exploration, a different type of creation and expression.

Therefore, in this, I express to you that creating within physical terms in physical dimensions is — in a manner of speaking — a playful, artful, creative expression for exploration. You at times within physical focus, as you have disassociated yourselves from your own remembrance, are forgetful of this element of your creation. But presently, as you move into more of the action of this shift, you begin to offer yourself the remembrance of all of these elements.

Now; as to probabilities, they are — in a manner of speaking — an element of exploration and experimentation. You insert into physical realities for you have chosen to be creating physical realities, and in this, you create within physical realities what is natural to you. Within all of consciousness, probabilities are continuously being created, for probabilities may be expressed as merely another term for choice. Therefore, as you are creating continuously within consciousness and within essence, you are also continuously creating choice and probabilities.

In this, you create in like manner within your physical dimensions, but within physical dimensions, you have purposefully created a singularity.

You have directed your attention singularly to be experiencing certain types of creations. In this, you choose certain probabilities and you insert them into your reality, individually and collectively.

Be remembering that physical realities, in a manner of speaking, do hold their limitations, for they are physical and you are creating within a specific medium, so to speak, in like manner to different expressions of artists. They create within specific mediums. You may not be creating an element of pottery merely from paint that you shall apply to a canvas, for you are creating within different mediums. Therefore, you have chosen to be creating within the medium of physical matter and physical reality, and in this, you have also chosen to be inserting probabilities in a singular manner physically.

Now; be also understanding that although you choose a probability and you may be inserting one expression of that probability into your physical reality, it extends far beyond this throughout consciousness and is created and expressed all simultaneously.

Therefore, you are merely expressing one element of probabilities into your physical reality in singular manner of attention, which moves quite harmoniously and in like manner to how you are creating of all of your reality within this particular dimension. You do not physically create the expression of all the aspects of yourself visually, and you hold countless aspects of yourself. You create one physical form. In like manner, you choose to be creating the choice of one expression within each moment of a probability, and allow all of the other expressions of that particular probability to be actualized within other areas of consciousness, inserting merely one into this physical reality, but you are continuing to be experiencing all of these aspects of probabilities and all of the realities, physical and nonphysical. This is just merely one area of attention. (#408)

Q: What is the nature of choice, in regard to the differences between choices we're aware of versus choices we're not aware of?

ELIAS: Ah, so you hold choices that you implement that you are NOT aware of? (Grinning)

Q: It appears so! (Laughter)

ELIAS: And I may express to you, what choices are you implementing that you are not aware of, that some other entity or hidden aspect of yourself is creating of without your permission?

Q: Well, I believe I was referring to objective awareness. For example, you choose your parents, you choose your probabilities ... things that a lot of us are not objectively aware of within the concept of choice.

ELIAS: As I have stated previously, your objective and subjective awarenesses, although [they] may be separated by a veil, DO move in harmony with each other and are not independent of each other.

In this, I have also expressed to you previously that if you are manipulating your attention within the moment of the now, you also shall offer yourself the awareness of your choices, be they what you may term to be subjective or objective.

You are assuming that there are choices that you create within physical focus — and probabilities that you create — that you hold no objective awareness of, and these are created within your subjective awareness only.

This would be where your belief in your subconscious stems from — that you believe there is an area of yourself which is removed from your awareness, that is inaccessible to you, and that may be controlling of your choices and creating of certain elements of your reality without your agreement — and this moves you into the aspect of your control and also moves you into the aspect of victimization, for these are elements that you do not control and that you do not create. Another aspect which is not within your control is creating of elements of your reality FOR you. These are all aspects of that there exists some element or aspect or entity outside of you that may be attained to.

In actuality, as I have expressed to you previously, if you are focusing your attention within the individual moments of your objective reality within the now, you shall offer yourself the objective awareness of what you are creating.

In like manner to our previous discussion that you have created automatic responses, you need not engage the action of manipulating energy in the area of creating thought in certain actions that you choose, for you have already created automatic responses. Therefore, you have provided yourselves with your "short cut," and you bypass your creation of your thought process. This, in your creating, creates within a time framework a faster response to elements within your reality.

In like manner, you do not pay attention to all that you are choosing within your objective awareness. This also be the reason that I have offered you your exercise in clarity, that you may attune your objective awareness more clearly, that you may offer yourselves the opportunity to be manipulating that which you automatically create that you do not perceive, for you bypass. You do not pay attention to what you are creating.

It is not that these elements of your creations, your choices, are hidden from you. It is not that you do not hold an objective awareness of your choices. You are merely skipping shells. You are bypassing certain elements of your creations and not paying attention to all that you create, in very like manner to your physical outer senses. You do not pay attention to how you manipulate your physical outer senses. You do not pay attention to your physical manipulation of your physical form. You do not create a thought process, "walk," you merely walk.

You do not objectively manipulate energy in the area of thought or direction in what you think of as an objective manner, for your thought process magnates to choices as thoughts. Your thought process in itself identifies by itself and with projections of itself. It offers itself its own translations.

Thought is reality. This reality identifies by itself, and in this, if you hold no thought process in the area of your choices, you assume that you are not creating your choices or that you are not aware of your creation of your choices, but you ARE aware of your creation of your choices, in ALL of your choices. You merely are not noticing. You are not paying attention.

And we return to our first word, noticing, which remains our banner word; that of noticing. You do not notice your breathing process. Therefore, are you not choosing to breathe? You ARE choosing to breathe, but you are not THINKING of your breathing, for you are by passing your thought process and you are creating an automatic response. You create many automatic responses within physical focus.

This correlates with energy vibration. What is familiar to you is faster vibration, for non-physical vibration of an essence is faster, and this is familiar to you. Therefore, even within physical focus and given your separation and forgetfulness, you hold the knowing of essence, and in this knowing you also mirror physical expressions of essence in many, many, many areas, which we have discussed many times previously. You hold many,

many examples of objective creations that are mirror images of what you know within your own abilities as essence — ALL of your inventions. You also mirror what you know within your creations of your expressions of self and your automatic bypassing of your own thought processes, knowing that you may manipulate energy in multiple areas simultaneously, freeing other areas of your energy to focus your attention upon, and you focus your attention upon your thought process.

Your thought process moves as an automatic response to your very creation of physical focus. It is a natural expression and byproduct of your physical creation within this dimension, a response to your emotional and sexual experience. It is the objective expression, that of the rational — the interpretation, the translation, the language — but although you may not offer yourself the language continuously, this is not to say that you do not offer yourself the awareness.

Therefore, in this I express to you that you DO hold an objective awareness of all of your choices and of your creating of your probabilities, which ARE your choices. You merely do not focus your attention upon your action of creating your choices. Therefore, within certain circumstances, you surprise yourself, for you have not offered yourself the attention to what you are creating. You hold the ability, as I have stated previously, to be objectively paying attention and aware of all of the choices that you are creating within every moment continuously. It is merely a question of focusing your attention and allowing yourself to be manipulating your own awareness in what you may term to be more efficient directions. (#331)

Q: At what level are the choices made? Because there are choices I'm sure I'm making that I'm not consciously aware of. And I'm wondering, is there a difference between conscious awareness and what we might call daily awareness? If it's true that everything happens to us as a result of our choices, I would venture to guess that those who are murder victims and those who are in car accidents and those who have terminal illnesses, in their daily awareness, aren't making those choices. Just as if I could tomorrow, or right now, in my daily awareness make a choice to change my reality ... The choices I make in my daily awareness are not reflected in my reality quite often.

ELIAS: Or so it appears! (Grinning)

- Q: I'm wondering at what level these choices are made, and how to access that level?

ELIAS: This is the reason that we discuss unofficial information presently, that you may more understand how you are creating your reality by witnessing and paying attention to all of your reality, not only what you are accustomed to paying attention to. I express to you that in reality, murder victims, murderers, accident victims, or any individual within any situation or circumstance, if you are truly viewing all of the information available to you, you shall see that you do indicate these probabilities. Just as you may, within quite objective obvious circumstances, view a pattern within yourself leading to a certain accomplishment, you also may view objectively, if you are noticing, indications incorporating unofficial information that shall express to you the direction that you have chosen within your attention, and the probabilities that you are leaning to be creating.

You also, as with the dream mission also, must be viewing creatively. Understand that you are creative beings. Therefore, an individual may choose a debilitating automobile accident, in your terms. This may occur quite surprisingly. In actuality, if you are noticing all of the information available within the reality of this individual, you shall see a "leading to" the drastic, dramatic creation for the reasons within the probabilities that this individual has chosen.

I understand that this is complicated, but if you are viewing closely you will view certain behaviors, certain choices, certain actions that are indications to you, clues of your own direction. You need engage your periphery and be understanding that all of your reality that you create is not within one narrow line. You pull from many, many angles within your probabilities, and you also interact and intersect with alternate selves. Much more is going on within your reality than you view!

In this, as you look to how you are creating your reality, you must also take into account all of reality and all of its angles, for there are many. Each action that you choose may not in actuality be directly related to the action quite previous to it. It may appear that the action is following within a line of probabilities or within a line of events, but this is not always the case; although simultaneously it shall also fit into the scheme of present motion, but it may hold ramifications beyond the present circumstances.

You do not think to yourselves of the influences that are pressing to you continuously. You hold many focuses within essence. You hold many alternates within one focus. Your future self, as you think of it, is also quite influencing of your present. This is not to say, once again, that you hold no objective control and direction, for you hold all. You only do not look to your own action.

I express to you that the smallest, to your way of thinking, actions that you alter within a daily routine are precisely chosen. You may awaken one morning and you may be choosing to comb your hair differently. You may choose to eat your porridge before your coffee or tea, as opposed to your normal routine of sipping your tea or coffee first. These seem to be insignificant alterations, but these also are conscious choices and affect you; for you have chosen, within this particular day, a different routine. You have chosen to alter your methods, and within this you alter the whole of you. Your perception changes. You may not notice a dramatic alteration of perception, but your perception shall alter. This is a very slight, small example which offers a very slight, small alteration of your reality; but it is an example of how each choice is created, which alters your perception and also creates your existing reality.

(Intently) It is all objective choices. You are not walking through this physical reality asleep! You are not engaging other individuals or your employment within your dream state! You are awake. You are objective. You are thinking. You are choosing. Your choices are made objectively. YOU ARE DIRECTING.

Q: Would you say that this is a trial and error process?

ELIAS: No.(Firmly)

Q: Which would imply that you know the results of your choices prior to making them.

ELIAS: In one manner of speaking.

Q: So if I choose to eat my porridge before I sip my coffee, I have some idea of what the implied change in my life is?

ELIAS: If you are allowing yourself to be noticing your periphery and noticing your reality. In one manner of speaking, yes; within essence you are aware, for all events are simultaneous. There is no future. There is no past. Therefore, you are aware of your action within its entirety. Within another respect you are not aware, for you choose to be singularly focused and you also choose not to listen and notice unofficial information.

Q: But regardless, you make choices. So those who are more aware of their subjective activity or unofficial information, whatever, make choices in light of that, at least arguably, and those who are not make their choices …

ELIAS: … the same. (Grinning)

Q: Okay. I guess that's not what I would have said!

ELIAS: YOU choose differently, for you choose to be engaging the action of widening … and you have asked!

Q: So the only difference is awareness. You make the choices with a result clear on some level to you, but your awareness of the results or the choices … you're either aware of them or you're not.

ELIAS: It is not necessary for your awareness. Many, many, many individuals engage physical focus, and do not hold an understanding of probabilities objectively, and move efficiently through their objective focuses. You have asked for this information. You have drawn yourselves to this information. You wish this information for your own widening, for the express reasoning of engaging the shift and engaging transition within physical focus. (#152)

Chapter 9

INTENT – DESIRE

"Your purpose, as we have expressed, is to experience;
but you are correct that within each individual focus you
also hold individual intents, and as you hold these intents
you create desires, and within this you create probabilities
to choose from within a pool aligning with your intent."

(#153)

Chapter 9

INTENT – DESIRE

Q: How do we determine our true intent? How do we become very aligned with the intent, and without all of the bombardment of mass beliefs but with our own true intent, our own true purpose for being here?

ELIAS: Many individuals look to this word of intent and become boggled and experience an overwhelming confusion and express, "This is so very difficult to identify!" I express to you, it is quite easy to be identifying your intent. Look to your entire focus and the directions that you consistently move within in all of your expressions, and this shall offer you the information of your intent. (#344)

What I am expressing to you is to examine the entirety of your focus, from what you recognize as being a small child to this present now, and allow yourself to discover what your individual theme has been; for each individual incorporates a particular direction in each focus, and that direction is what motivates all of your experiences.

Now; the reason that it holds significance and importance that you allow yourself to attempt to view your theme or your direction in this focus is that this offers you individually more of an understanding and familiarity with yourself. I may offer certain information to you, but the information that I offer to you in this type of questioning is incorporated merely as a concept rather than a genuine knowing of self; whereas, as you allow yourself to genuinely examine and discover your own movement, you also allow yourself validations concerning yourself, and you create more of a familiarity in your own relationship with yourself. (#918)

Understand that you create an intent within an individual focus as a direction of exploring your experiences. Therefore, you initialize and actualize your intent from the moment of your entry in manifestation. You are already expressing that intent. Therefore, it is expressed throughout the entirety of your focus, for were it not be that you were expressing your intent, you would not be creating your value fulfillment, and if you are not creating your value fulfillment, you disengage, for there is no point of continuing if you do not continue to express and create your value fulfillment, and this is accomplished through your intent.

Therefore, in allowing yourself to view what is your intent within a particular focus, the direction is not to be turning your attention in seeking what you should be doing or accomplishing or what you should be creating or what you wish to be creating, but rather what you have been creating and what you are already creating and continue to be creating, and many of your experiences shall bear that out. They are evidences of your intent.

Each individual may view their focus, from the remembering of their experiences and their directions, their drives, their movements, as an infant, as a child, through their development, so to speak, within their focus, and into what you term to be your adulthood. It is an underlying theme that continues throughout the entirety of your focus. It is not a purpose. It is a direction of energy.

Many individuals create a misinterpretation of their intent, and identify or define this movement to themselves as a purpose and as that element of themselves that is their reason for being.

In actuality, your reason for being is that you ARE.

Q: Very unromantic!

ELIAS: Ah! But in what you are, you do create directions, and you do create a movement in specifics in direction. This is another exercise in familiarizing yourself with yourself. (#733)

Q: I've been doing a lot of trying to figure out what my intent is, and I feel like at different times, it's different things. I would think that beliefs would be getting in the way as far as that's concerned, and that's why maybe I have different purposes at different times.

ELIAS: Let me express to you that within the lines of probabilities that are created in any particular focus, you shall be following your intent, although the actions that you choose to be creating may not always seem to you to be moving in the same direction. You may choose any number of avenues, so to speak, in different actions that shall all be connected with an individual intent. This is merely differences in the expressions of that particular intent.

Therefore, in this, do not confuse yourself in the area of thinking that you must be proceeding in one particular direction to be accomplishing of your intent. Many individuals move and sway into many different expressions and directions throughout their focus, but they are accomplishing of their intent for the larger picture, or the whole of their intent encompasses many different expressions. It is merely the base line that you are following that shall remain constant.

Q: So basically, just live in the present.

ELIAS: Absolutely, which I have stated many times to many individuals, and yourself also, that your concern need move in the direction of focusing your attention within the present now and allowing yourself the accomplishment of all of your interactions and expressions within the present now, not looking to future or past events or creations and moving into the direction of projecting yourself outside of what you are creating within this now. For let me express to you that all of your creation for past and future is created within the present now, for no other element exists.

All of your time, so to speak, is simultaneous. Although you look to your time as moving linearly and you look to the line of past and present and future, in actuality all exists presently and is all created presently. Therefore, where shall you be projecting to within your future and past? For it is all existing NOW.

Let me express to you that within the action of this shift and within this particular time framework that you participate in within this particular dimension, ALL individuals upon your globe are moving in the direction of an element of each of their intents, which is that of acceptance, as being in conjunction with the action of this shift. This is all individuals' intent individually, but also globally and collectively.

This is not to say that this is the only aspect of your individual intent. It is an element of your intent in conjunction with this shift, as I have stated, but you also each hold your own individual intents for yourselves that is in keeping with the line of probabilities that you have chosen as your pool of probabilities for this particular focus.

Now; you may be choosing to alter some of those probabilities, and you may also move outside of your chosen pool of probabilities and pull to you new probabilities that are not encompassed within your pool of probabilities, but you shall in doing this stay in keeping with your original intent within a particular focus.

I may also offer to you that there are times that individuals may be choosing to change their intent within a given focus, but this would not be the situation with yourself. You have chosen a particular intent within this focus and you are following within those probabilities and not altering of your intent chosen. (#289)

Q: What's the difference between intent and desire?

ELIAS: Answer!

Q: My opinion is that desire is ever-changing. Intent is constant. Intent is what best describes your focus. Desire is what drives the intent.

ELIAS: Reverse. Your intent will be driving your desire. Therefore, as you do not understand or know what your intent is, your desire fluctuates and changes, for it is searching for the other half. Your desire allows you information about your intent, for as you view your changing desires of your focus, this will illustrate to you a commonality which will point to the direction of your intent.

If you are viewing your experiences and your desires of not only this present, but of all of your present moments, from your birth to this present moment, you will see that your desires have taken different roads, but generally incorporate a basic theme. In this, you offer yourself information of your intent. This also offers you your clues of yourself; who you are, what you are, how you create your reality, and that you possess all knowledge already. You need only remember; and as you are looking to yourselves and you are discovering your desires, you will also be discovering parts of yourself; how you create your reality; for you already possess your own answers. (#59)

Q: The relationship between purpose, intent, attainment, value fulfillment, and belief systems. Is it the case that we decide to manifest and to attain, or we're attempting to attain, value fulfillment within a certain set of belief systems? Is that a succinct way of stating why we are here, or is it inclusive?

ELIAS: You manifest physically to experience.

Q: Right. And there's no preconceived value fulfillments and belief systems?

ELIAS: You shall be accomplishing your value fulfillment, or you shall not be within this manifestation. If you are not accomplishing your value fulfillment, you shall disengage. There is no purpose for continuation without value fulfillment. Therefore, if you are not accomplishing value fulfillment, you shall disengage. You shall not continue. *All* consciousness exists with value fulfillment. Every link of consciousness exists with value fulfillment.

Q: Is value fulfillment modified during the manifestation? The set of value fulfillments?

ELIAS: No. You are viewing value fulfillment in the terms of moral values and objectives. Value fulfillment is independent of these. A link of consciousness holds no moral value. It also holds no objective. It accomplishes value fulfillment in being its most excellent expression. Value fulfillment is within the being and creativity. It is not an objective. You do not strive for value fulfillment. You accomplish. You do not move towards value fulfillment. You be.

Q: Then how could you not fulfill value? If value fulfillment is simply being, how could you not fulfill value?

ELIAS: Being within your highest expression and fulfillment, not only to self but to all consciousness. Innately, you know if this is not being accomplished. Objectively, you may not understand that this is what is occurring, but you shall act upon this innate knowledge. As a member of your species, you shall disengage by means of suicide or you shall create disease or you shall merely not awaken, but you shall not continue within your manifestation. This is common within all manifestation physically. If a flower is not creating and accomplishing its value fulfillment, it shall not be.

Q: Is value fulfillment different from intent?

ELIAS: It is moving with your intent.

Q: Is intent an objective?

ELIAS: Partially. To your way of thinking, you may express that intent may be described as an objective, for it engages probabilities that succeed each other. It creates a design; a pattern; a mosaic.

Q: A pattern by which value may be fulfilled?

ELIAS: Correct; but value fulfillment is not dependent upon intent, for not all consciousness must hold intent.

Q: But we have a set of belief systems. What is the value of the belief systems in the experience? Is it true that we attain value fulfillment within a set of belief systems, and that is part of the experience?

ELIAS: You achieve value fulfillment within all of consciousness, within every experience and within every area of consciousness, regardless of belief systems.

Q: Do belief systems add to our attainment of value fulfillment?

ELIAS: No.

Q: But they are valuable.

ELIAS: They are relevant to physical focus, for they are influencing of your creation of your reality.

Q: They're necessary.

ELIAS: Within physical focus.

Q: And that is the experience.

ELIAS: Correct.

Q: We don't choose this prior to the manifestation of the focus in any way?

ELIAS: Within your belief systems and your creation of time framework, this question may be answered affirmatively, although in actuality, all events are simultaneous. Therefore, how may you choose before? But within your reality, which is reality, of your time framework, yes; you choose before. (#166)

Q: I am trying to understand what my ... or maybe other people have the same question ... what our individual jobs are at this point in time, in assisting ourselves and others through the shift. For me, I perceived my work to be what it apparently is not, because it never works the way I think it's going to. Can you comment on that?

ELIAS: And although you each distort this imagery within your belief systems, expressing that some outside force is thwarting your efforts, you are in actuality correct anyway ... except it is not an outside force thwarting you! It is self, which is aware and knows the direction of your probabilities that are most efficient; and if you are choosing to be deviating, you shall also create conflict for yourself. In this, you shall be recognizing when you are deviating from your intent within any individual focus and when you are moving off of your track, so to speak, for you shall not be running on your rails any longer. You shall be bumping through your fields!

You direct yourselves within essence in the area of your intent, and you draw yourselves to situations and circumstances to be offering you information and direction in your intent. Many times you choose not to be listening! Many times you may be presented with your information of your direction and you do not listen and you turn away, but quite fortunately for all of you, your boat does not dock only once! It returns and returns and returns to your port, until you are ready to climb aboard and heave ho! (Grinning)

Fear is the most powerful element that is blocking of individuals within the following of their intent. In actuality, as I have spoken previously, within any given focus you are always following your intent to an extent, although you may be following your intent in the manner of my analogy of crossing your street directly, or crossing your country and returning to cross your street! You shall cross your street, but within one action you shall exert much energy out of your way to be crossing your street!

This also involves the acceptance and trust of self. This is the most difficult element that you may grapple with. Each of you struggles with this trustfulness of self. Each of you listens to this small little voice within and at times express to yourselves, "Which little voice am I listening to? Are you the right voice or the wrong voice? Shall I be listening, or shall I not be listening? I shall be suspicious of these little voices!" (Laughter) Then you may express to yourself that you are insane anyway! (Humorously)

Therefore, I express to you that you find it difficult to be trusting of self and following what you view to be your intent within an individual focus. In actuality, trusting of self is so much less complicated than not trusting of self! It is so very easy to be accepting of self and your own expression and freely offering this, than to be battling continuously as a knight on a horse in much armor, falling off continuously and climbing clanking back upon your horse! It becomes quite tiresome! (Laughter)

You, as I have said, shall not betray you. You shall bear yourself out. You need only evaluate the belief systems which color your perceptions; and within these belief systems, as I have stated this day, if you are indicating strenuously to yourself within any direction, you may be assured you are dealing with a belief system! The more and the harder that you struggle, the more you are facing yourself with belief systems; for within acceptance of belief systems and self, there is effortlessness. There is an ease of movement. It is unnecessary for such struggling, although it is entertaining as you are creating of your dramas! But as you have come to this time period within your time framework you become weary of this game also, and have chosen to be more creative within consciousness and allow yourself new freedoms without the constraints of your belief systems.

Pay attention to those elements which present themselves within your lifetime. These are elements that you have drawn to yourself for your purposes, and your fulfillment of your intent, and your value fulfillment; this being how you confuse yourselves, that you do not pay attention to what you draw to yourselves. This essence speaks to you not in accident.

Q: Are you saying that it matters that we have an experience, but that we should take the experience as it comes along, and whatever that experience is doesn't matter?

ELIAS: Within your choices of probabilities, you choose a direction that follows your intent and your desire within a particular focus. This matters. You have chosen this for your value fulfillment; but within the recognition that all probabilities are probabilities, that all probabilities are actualized and that you are creating for the experience, it does not matter. This seemingly is a contradiction, although it is not a contradiction; for within your belief systems, you place value upon elements that do not necessarily hold value.

You hold seriousness instead of playfulness. You focus to judgment instead of acceptance and you create confusion and conflict, and then you express to the cosmos, to your universe, "Why must I experience such conflict?" But you have created this conflict because you have created such seriousness and eliminated your playfulness, and you have created confusion by placing ultimate importance upon belief systems instead of truths, and you cry within confusion that you wish your experience to be different and you wish your existence to be different. I express to you elements to consider to be offering alternate perceptions to be creating your existence and your reality differently without conflict, and you roll within your conflict and express back to this essence, "But this cannot be!"

All things are reality. All things that you create physically or non —physically matter, for there is no element that is any less than any other element within consciousness; but within the experiences, no experience is more important than another experience. I have expressed to individuals previously, the action of creating a sandwich for yourself to be consuming is no less important than the erection of a monument, or the fighting for a cause, or the viewing of a flower. They are all experiences. They all matter, but they all do not matter within belief systems. They matter within experience. They do not matter within belief systems. (#137)

Q: Do we each have a higher purpose than this thing called physical reality? I've always had a sense that I do, but I haven't quite figured out what it is yet. And if we do, can you offer suggestions as to how we can get clear on the contribution we're supposed to be…

ELIAS: Let me express to you, as to your question — do you hold a higher purpose — no, you do not. But I shall express to you, the reason that you feel that you hold a higher purpose is your recognition and your knowing that you DO hold an individual intent.

Each individual within their manifestation in physical focus holds an intent, and this is the direction that that individual has chosen to be creating its reality in conjunction with. It is the expression of their individual creativity, and this is the motivating and directing force of each individual within physical focus.

This is translated into an identification of purpose, but I express to you, there is a difference.

Purpose is what you are accomplishing within every moment in every movement that you create in your exploration. You are purposefully creating your exploration. Your intent is your direction.

And in this, what may be helpful to you in your identification of your intent is your desire, your creativity, and what you identify physically or define physically as your "contribution." Your contribution in actuality is merely your expression of yourself in the fullness of your creativity individually, and this is the expression of your value fulfillment.

Therefore, as you look for your purpose, merely look to your genuine expression of self in what creates joyfulness and fun within you, and this is the direction of your desire. As you move in this direction, you are creating of your purpose. (#475)

Chapter 10

IF IT ISN'T FUN, DON'T DO IT!

*"If you are incorporating action that is pleasurable to you,
you are incorporating what we would express to you
as value fulfillment. Your essence does not manifest
for the purpose of experience for some mystical reason!
Its fullest value fulfillment is expressed through pleasure."*

(#74)

Chapter 10

IF IT ISN'T FUN, DON'T DO IT!

ELIAS: If it is not fun, don't do it! This seems to be a very blanket statement, and indeed it is, and indeed I mean this literally!

Q: Well, my question has to do with your blanket statement.

ELIAS: Ah!

Q: So, if a teenage child decides that going to school just isn't fun anymore, then he should just stop going to school?

ELIAS: Yes.

Q: And wouldn't that be incorporating of not fun, possibly for say his parents?

ELIAS: Each individual incorporates within their own focus their own choices. Therefore, you do not base yourself upon the actions of others, and if you are not incorporating fun, you have choices also, to eliminate what is causing you conflict. I believe you will find that if a child is not experiencing fun within their learning years, that there will be reasons for this that may be eliminated to allow the incorporation of fun. Also, this same individual may choose not to incorporate with school, so to speak, but this does not mean that they will be experiencing fun NOT in school.

Each individual incorporates an identity, which within physical focus, this aspect of consciousness rebels against all others temporarily, therefore attempting to establish its identity. Within this, you will find that individuals who are not allowed their expression of their identity push harder against any individual who will be threatening this by posing as authority. Authority symbolizes to you another individual who will tell you what to do or how to do this, or what to think or how to be. Within this, if you have established your own solidity within your identity, you will encounter many individuals who will assert this on you, but you will not care for it will not affect you, for that part or that aspect of your consciousness will be connected and not threatened within its identity.

This brings us to my expression to you that if you are incorporating essence consistently, you will be eliminating many conflicts and you will be incorporating fun much more, if not continuously! You may say, "What if an individual does not wish to be tilling the fields? How will we eat? For they will not grow the food." Incorrect! There are ALWAYS other individuals who DO find pleasure and fun within this work. There are ALWAYS individuals that DO incorporate fun within the learning process. Individuals who do not incorporate fun within the learning process are also not learning! Therefore, you defeat your purpose!

You incorporate into your reality that which you find to be pleasurable and positive. You decide to incorporate what you believe to be negative or not pleasurable when you have convinced yourself that you are not capable of accomplishing the other. Therefore, you accomplish and create quite efficiently within what you term negative aspects. Either way, you are creating quite efficiently. You are effective in both aspects. There are always essences which will incorporate themselves in ALL areas of physical focus to accomplish your necessities.

Within the area of education, this is completely limited to a physical focus issue; for within essence, every essence manifesting physically incorporates a natural desire and passion for learning. This illustrates itself within the very first moments of breathing life. Even before breathing life, the essence, within growing within the womb, incorporates learning and a desire and growing. Therefore, the issue of an individual physically focused NOT incorporating fun within the area of learning is a direct effect of physical focus and the rules that you have incorporated within your societies and within your communities. You have stifled yourselves and your small ones, and you encourage separation. Within separating, you also encourage conflict and a lack of fun! Within the focus of connecting, you will notice that there ARE individuals who are not encouraged as much to separate, and their essence expresses itself with a thirst for physical knowledge; this being where you differentiate.

As to your question of, "Then what do you do after this has already been accomplished?" This is all fine and good if you were all raised perfectly, and you all have not been! And, "If a child is wishing to not continue within school, then what?" That is that individual's choice, and that individual will deal with that choice within the accepted official reality that all of you have created, and you as a parent incorporate choices also. If you are not in agreement, then do not be in agreement! If you are not experiencing pleasantness with this child that has not continued, then you have your own choices to make, one of which obviously may be to disconnect from this situation; this being much easier for me to express to you than you will find this to implement! But if you are truly trusting within essence and you are truly understanding that each individual creates their own reality, then you will experience no conflict with this.

The most difficult sentence I have ever expressed to you is that you create your own reality, for this not only incorporates you but every other individual separate and apart from you, as they do all create their own reality, and in your reality you have each created belief systems of right and wrong, and within that you create your reality accordingly. (#44)

I will say to you all — it has been said by another in words of your time now that you may understand — if it is not fun, stop it! This would be including Elias' sessions. If you are incorporating conflict, do not incorporate Elias, for if I do not offer what you are considering to be positive or fun, then you should not be here. You should not be doing or participating in this or in anything. If anything is creating conflict with you or separating you from you or creating unhappiness within you, then you should not incorporate that.

Each individual's truth is their own. It all in essence is the same, but each individual manifests this truth within their reality their own way. Each individual incorporates no conflict within their own way.

Each individual connects with love and joy within their own way. What may be comfortable or non-conflicting for one may be creating of conflict for another. Your focus is to focus on you. It is not important what others view of you. It is not important what others' opinion is of you. What is important is that you are true to you, and that you are happy with that. (#40)

Do not be discounting of fun! It lends less thickness to your focus and it also is quite validating of you, and I am quite encouraging of individuals to be creating of fun and to be moving in the direction of pleasure, for pleasure is your natural inclination of essence and provides you with the greatest ease in moving through your focus ... and no conflict! Conflict creates thickness. Confusion creates thickness. Pleasure does not. Therefore, I am encouraging in this direction! And do not allow your belief systems to be limiting you in this area and expressing to you the rightness or wrongness of these areas, for in actuality, there is no right or wrong. It all merely is, and all of your experiences are merely experiences. (#324)

It matters not what you choose. The reason that I interact with you is that you HAVE created a choice within your preferences, which are also influenced by your belief systems, that you choose to not be experiencing trauma within the action of your shift, for within your belief systems you view this to be negative and undesirable, but this also is viewed by your belief systems.

As for myself, within the area of consciousness that I occupy this is not an element, for I do not hold belief systems, and therefore any experience, regardless of how YOU view these experiences as pleasurable or not, are merely experiences for my viewing. But I shall express to you that within your physical focus you HAVE created an officially accepted reality, and in this you DO create the reality of thickness or not within your energy, based upon your belief systems. Therefore, if you are moving in directions within your physical focus of hurtfulness or judgment, you also create a thickness with the energy that you receive and that you project, and this creates what you may term to be — although in actuality it is not, but what you may term to be — a slowing of your motion. I may also express to you that in seeking pleasure or in moving in the direction of pleasure in ANY area, you eliminate this thickness.

Now; here shall be your paradox in your duplicity, for you view those elements that are positive to be good and acceptable and you view those elements that are uncomfortable or hurtful to be bad, but you also view those elements that you view to be positive and good as pleasurable and you view them also to be bad! (Laughter) There are only certain conditions that your pleasurableness may be accepted, and if you move outside of these conditions, you place yourself right back into your duplicity in expressing, "Now this pleasure is bad!" It is acceptable to be experiencing pleasure in certain areas. It is acceptable within your officially accepted reality to be experiencing pleasure if you are not abusing pleasure, which is ANOTHER belief system, another bird in the cage! You may be experiencing substance if you are not abusing substance, for this may be pleasurable, but it is also bad. You may be experiencing sexuality, but you may only experience this within the confines of your belief systems and the mass belief systems, for if you move outside of the mass belief systems and engage this action of pleasure, it is bad and it is no longer acceptable.

You may move in the direction of many pleasurable actions, but once you move in the direction that is not compliant with the mass belief systems, that pleasure automatically becomes unacceptable and bad, and no pleasure — we shall rock your world with this statement — no pleasure is bad! ALL pleasure is acceptable and ALL pleasure lends to the ease of your movement through your focus, for you automatically within essence magnate and move in the direction of pleasure, and this eliminates your thickness ...but you limit your pleasure tremendously!

You shall at time periods be witness to this essence express acknowledgment of individuals inquiring in the area of pleasure. "But Elias, shall I move into this direction of engaging another individual in pleasurable activities when our mass belief systems are so very far against this?" And I shall be expressing, "Yes. Shall you not?"

You shall express to me, or other individuals may express to me,

"Shall we not place judgment upon individuals that engage in popular substances?" What is your present substance, which is so very popular, of smoking?

Q: Marijuana?

ELIAS: Ah, very good! Very bad bad bad! (Laughter)

Q: Or the new sex drug ... what is it? Viagra!

ELIAS: Very bad bad bad! (Laughter) These are pleasurable items — very bad! — for you hold very strong belief systems in these areas, which are very reinforced by your mass belief systems.

Ah, another area which has become a very strong mass belief system — and we shall rock your world again — your [tobacco] smoking. Individuals have inquired previously, "Is this harmful to me?" Yes, it is harmful to you, in relation to your belief systems. If you are in compliance with the mass belief system and you hold the belief system also that this action is harmful to you, yes, it shall be, for you shall create that; but in itself, no, it is not.

It is merely your belief systems that dictate what you create, but the things in themselves do not hold belief systems. Therefore, how may be they affecting of you in any harmful manner, for nothing that you create is harmful to you. It is merely your belief systems that create the harmfulness, for you do not create harmful elements, for essence is not harmful to self and is not intrusive to any other essence. Therefore, how shall you be creating of any element that is hurtful to you, except within the expressions and the influences of your belief systems.

Therefore, I answer to you: Yes, to you there are actions that are acceptable and there are actions that are not acceptable. There are directions to be followed and directions not to be followed. You shall not be harmful to another individual and murder them, for this is unacceptable. I express to you, if you shall be engaging the action of murdering another individual, you are in agreement to be experiencing a role of perpetrator and victim for that experience, and it IS a choice and it IS an agreement. (therefore) what is the right or wrong? There is none. It is merely an experience, and each experience is purposefully chosen by each individual for their own benefit; not necessarily pleasure, but benefit.

Q: So people choose to be a victim?

ELIAS: Absolutely. All of your actions within physical focus are a choice. You choose what you desire to be creating within your experience in conjunction with your intent that you have created within each focus, and for its purity of its experience

Q: So somehow that will be beneficial to that person that chooses to be a victim?

ELIAS: Yes. If they are surviving, they may be...

Q: But there is no death, so...

ELIAS: You are correct. I use this word of survival in conjunction with your belief systems of physical survival, and if they are surviving physically, they may be using this experience to their benefit. If they are not, they have chosen to be disengaging in this manner, which is not bad, for they are not within death. They are merely creating a choice to move into a new emergence in that moment.

It is all a choice. Your choice of disengagement is yours. You may be murdered. You may be eaten by a bear. You may disengage within your dream state. You may choose to be creating of tremendous disease, and in that...

Q: Or you could choose pleasure!

ELIAS: And you may! It is all your choice. You may choose to engage disengagement as you are experiencing pleasure within your sexuality! Quite fun! (Everybody cracks up) It is your choice. (#284)

Q: How do we experience natural time? I get the sense that we've lost what it is to experience natural time. Which, when I think of natural time, for me, is when I'M experiencing fun, enjoying myself.

ELIAS: You have created your cultural time; therefore, this supersedes your natural time within your perception. You have created your civilizations and your societies to be revolving around your cultural time, your "time slots." You have distorted your appreciation of time. Originally; once again, a time-oriented word; you have originally created your dimension of time for specific experiences. In your appreciation of your time element, you have chosen to be focusing upon each moment of time, with a desire to be appreciating of each moment of time. You have distorted this desire into the area of attaching a production level also to these moments of time. Therefore, to be appreciating of time, you must be utilizing time. You must be incorporating action "doing something" with it. Just as you view [that] you spend "quality time" with your children, you do not view spending "quality time" with your children ignoring them! You are interacting with them. You are "doing something" with them. In this same way, you view that you must be interacting with time itself, placing a value on each moment. Your distortion has come by equating value with action, with productivity. You may be incorporating action, in your appreciation of time and moments, simply by noticing time itself and experiencing your time element, but this is not sufficient within your belief systems now.

Your animals do not incorporate this perception of time. You may view, within your domesticated animals, they do not incorporate time in the same fashion as you. They are not focused upon filling each moment with the production of action. They experience each moment. In this, the moments collide and intermesh with each other, being indistinguishable, one from the other. An animal does not incorporate seconds or minutes or hours, for these are unimportant. They simply experience the element of time within physical focus.

You ask, "How do you experience natural time?" Allow yourself to be natural. If it is not fun, do not do it! If you are incorporating action that is pleasurable to you, you are incorporating what we would express to you as value fulfillment.

Your essence does not manifest for the purpose of experience for some mystical reason! Its fullest value fulfillment is expressed through pleasure. This is what your self strives toward, this being why you also incorporate positive and negative; negative being all elements that do not incorporate pleasure, positive being what you strive for, being pleasurable. This is your choice. (Pause) You may experience effortlessness and a pleasurable existence if you are fulfilling your desire. This is why I say to you, if it is not fun, do not do it! Incorporate fun only, and you will experience natural time.

You incorporate a perception of "needs." You perceive your existence to be surrounded by needful demands upon your time, elements of accomplishments that must be met. Therefore, you will incorporate action, to be fulfilling of these elements, which does not incorporate fun; for you believe that necessary is more important. What you do not understand is that all that is necessary to your existence may be fulfilled in fun!

You will find that when you are following your desire and your intent, you will experience the effortlessness of which I speak, and you will incorporate fun, and you also will not feel so "locked into" your cultural time. This is not as easily attained, within your time period now, as it sounds; for even those who follow their individual intent and desire are quite influenced by cultural time. You may discover an occupation to which you are fulfilling your desire and your intent, but you have locked yourself into your cultural time element.

You must appear on time. You must depart at a designated time. You will be incorporated with other individuals to which time is important. Unless you are removing yourself completely from this framework of cultural time, you will incorporate cultural time to some extent, although you may quite efficiently move through your focus effortlessly, and also pleasurably, and appreciating of both time elements.

Q: The conflict we have with cultural time could be influenced by your perception?

ELIAS: Absolutely, but then your perception is influencing of all things. Therefore, in altering your perception, you also alter your existence.

Q: Which all of us can attain.

ELIAS: Correct, and more! (Smiling) It is only dependent upon your desire, and [your] motivation to be accomplishing.

Q: Right, and my desire and motivation get tweaked when I think of having to pay the bills, and then it lessens.

ELIAS: In this, I am realizing that you look to me and express, "Well! Elias does not incorporate money, or housing debts, or commitments. Therefore, he is not understanding of physical focus!" Incorrect! I have been physically manifest many, many, many times! I am quite familiar with the demands of physical focus. I am also quite familiar with the reality that through the engagement of trust within oneself, and within truth and essence, effortlessness may be achieved within physical focus; and you may acquire all that you desire pleasurably, and incorporate fun, and satisfy your "perceived" physical needs! (Pause, smiling)

An old saying: Where there is a will, there is a way! Many individuals accomplish great feats against insurmountable odds, and are quite happy!

Q: Is there a common element amongst these people, that they do that, that I'm missing the boat on?

ELIAS: (Accessing) Each individual is unique. You may view that you perceive commonalties, within individuals who seem to be motivated and those who seem to be unmotivated, but within these elements, each individual incorporates their own (?) which serves to influence their desire and their motivation. Therefore, it would be incorrect of me to be generalizing and expressing that individuals, who all accomplish against all odds, so to speak, bear this or that element in common. I will say to you that the one element that they all do possess, fairly, and that you do also, is to be reaching within and connecting within themselves, and offering their own direction, and trusting themselves. (#74)

Q: How do we return to the playfulness?

ELIAS: Choose! Be! And if you do not experience fun, discontinue! (Laughter) Do not be forcing slavery upon yourself in creating bondage of unhappiness and anxiety in that which you do not wish to be creating! Create what you wish. (#137)

Chapter 11

YOU SHALL NOT BETRAY YOU

"Be trusting of yourselves. Do not be looking to other individuals and their belief systems and their judgments and their evaluations upon your choices. Merely be trusting of yourself, and you shall not betray you."

(#216)

Chapter 11

YOU SHALL NOT BETRAY YOU

ELIAS: You create your reality. You create all of your reality! If you are accepting of self and trusting of self, you shall materialize that which you set before you to create.

This is sounding quite simple! This is truly one of your most difficult tasks, for you do not accept and trust yourselves. If you are trusting of self you may say, "I choose excellent health," and you may give no more thought to this choice and it shall be, for you believe and trust that it shall. You hold no doubt. I wager to say, no individual within this forum may express that they hold no doubt! This being the area that you may practice your affirmation, but not in the manner that you are accustomed to, as you are reciting to yourself phrases over and over as a machine, hoping that within yourself eventually you shall believe yourself and your affirmation. I express to you, you may affirm anything to yourself, and then, believe this.

You, once again, shall not betray you. You are your highest expression, and you shall always look for your highest value fulfillment, and you shall accomplish this! You may express that you experience conflict, for you are striving and striving and you are not accomplishing what you choose to be accomplishing and your existence holds much struggling and conflict, and you may even express that you do not understand your purpose or your point. If you are allowing yourself the freedom to accept self and to know that you have manifest to experience and that no experience is worse or better and that you are perfectly creating within every moment of your focus, you shall eliminate much of your conflict.

I have expressed this many times, although to this present now within your physical focus, you do not understand. You wish to be seeking out individuals that shall map your road for you, that shall express to you: "Move this way. Accomplish this. Occupy yourself with this job. Be creative within this area, and you shall be successful." You shall be successful when you are believing in you. When you are allowing yourself to loosen your hold upon the duplicity of self, then you shall be accomplishing, but as you continue to view better and worse and you are striving and not addressing to the belief systems that you hold, you shall continue within your conflict. Do you not think that if this were not so, that throughout your ages individuals upon your planet would not have already formulated the method for complete, ultimate successfulness in every area?

You are inventive creatures. You are extremely creative. You may build machinery to explore your physical space, but you may not solve these tiny individual problems of successfulness within individuals, for no prophet or psychic may express to you a method for accomplishment if you are not trusting of you. (#165)

You hold the concept that you may be trusting yourself and that you may be moving in whichever direction you choose, but this remains a concept. You now challenge yourself in the area of creating this concept into your reality and trusting yourself that you truly DO create your reality, that it is not accidental or coincidental or thrust upon you, but that you are orchestrating all of your reality and that you hold the ability to be orchestrating of all of your reality.

Let me offer to you that which I have expressed much time ago, in your terms. You are a symphony. You are all of the instruments within the symphony, and you are also the conductor. Now; you accept yourself as the conductor of the symphony. You conceptualize that you are also all of the instruments, but you do not accept that you are all of the instruments. You do not trust that aspect of yourself, and in this you may be conducting of your symphony, and some of your instruments may be playing by themselves and they may not necessarily be following your direction, for you are taught that you are not orchestrating all of your reality, but you are.

In this, you are also taught that you hold needs, and that there is a specific direction you must be moving into to be accommodating those needs. You NEED food. You NEED shelter. You NEED garments. You NEED currency for exchange. You NEED to be engaging payment upon debts. You NEED be physically accommodating yourself, and to be accomplishing this, you NEED specific types of employment that shall be generating of the revenue that shall be affording you the exchange to be addressing to all of your needs.

And many individuals within this forum, I am quite aware — although not necessarily addressing to myself — express outside of our engagement together, "Oh, very well, Elias. Well that you may entertain the idea that there are no needs, but you do not occupy physical focus, and I hold physical expenditures that need be attended to! You are a non-physical essence. Therefore, what needs do you hold? I am engaged within physical focus and hold very definite needs!"

It matters not that you occupy physical focus, and I AM quite understanding of what you perceive to be your physical needs, and I express to you that within physical focus, there is NO THING that you need, and there is no thing within your physical focus that you WANT that you may not provide yourself with in trusting yourself. This may appear and sound to you quite oversimplified, but I am quite aware of the difficulty that you hold in implementing this concept, creating it as a reality.

In actuality, if you are trusting of yourself and moving into the directions of your desire and what is creating of your fun and your pleasure and that which you identify as your happiness, trusting in yourself in these areas, you also create an ease and amaze yourself and express to yourself, "How may this be, that elements merely come to me?" But they are not merely coming to you, for you are automatically creating that to be drawn to you. This is the aspect that you do not understand!

Look to your creativity. Look to your wants. Look to your desires. Look to those aspects of yourself that create your fun, your happiness, your pleasure, and as you look to those elements, you may also turn your attention to the vast well of creativity that you hold within you to be manifesting in those areas; not necessarily in the areas that you think you MUST be accomplishing, but in the areas that you WANT to be accomplishing.

Let me also express to you another aspect of your reality that may be helpful to you, which I have expressed this also many times, but individuals many times are not listening.

Occupy your attention within the now. You turn your attention to projections of future, and you automatically set yourselves in motion for disappointment and conflict.

Individuals within your time framework presently hold a usage of your language, of "setting up." You express this to yourselves, to each other, quite often — setting up: setting up of situations of circumstances, of other individuals, of yourselves. Let me express to you that as you project yourselves futurely or pastly, you are NOT focusing your attention within the now and you are NOT offering yourself all of your choices which are available to you. You are also NOT allowing yourselves to be trusting and accepting of yourselves, for you are always moving in the direction of futurely or pastly, and you shall not be accomplishing if you are not attending your attention to NOW.

For in reality, there is no futurely and there is no past. All is now. All that you create is now, all that you shall create is now, all that you have created is now!

You may look to yourself and you may set yourself in motion. You may "set up" yourself in expressing to yourself within this now, "An event shall be occurring next week. I am quite worrying of this event." Why shall you worry of an event of next week? It is not now!

As inadequate as it may seem to you, you may not be engaging physical focus next week! (Laughter)

Therefore, it matters not as you "set yourself up" in the motion of expressing to yourself, "I may relax now, for I anticipate next year."

I am quite encouraging you to be focusing upon now and creating your choices within the now. (#335)

There are no limitations to what you may be creating within this physical focus. You present yourselves with your own obstacles, but you also hold the ability to move all of the obstacles that you place before you, and they are not so very difficult to be removing from your path, so to speak.

You are quite efficient and accomplished at offering yourselves obstacles and reinforcing yourselves that you may not be creating what you desire to be creating, but I express to you that you hold the ability equally to be removing all of these obstacles, or to not be creating them at all.

In this, there is one key, and holding this one key is the element that shall provide you with the objective ability to create all that you desire.

Now; this one key may appear in your language as very simple, but in actuality, applying it genuinely within yourselves is another matter entirely. The key is trusting yourselves and your own abilities, and knowing — not doubting, knowing — that what you set into motion within probabilities you may accomplish, regardless of how very impossible it may seem.

There is no impossibility, even within your physical focus. You, if genuinely accepting and trusting yourselves and KNOWING that you hold the ability to move in whatever direction you choose, may even move your physical form through objects of physical solid matter.

There is NO element within your focus that you may not be creating. You merely BELIEVE that you may not be creating.

Let me express to you also that there are examples of individuals that create amazing events and materializations within their focus, and you may be amazed at their accomplishments, but you also discount them by expressing to yourselves and to other individuals that these individuals may be participating in cults, or that they are not viewing reality realistically, or that they are experiencing lunacy. But these lunatics are creating their reality quite efficiently and not creating conflict in the areas that you create conflict, for you do not allow yourselves the same abilities for fear that you may appear to be a lunatic also!

In this, you limit your own creations. You dare not be expressing an impossible feat to another individual, for you may not hold the ability to actually be creating of this, and other individuals shall surely see this and shall surely deem you a lunatic. And what does it matter, if you are creating efficiently and effortlessly?

I express to you that I shall heartily advocate ALL of you creating lunacy for yourselves, and in this quite joyfully creating wondrous actions and events within your focus, within your reality, be it far removed from the officially accepted reality of your societies. It matters not! You each may be creating of wonders, and the key is merely the knowing and the trusting of yourselves.

Let me offer you, hypothetically, a small example. (Elias was very funny and very "on" throughout the rest of this session)

(Humorously) Within the cosmos, we essences, as you know and are fully aware, are floating about and watching you all within physical focus, for you are so very entertaining! (Laughter)

Therefore, as we sit upon our clouds and view you all scurrying around, we are aware of listening to the moaning and complaining continuously of how you are not creating enough currency and financial aspects within your focus to be providing you with all of your desires! Blah blah blah blah blah! (Laughter)

And as we are watching all of you and being quite amused at your tremendous moaning of what you do not have, we also turn our attention, upon our clouds, to some individuals who ARE trusting, and within THEIR reality, events, objects, desires, wants, seem to merely come to them. They are little magnets attracting all of the joyful and wondrous elements of their focus that merely fall upon them.

And all of YOU are continuing to be moaning and also creating angriness within you towards these other individuals, expressing,

"Why shall you have all that you desire, and I am struggling struggling struggling, and I am not accomplishing?" (Laughing) And you continue to not be trusting yourselves!

And the other individual may express to you, "You need merely trust the universe. It shall offer to you. Chant a mantra and believe in this, and it shall come to you!" And you shall shake your head and express to yourselves, "No, no, no! You are a lunatic, and I must be creating much work and struggling to be accomplishing within my focus!" I express to you, very, very, very, very, very incorrect! (Laughing)

You need not struggle. This is a choice. If you choose to be struggling, we shall be viewing you from our clouds within the cosmos and being quite amused at your whining and your struggling and your complaining of how you are not creating what you choose and wish to be creating, for we are quite aware that your reality is quite removed from you! It is all "subconscious."

THIS is what is creating of your reality, this elusive element of consciousness that is beneath some other area of consciousness that you may not tap into and have no control within these areas. Some other energy element is creating for you without your permission! (Laughing)

There is no subconsciousness! There is no lesser consciousness! ALL of consciousness is available to you. It is merely a situation of your own choices as to whether you choose to be accessing all of your consciousness.

Ah! But let us not be forgetful that you are only engaging ten percent of your physical brain! Therefore, you also are quite inefficient at creating your reality, for this mass of organ which resides within your physical head is not being accessed!

I shall express to you that you may remove physically half or more of your physical brain, and continue to be creating within your physical focus as efficiently as you are now ... or as inefficiently! (Laughing) And you may manipulate your reality in the same manner.

Your physical brain is not creating your reality! It is merely communicating impulses to your physical body. This is not what is creating of your thought processes. YOU are creating your thought process, YOU as consciousness, in cooperation with your physical form as your outward expression. Therefore, I do not accept the excuse of your brain being inefficient to be creating your reality or that you hold some element removed from you — as this elusive sub-consciousness that is such a demon — creating undesirable elements within your focus that you are not choosing ... for YOU do not create your reality! We are aware of this! (Laughing)

From its cloud upon this elusive cosmos! (Laughing) We are all quite amused! (Laughing)

Now! I express to you to be altering your moping and your frowning and your complaining of what you do not possess, and to be offering yourselves laughter and joyfulness and the acknowledgment that you DO hold the ability to create ANY element that you so choose!

Q: You spoke a lot tonight about that we could perhaps choose what we wanted, and that if we believe or we know that we're gonna get something, we will get it. I hear what you're saying, but I guess what I'm wondering is, if you intrinsically don't feel like you're gonna get something but you want to get it, how do you create a belief that you will get it?

ELIAS: It is not necessarily creating the belief that you shall receive, but allowing yourself to recognize and genuinely hold the trust in self, which allows you the knowing that you shall be creating. You do not trust yourselves and therefore you doubt what you may be creating, and as you doubt, you block your own creations and you block your own ability.

Therefore, ALL stems from the basic building block, so to speak, of the trust within self, the trust that you truly may create ANY element within your physical focus, KNOWING that you ARE magnificent creatures and that you need no other individual to dictate any element to you. You are quite efficient and hold the ability to be creating in ANY direction that you choose. It is merely a question of your own trust of self, and as you are trusting, you shall not doubt.

You trust that you hold the ability to walk, do you not?

Q: Yes.

ELIAS: And therefore, you walk, and you do not allow yourself a thought process concerning your walking. You merely create it. You merely implement it effortlessly, thoughtlessly. You do not concern yourself with its mechanics. You do not concern yourself with the dissection of the probabilities that enable you to enact walking. You merely trust that you hold this ability, and therefore you do.

In this manner, as you trust within all of your creations that you hold the ability to be accomplishing, it is unnecessary to be lending any energy in obstacles, and your obstacles are created by doubt.

As you allow yourselves to be genuinely trusting yourselves, you also shall be much more attuned to your own voice, which quite clearly offers you directions each moment. Each day — each MOMENT of each day — you are offering yourselves communication, but you are not listening and you are not paying attention. You are not noticing.

YOU ARE NOT NOTICING!

Q: I know, I know, I know!

ELIAS: This is not to say that you are not creating or speaking to yourself or offering yourself information! You are merely not noticing, for where are you? You are not within the present! You are noticing myself, for you are present now. And within your moments, your days within physical focus, are you so very present? You are projecting pastly, futurely; five minutes from now, five minutes ago; two weeks ahead…

Q: A whole lifetime!

ELIAS: Next year, last year! And you are not noticing now, and your communication is now, for your reality is now! Your reality is not next year. It is now! ALL of reality is now! There is no past, there is no future. There is merely now!

Q: How do we live more in the now?

ELIAS: Remind yourselves. Practice, and as you practice with your attention, you allow yourself more acceptance of self. You allow yourselves to trust yourselves within the now. You do not create massive conflict in projections, and you eliminate much of your confusion, and you allow yourselves the ability to LISTEN to self and to HEAR self. How shall you be hearing self if you are listening to all other elements? Think to yourself of your mirror images that you create within physical focus. Every behavior that you create within physical focus is some type of mirror action of subjective movement.

If you are choosing to be concentrating upon a communication with one other individual, how shall you be attentive to this communication if you are also listening to twenty other individuals speaking to you simultaneously and thinking about what you shall be creating tomorrow and what you are not very efficient at creating yesterday? This one conversation with this one individual shall become dimmer and dimmer and dimmer and quieter and quieter, and you shall be expressing, "What? What have you expressed? I was not hearing what you have expressed. Speak up!"

The voice is quite loud enough, but you are not listening. You are not noticing, for you are allowing your attention to move in many other directions, and you are not holding to the now.

All of these expressions that I offer you are so very simple. They are so very easy, but you complicate them so immensely, and you allow your belief systems to manipulate you in this direction and in that direction, and you become a bouncing ball all around your field, and you know not where to move. (Smiling)

Begin in the now. Begin to be trusting YOU — not what other individuals view, not what other individuals express, not the expectation of other individuals, not YOUR expectation of THEIR expectation, but your own trust of you, NOW — and this be the manner in which you shall begin to be accomplishing all that you desire effortlessly, not questioning.

Q: Trusting self in the now. I'd like you to comment on the relationship between what people term centering — and I don't know if you've used that term or not — and being in the now.

ELIAS: Many individuals express this terminology of centering. There are many different definitions within physical focus of this terminology of centering, but...

Q: Have you ever used it?

ELIAS: I do not express the expression of centering, so to speak.

Although it is merely another term for balance, which I have expressed previously, and acceptance; focusing upon self, not upon all that you view to be outside of self, but upon self. In focusing upon self, you allow yourself an acceptance of self, and in this you practice your trusting of self. This may be accomplished in many different manners.

You are quite efficient at developing methods. Therefore, you may choose any of your methods that you find acceptable to yourself to be engaging this action of looking to self, may it be brushing burrs within a creature's fur, may it be sitting and participating in what you term to be meditation, may it be exercising and involving yourself in much physical activity. It matters not.

Each of you shall find your own manner in which you allow yourselves to be connecting with self, and this is your quietness, and in this quietness you shall allow yourself the acceptance, and this shall provide you with your trust.

You do not create outside of yourself. You BELIEVE that you create outside of yourself, but you do not. You create within, for each creation that you engage begins with the creation of a probability, and that probability comes from within. (#345)

Q: Well, it seems that if trusting self and allowing yourself to physically manifest what is in alignment with your intent and your value fulfillment is really the most efficient way to eliminate conflict, it seems that wants would be in opposition to that.

ELIAS: Not necessarily, but if your wants become obsessive or if your wants are occupying the majority of your thought process, then you are thwarting yourself.

Q: Wouldn't a trusting of self and a belief and an understanding that no experience is better or worse lead to an acceptance of, "Any experience is okay and in alignment with intent?" And if I were to put myself in a position of that kind of trust and acceptance of whatever happens, it seems that that would eliminate wants.

ELIAS: You shall have desires which are in line with your intent. Your wants shall become temporary.

Q: Temporary until they're fulfilled? Why would they be temporary?

ELIAS: In this, I may express that within reality your ongoing wants are also temporary, but within this context I express that they shall be very temporary, for you may desire movement into new areas as you are always becoming and exploring, but you shall not experience conflict with these wants which are connected to the desire, for you shall allow yourself within trust to manifest. Therefore, these shall be temporary. You experience conflict for you do not manifest. Therefore, you continue your cycle over and over. You do not manifest. Therefore, you concentrate more. Therefore, you experience more conflict, and as you experience more conflict, you concentrate more, and you experience more conflict!

Q: Would wants that are not in alignment with our intent be a result of belief systems?

ELIAS: Absolutely.

Q: If I want to apply what you're talking about, the first step for me would be to concentrate less on my wants and just have more of an allowance of action, whatever that action is, without judgment about it?

ELIAS: Partially.

Q: Okay, what's the other part?

ELIAS: You look to your concentration as a means of manifesting. You concentrate upon these areas that you wish to manifest, which the more you concentrate upon these, in essence what you are accomplishing is reinforcing the underlying belief systems, for if you do not hold these belief systems that you may not accomplish, it would be unnecessary to continue to be concentrating upon the objective, but as you doubt and do not trust, you continue within your concentration and you continue to reinforce the belief systems.

Q: The conundrum that I have with this whole situation is that if we ultimately accept and allow action to occur naturally, it's very possible that the action that occurs and which is in alignment with our intent is not in alignment with what we objectively think we want. It may be completely opposite, and it's the letting go of belief systems about some things being good and some things being bad that is the tough one for me, and the reason why it's really hard to let go and trust. Because it's almost like setting a boat to sail and just letting it go wherever the tide takes it and trusting that even if it crashes against the rocks, that's okay because there is no good or bad. But it's this fear of crashing against the rocks that keeps me at the rudder of the boat, steering it in the direction I want to go, even if the wind is in another direction and I'm fighting it the whole way. So it's a real puzzlement about how to let go of these belief systems about good and bad and just be accepting of whatever happens.

ELIAS: Your attempts to this present now are unsatisfactory to you. Therefore, why do you not choose to explore another avenue? (Pause) Fear!

Q: All of us would like to be in line with our intents, naturally. But some of us have never developed an instinct or an intuition to trust ourselves to know that intent, and perhaps we'd all like to know sooner instead of later what our intent has been so we can accomplish these things. Can you give us a few ideas on developing an understanding of our intent, or of ourselves and our belief systems?

ELIAS: Look to yourself and examine the entirety of your focus. Look to the commonalties throughout your focus presently. Your intent shall be manifest from the beginning. You shall be following with this throughout the entirety of your focus. Therefore, look and view the events and the desires within you throughout your focus, and you shall arrive at the intent that you hold.

Be understanding that regardless of whether you realize objectively what your intent is, you shall manifest in line with this intent. You may experience conflict, for you hold fearfulness and you allow belief systems to block you within your movement, but you shall be manifesting within the designs of your intent.

Q: If I were to follow my inner feelings, I would really believe that I know most of my intent, but I would say the conflict comes when I do not allow myself to go that way or when I allow others around me to discourage me from that.

ELIAS: Quite; for I express to you to look to self. Trust self. This is of utmost importance; not to be following of another or allowing conflicting influence of another, but to be a straight little sapling and to be concerned only with self. You shall not betray you! You know within you which direction you wish to proceed within.

You allow yourselves, as you do not trust yourselves, to be swayed by other individuals and circumstances and belief systems. It is quite difficult within physical focus to be trusting of self and knowing that you shall not betray you.

Individuals express, "Trust within the universe and it shall provide for you." I shall express to you, this is not quite so far off. Trust self, and you shall provide for you!

Q: Is that why at times when, I mean on a small scale of this grand idea, if you let something go, you have something on your mind that you want to find or that you want to do, you just let it go and trust that "It'll come up, I'm not gonna make a big deal about this," and then in my experience, it just shows up. You know, something in my mind says, "Oh, look under there," and I find it. So basically you're just saying that we can do this very same thing on a grand scale, and that's what this goal thing and the purpose thing all comes from. Is that right?

ELIAS: Absolutely. Effortlessly!

Q: So we really don't have to do anything.

ELIAS: Your belief systems dictate to you that you must do much, that you must be striving, that you must be expelling tremendous effort or you shall not accomplish your goals. I have expressed to you ongoingly, you may accomplish all effortlessly. You create effort with conflict, for you do not trust.

Q: Effortlessness doesn't necessarily imply non-action, though.

ELIAS: Correct.

Q: So to use the example of the boat, you don't just get on the boat and wait for it to float someplace, whether that be on the rocks or out to sea. It's still appropriate to be at the rudder. You just have to trust that you're going to steer the boat in the proper direction and have some sense of where you want to go.

ELIAS: Trust your directions. You are the director. You are the captain of the boat.

Q: So not steering the boat would be not accepting or trusting.
It would be simply giving up. (Elias nods) But it is true to say
that your intent, or the experience you've chosen for this life, is
to crash into the rocks, is it not?

ELIAS: If you are choosing! (Laughter)

Q: But we are where we're supposed to be at this moment, and
everything that's come before was supposed to have happened,
and everything is okay.

ELIAS: Quite, this being how you may look to yourselves and
be accepting of self. There is no difference with "supposed to
be" or "choose." It is the same, for all things are choice. All
actions, all probabilities, are choice. You have chosen every
action within your focus. You are where you have created
yourself to be. If you are experiencing conflict within what you
have created, you may look to yourself inwardly and explore the
belief systems that hold you, that do not allow your movement
and cloud your choices, to be experiencing no conflict.

You hold many, many belief systems, many of which are in line
with obligation to other individuals. You create your reality
dependent upon your belief systems of the expectations of
others. You must be appearing at your work place at a specific
time. You must be accomplishing a specific task. You must
speak within a certain manner, as to not be offensive to
another individual. You must be caring for another individual.
You must, you must, you must! All of these musts are belief
systems. You may choose to hold these belief systems, and they
may be efficient, and you may not experience conflict within
them; but you also may experience conflict, and as you do, then
you may evaluate these belief systems, recognizing that all that
you accomplish, all that you do, is filtered through belief
systems. Some of these belief systems are efficient for you;
some are not. (#165)

I am quite aware that individuals grow weary of my continuous expression in this area, over and over, in this acceptance of self! And I shall continue to be repeating of this concept until the point that each of you converts this concept into an actual reality, that you recognize that you are not creating this acceptance of self, and that within the actual action of widening your awareness and accepting and trusting of yourself, you are automatically creating of new, amazing liberation, that you shall actually experience in what you attain to experience now! But you SHALL experience and amaze yourselves in each movement that you allow yourselves in the area of the acceptance and trust of self.

All that you may imagine within your physical focus, of your spirituality or of your playful creations, may be actualized in reality within your physical dimension, merely in the action of trusting and accepting self. But this continues to be merely a concept within you that you attain to, and you have not realized that there is no attaining to this. You already hold it. You need merely discover what you hold! But you have blanketed this with your different aspects and expressions of your belief systems. Therefore, you are covering your own awareness and your own periphery, but as you peel away all of these blankets, you allow this shining ability, and you amaze yourself with your own creativity.

The word "creativity" means little to you each, for you do not understand the implication of what you may create in allowing your creativity. You do not understand the ability that you hold within your expressions. You fascinate yourselves with the miraculous expressions of certain individuals throughout your history, within this dimension, that possess strange and wondrous abilities to alter physical reality in amazing manners, but you ALL hold this ability.

You ARE your own channel, so to speak, for you may channel your energy in any direction that you are so choosing, and your physical focus is not so very limited as you view it to be!

(Humorously) You BELIEVE that your physical manifestation is quite limited, for you of course are within a working, learning dimension upon a working, learning planet upon a working, learning plane, which shall we not forget is a very lowly plane, that you need be learning your lessons quite well, that you may attain to your higher planes and move into your greater abilities with your "higher self."

You do not hold a higher self! You ARE your higher self! You are your highest expression! You are all that you may be, and your physical dimension holds the ability to accommodate much more of your expressions and your creativity than you allow yourselves to view. You may channel energy through your physical self, through your physical expression, in countless different directions that you do not even allow yourselves to imagine.

Q: So for me personally, what is this huge blanket I hold up to myself, that I will not allow myself to know this already?

ELIAS: Your expression is quite similar to many, many, many other individuals within physical focus. For yourself individually, I shall be repeating to be focusing your attention upon the acceptance of self, WITHIN REALITY. You may move throughout your focus continuously, and you may express to every other individual that you physically encounter upon your planet that you are a wondrous, glorious being: "Look to me! I shine like a star! I am a glorious being, and I adore myself!" (Laughter) And you may project this false personification, but in actuality, as you quietly, individually turn your attention inwardly, the star becomes quite dim.

Q: We have an amazing belief in practice makes perfect!

ELIAS: Ah, for you are not perfect! You are flawed! And you have created mistake after mistake after mistake within your physical focus, and you also are the victim of your very self and your mistaken creations! (Grinning)

Q: I'm my own worst enemy!

ELIAS: Quite! And suddenly, this bright, shining, glorious star becomes this black hole of inverted energy that you are lost within, screaming to yourself that you may not find the light! (Grinning) And THIS is the blanket that you cover yourself with!

I am not expressing to you that your practicing within your outward expression may not be influencing, for within your physical expressions and creations within physical manifestations, you DO allow yourself to assimilate information that you repeat to yourself, regardless of your belief within it.

Therefore, this be the reason that many essences and many individuals shall express to you that you affirm to yourself some element that you do not believe over and over again, and you shall believe this.

In part, there is validity to this action, and I myself have offered this suggestion to certain individuals in certain situations, knowing those particular individuals, and in this, knowing their acclimation to this type of action. This is not an action that all individuals within physical focus shall allow themselves an acclimation to, but there are some individuals that respond to this particular type of action quite efficiently.

With yourself, this may not be an efficient expression, for you may move about your day and you may express to yourself ten thousand repetitions that you are a glorious being, and you shall merely be expressing physical words and you shall continue within this expression of the words, but the belief does not accept the words. "I am a glorious being." "No!" "I am a glorious being." "No!" "I am a glorious being." "No!"

Q: Yes, but I can use that to make it so that I don't spend time actually going inside and thinking about it!

ELIAS: Ah!

Q: Ah! (Laughing)

ELIAS: Therefore, you may distract yourself!

Q: It's a wonderful tool! Yes!

ELIAS: And you may offer yourself a different direction within your distraction, which is quite efficient in NOT occupying your attention with self and the acceptance of self, but distracting yourself in another area, that you may not occupy your attention with those elements that you look to as unpleasant or distasteful.

What is so very awful of yourself?

Q: God knows! (Everybody cracks up)

ELIAS: This be YOU! Therefore, answer MY question!

(Grinning) I express to you, God, how are you such a terrible little devil? For obviously, God is creating of the devil also!

Q: Hmm!

ELIAS: And as you are God, where be your devil that you are so displeased with? And what may you possibly create that is so very black — I am quite fond of black! — that may not be viewed? Be remembering, there are no secrets within essence. There is no element of you that is unknown within consciousness. Therefore, you delude yourself within your thought process that you may be hiding so efficiently behind your camouflage. You are accepted within all of consciousness, so why may you not accept yourself?

And I may express to you also, as I have expressed to other individuals previously, this may be your most difficult word within your objective language, of acceptance, that this be the reason that I express this concept over and over, that you may each understand the grave importance of this one action. And within the action of this shift in consciousness, you ALL within this dimension ... every individual physically focused upon your planet is within agreement to actualize this shift in consciousness.

Therefore, this action SHALL move, and you SHALL be accepting of belief systems! It is merely a question of how. Shall you be accepting them within trauma, or shall you be accepting them without trauma, within ease? And this be the reason that I speak to you, to be helpful in lessening the trauma associated with this acceptance. And I say to you, there is grave trauma that may be associated with this action. It is unfamiliar to you within physical focus.

You have created your physical focus within this dimension from the onset in the direction of moving through, holding to, manipulating around, and changing belief systems, not accepting belief systems. This is an unfamiliar action; a chosen action, but an unfamiliar action within your objective creating within this particular dimension. You move into an entirely new expression of this physical dimension, and in this, you are altering your reality. You may physically appear visually the same, but all your reality shall be different.

You may engage your imagination, which is also reality, and you may imagine to yourself of the trauma associated with this type of action. Think to yourself of your own experiences. This is quite similar to a physical birth, as I have expressed previously. You are within your labor within the action of this shift, and you are pushing to be giving birth to a new expression.

Q: Breathe!

ELIAS: And relax! And as you tense, you create painfulness. As you hold to energy, you create conflict and trauma. As you relax, you also ease your painfulness. As you let go of your energy, you create easement and no conflict. (Pause) And you shall be accomplishing! (#332)

I am expressing to you quite often to be addressing to belief systems, but I have consistently expressed to you all that the first action that shall be addressed with you all is to be looking in the direction of self and acceptance and trust of self FIRST, for in this action there are many automatic byproducts that lend themselves to the easement of all of the other directions that you may choose to be moving into, and this shall also lend much to the easement of your movement within the action of this shift, in acceptance of belief systems and the acceptance of other individuals and of all of your situations.

The acceptance of many, many, many aspects of your reality hinges upon your acceptance of self, but you automatically move in the reverse direction, for this is the type of creating that you are accustomed to. You are familiar with creating in relation to all aspects that you view to be outside of yourself first, and looking to self last, so to speak.

This be the reason that these concepts are so very difficult for you within physical focus, for I have presented them in reverse, and although they seem to be within your language quite simplified, they hold extreme difficulty, for you automatically move in the reverse direction: in looking outside of yourselves or looking to other aspects of your reality first, before looking to self.

Within the very context of this information, you automatically focus your attention upon your belief systems and all of the aspects of the belief systems first, and attempt to be altering of your belief systems or manipulating them in EVERY direction that you may think of and NOT addressing to your own issues in duplicity and addressing to self and your self—acceptance and your self—trust, which in looking to THIS element FIRST, you automatically create byproducts of accepting many aspects of the belief systems that you hold, and you automatically move in the direction of elements of acceptance of other individuals.

But you are QUITE insistent upon the continuation of playing with this dead mouse and moving in the direction of the reversal of my information to you!

Therefore, I move in the direction of becoming quite redundant, expressing to you over and over and over again: look to self and the acceptance and trust of self, and this shall automatically lend itself to your other accomplishments, and in this repeated statement I hold great hopefulness that eventually, within your linear time framework, you shall HEAR these words and you shall heed them also and offer yourself a slight turn in your perception within your focus, and in this slight turn you shall allow yourself the ability to view the ease in which you may be accomplishing, as in difference to the difficulty that you create that is unnecessary! (Chuckling) (#325)

Q: What else can one do to change their core belief systems and learn more about themselves and trust themselves? It seems like I've been trying for so long to do what you're talking about doing. If I'm not doing it right yet, what should I be doing that I'm not?

ELIAS: Ah! First of all, you are not "not doing it right," for you are not doing it wrong! But I shall say to you, many individuals endeavor to be exploring many areas of consciousness and never engage their own core belief systems. Many individuals that you may physically view and call " master" engage many activities within many areas of consciousness and do not widen belief systems and do not acknowledge belief systems and continue within their belief systems. You may explore many areas and experience these areas. If you are holding a desire to be moving within consciousness to widen your awareness, then you must be looking to self and examining these belief systems and understanding, recognizing and accepting of belief systems. In this, you also shall be influencing of how you are creating your reality. Individuals presently within this time period have incorporated, as you express this, your "new age" type of thinking. They have created their new religion of "metaphysics" and continue only with new terms, but continue belief systems that have been in existence throughout your history.

The point of this interaction is to be allowing you to recognize the belief systems that you hold within physical focus, and in recognition of these belief systems you may also be accepting of these, and therefore diffusing them.

Q: And I'll recognize these through my actions, through what I manifest? If I'm not currently aware of them, what's the best way to become aware of my core belief systems?

ELIAS: You shall, as you ask, present yourself with examples frequently. As has been said in ancient times, "Be watchful of what you request, for you shall have it!"

As you ask to be widening your awareness, you shall. You shall draw to yourself information to be challenging of yourself. You shall notice your own actions. You shall notice within individuals around you. You shall notice in everyday life all about you. Those belief systems that need be recognized and accepted shall be presenting themselves to you, for you shall present them to yourself.

You may not initially recognize automatically and identify the belief system. You may view similar actions occurring repeatedly before you, and you may view these actions for a time period before you recognize what you are presenting yourself with. You may engage individuals within this forum and exchange also with them, for they experience this also and may offer helpfulness and instruction as they have experienced this phenomenon of identifying belief systems. This is not as simple as it sounds!

Q: It doesn't sound simple!

ELIAS: As I have stated, you have carried belief systems for centuries and have worked with them. You are not so willing to be accepting of these belief systems and disallowing their power! Many are very, very strong. You do not even recognize that all that you do within physical focus is related to a belief system. Every action that you take within physical focus is related to a belief system. This is not "bad." It is what you have created. It is now only inefficient. As I have stated this evening, you shall continue with your belief systems even within your shift, but you shall understand and accept these. Therefore, you shall not be influenced or blinded by them as you may be presently. (#146)

I have offered you much information as to the identification of your self, and as you are listening, even the act of recognition that you are confused is an exhibition that you are attempting to be listening to self. I have expressed to you all many times that your self shall not betray you. You, regardless of what you may express to me, do NOT believe this! You hold a very strong belief system of the duplicity of self. Therefore, you do not believe when you are told that you will not betray self. But I express to you, in complete immaculate sincerity, you shall not betray yourself! You shall move to your own value fulfillment, and you shall also, as does all consciousness, add to the value fulfillment of all consciousness simultaneously. (#153)

Chapter 12

BIRTH–DEATH–TRANSITION

"There are many questions concerning what you term death.
This does not exist.
It is only birth, a moving timeline of one birth to another."

(# 4)

Chapter 12

BIRTH–DEATH–TRANSITION

Q: I'd like to ask you about death. Like what happens when we die. There's a ton of information out there already, many books on the subject. I'm just curious as to what you have to say about it, from the moment we die. Then what?

ELIAS: As an individual focus disengages from this physical dimension — or what you term to be dies — that focus, that individual enters into the beginning throes of an area of consciousness which is identified as transition.

In this action of transition — for it is not a place — but in this action of transition, initially the individual retains their objective awareness in very like manner to physical focus.

They have not yet moved into the area of the presentment of all of their focuses simultaneously. They merely project singularly their objective awareness and materialize the scenarios of their belief systems.

Now; this you may liken to a hologram, for it does not hold the solidity in quality that your physical dimension holds, although it may APPEAR that it holds that same type of solidity.

In this, think of your concepts that you present yourselves with presently in your science fiction. In your technology of your science fiction presently, you project the idea of holograms as holding the quality of such solidity that they appear to be actual reality.

In this, what I am expressing to you is that an individual focus that has disengaged or has died within physical focus moves to the action of transition, in which they continue to hold temporarily the same — or almost the same — quality of objective awareness as they held while they were participating in physical focus. Therefore, the area of transition appears to them to be quite similar.

In this, they shall create the imagery or the hologram, so to speak, of very similar creations — the same earth, the same human beings, the same creatures, the same vegetation, the same structures. All of these elements are familiar to them and they are all intimately involved with their belief systems, and as they are continuing to project through an objective awareness, they create a type of holographic imagery that appears to be solid and appears very similar to your reality within physical focus.

Now; an individual may continue in this type of creation for some time framework, in your terms. Be remembering once again, this is figurative, for within nonphysical areas of consciousness there is no time framework, but within your concept it may translate into a time framework.

Therefore, the individual may continue in this type of creation of this holographic imagery for an extended time framework appearance, not yet moving into the actual action of transition, which is the shedding of belief systems, for the actual action of transition initiates and continues the viewing of all focuses simultaneously.

This action, incorporating the individual's belief systems which have not been shed yet, would be creating of tremendous trauma and confusion were the individual to project themselves entirely into the action of transition immediately following their disengagement of physical focus.

Therefore, individuals do not engage this type of action. They move into the action of transition as they allow themselves an acclimating time framework, in a manner of speaking, for as they continue within the initial throes of transition, they also hold a realization that what they are creating in objective imagery more and more deviates from the type of objective creations that were created within physical focus. They become less and less solid and more and more changeable.

In this, as they realize that their reality holds much greater suppleness and changeability, they also realize that what they are creating in their holographic imagery is directly based upon their beliefs, but in difference to physical reality. You may hold an awareness that what you are creating within your reality is directly influenced by your belief systems to a point, but it holds a very different quality, for your physical dimension holds a solidity.

You do not question your belief systems as you view a wall. You do not question your belief systems as you view a structure. You do not view the structure and express to yourself that this is a projection of imagery based upon your beliefs. You merely accept that this is what you create within physical focus and that it is solid.

In this, you create another belief which expresses to you that solidity is absolute.

Within nonphysical projections of imagery, the individual becomes quite aware objectively that their creation is not as solid as it appears initially. They also become aware that the form of a thing is based upon their perception, which filters [through] their belief systems.

Therefore, as they alter their attention with belief systems, and move from one aspect of belief systems to another or examine their belief systems from one angle or another, their physical imagery also alters. In this, they demonstrate to themselves the lack of absoluteness and allow themselves a gradual ease into more of an understanding of their reality beyond belief systems. (#436)

Q: So what I am understanding, from what you're saying, is that what an individual shall experience after disengagement of physical reality, shall be determined by what beliefs they hold, as in the area of what they believe happens after one dies?

ELIAS: You may be an individual physically focused, expressing you hold no religious belief systems. You do not believe in God — you do not believe in heaven or hell — and at the moment of your death you may find yourself in heaven facing God, for your underlying belief systems lie in this direction and this shall be what you create.

Some individuals are creating of familiarity, or what they think of as familiarity objectively. Therefore, the scene does not change. They view life moving about them as it always has, but with a strange quality to it; but they may be functioning within this quite well for a time, for they are operating within their belief systems and their objective awareness.

Another individual may hold no religious belief systems in their opinion objectively, but they may view themselves within the strength of their own duplicity as inadequate and bad throughout their focus, and at the moment of their death they may find themselves in this burning place called hell. It is a temporary experience, one that they have created themselves within the strength of their own belief systems, but it is quite possible to be creating this objective imagery and it shall be very real!

Q: Is there more of a probability that you will create one of your underlying core belief systems that you may not objectively be aware of?

ELIAS: Yes. (#258)

Q: How do belief systems work in with transitioning? Is the act of transitioning, or choosing to have this be your last physical focus, how does that work in with belief systems? Because we have to have belief systems in order to be able to be functioning here in this physical focus. Is it an exchange of belief systems that brings us to a point of transition, or is it not connected at all?

ELIAS: Within the action of transition, this is different. You are moving from one manifestation within consciousness, one focus of attention which holds belief systems. These are unnecessary within non-physical focus. Therefore, you create the area of transition to be allowing the disengagement of objective awareness and the detachment from belief systems.

Belief systems are relative only to physical focuses within each dimension. They are not relative to non — physical focus. Therefore, transition is that area of consciousness which allows you the opportunity to discard or shed these belief systems, acclimating yourself to subjective awareness. You presently hold basically an understanding of objective awareness. As you move into transition, you transition from objective awareness into total subjective awareness, for objective awareness is also relative to physical focuses.

As I have stated previously, do not fool yourselves with the belief system that as you disengage physical focus, that you automatically disengage objective awareness. You do not! You carry into non — physical focus objective awareness. You are aware of belief systems. You are aware of physical body consciousness. You are aware of objective reality. Your physical form is that physical projection and expression — not a vessel — of your essence. Therefore, it is also you. (Emphatically)

The consciousness of the physical body, the physical form, is a projection of your consciousness, and as it retains its physical consciousness, in your estimation, after ... for there is no time framework, but within your physical reality there is, and your body consciousness holds its consciousness, at times, objectively beyond your physical choice to disengage. As we have spoken, this varies within your choice of how you shall disengage, and what you choose to be engaging with your physical form after your disengagement.

If you are choosing, as an example, cremation, your physical body consciousness moves into transition with you, in your terms, more quickly. If you are eaten by a bear, your physical body consciousness travels with you to transitional areas of consciousness immediately, for the energy is immediately reconstructed and absorbed by the creature and rearranged, and your consciousness of body or physical form is immediately projected also into transition. Therefore, you hold this awareness also for a time period, within your interaction in transition. As you shed your belief systems, this dissipates and reconstructs into different energy; therefore not existing any longer within the terms that you understand.

Within transition, the objective is to be eliminating — not within physical focus but within transition non-physically — to be eliminating of belief systems which are connected with an individual physical reality. You may not accomplish this without objective awareness, for objective awareness is belief systems! Your body consciousness is affected directly by belief systems. It also holds objective awareness. Therefore, that aspect of your consciousness that must be transposed or shed to be completely subjectively focused must also include physical form, which is an element of your projected image of essence. It is consciousness, no different than that which you recognize as the you of you.

You are not a shell! You do not possess a vessel! You are not a boat floating upon a river! You are not a vase containing flowers! You are a magnificent expression of extremely complicated arrangements of links of consciousness which physically manifest into matter of atoms and molecules that you manipulate. (#185)

Q: Well, what's the point of us being here then, if we have to go and get rid of everything? Sort of like you have to go like clean yourself to move on to the next... (Elias is shaking his head)

ELIAS: No, no, no, no, no! You are not rejecting or throwing away! You are holding to the experiences, which are creating an addition to your state of becoming, but it is unnecessary to hold to the belief systems that are connected to the experiences. The belief systems have been created within this dimension as explanations to yourselves objectively for concepts and behavior that you create that you have forgotten the truths within essence of. You hold elements of truth within your belief systems, but the belief systems have distorted these. Therefore, you shed the belief systems and return yourself to the knowing and the remembrance of essence, but you continue to hold the experience. (#288)

Q: Some one close to us all passed away recently. Is he engaging the action of transition presently?

ELIAS: Presently, James, or the focus of James which you know to be as that individual that you have called Tom, has not entered into the area of transition yet, but occupies another area of consciousness which is quite common to individuals disengaging that continue to hold very strong belief systems and emotional attachments to physical focus. He shall be eventually moving into the area of transition, but at this present now is not within that area or action yet.

It is not always automatic that you immediately move into the area of transition, into this action of transition. Even if you are engaging the action of transition within physical focus, you may move yourself into a temporary state of consciousness which is outside of the action of transition once choosing to be disengaging from physical focus, dependent upon your issues and your belief systems which are held within physical focus.

Q: Not long after Tom's death, his girlfriend had some kind of experience where she saw him. Had a visual of seeing him. Did she in fact see what some would term the spirit of the deceased?

ELIAS: Many individuals in the action of disengagement choose to be allowing energy deposits to be remaining within the area of Regional Area 1, physical focus. This is actual, physical, moving energy; that which you may term, in your language and in your terms solely, as living energy. It moves and it pulsates, and it holds elements of the personality of that particular individual which has occupied physical focus.

Now; within this energy deposit, the individual engaging disengagement from physical focus may also insert into this energy deposit any imagery that they are so choosing to be connecting with any physically focused individual.

You will find many times throughout your history, in individual situations or stories of physically focused individuals that hold great affection or connection to each other within their focus, they may be creating of an agreement objectively that at the time period of the disengagement of one, there shall be offered a symbol or imagery to the other individual which is remaining within physical focus that shall be recognizable to the remaining individual within physical focus. Throughout your myths, these may be termed to be " signs" of the continuation of the disengaged individual for the benefit of the remaining physically focused individual.

These "signs" have been romanticized throughout your history. In actuality, it is not an actual interaction of the individual focus disengaged with the individual physically—focused focus, but rather it is an energy deposit which remains purposefully by the individual who has chosen to disengage. This is left, so to speak, to offer encouragement and validation and also comfort to those individuals that remain within physical focus.

In this, let me express to you that regardless of challenges, issues, shrines and belief systems that any individual holds within physical focus, regardless of any of the experiences or actions that they choose to be engaging within, at the moment of disengagement there is an objective awareness that there is presented the opportunity to be offering of these energy deposits, and many times individuals move in the direction of engaging this action.

Therefore, there are individuals within physical focus that you term to be psychics that may engage these energy deposits and relate to you in translation that they have been within contact of this individual that you term to be "lost" or has moved to the " other side," so to speak … which there is no other side! In this, what they are accessing is the energy deposit, the personality which is attached to the energy deposit, and any imagery that the individual has placed within the energy deposit which shall be recognized by the individual inquiring of them.

The energy deposit which has been offered to you is that which has held a fascination or an attention to the individual of Tom before the action of disengagement. In this action of placing this particular type of imagery into the energy deposit, it is a recognizable symbol to you, therefore offering you a validation of the continuation of energy, also offering you a comfort that no thing has been lost, for although you do not objectively physically engage the individual any longer, the energy deposit remains and has been offered to you to be comforting to you in a manner that shall be recognizable to you personally.

Q: Did Tom accomplish his value fulfillment?

ELIAS: Every individual is accomplishing of their value fulfillment throughout their physical focus, and when they are not fulfilling their value fulfillment, they are choosing to be disengaging. This individual of Tom was not creating of his value fulfillment any longer, and therefore was choosing to be disengaging of this physical focus.

Q: Is Tom aware of our interaction today?

ELIAS: Not objectively, for the individual occupies an area of consciousness, as I have expressed, which you may term to be between physical focus and non-physical transition action. Therefore, in this state of consciousness, what shall occupy the individual's attention and interaction shall be the creation of their own belief systems and strongly held issues.

This is NOT a negative action. Be understanding of this! Energy must be expressed. Energy is ALWAYS expressed, and if it is not allowed its natural expression, it shall express itself in other manners. Once disengaging physical focus, the energy shall be expressed in a natural manner which shall be creating of imagery in alignment with those issues which have not been addressed to within physical focus.

Now; I express to you strongly, this is *not* a reviewing of your lifetime, so to speak. It is NOT karma. It is NOT punishment. It is NOT an automatic action that is created by some outside force which moves you into the area of accountability. It is a CHOICE which is automatically entered into after disengagement to be releasing objectively held energy in the area which has been held in shrines and issues which were not chosen to be engaged or moved through within physical focus.

Therefore, there is engaged a *temporary* situation with these individuals that they shall engage before the action of transition, a shedding or a releasing of this held or pent—up energy which is directly related to one individual focus, therefore allowing more of an ease and a balance once moving into the area of transition and the action of viewing all focuses and of meshing all focuses in the shedding of objective awareness.

Now; within a final focus, if issues are held tightly and not chosen to be addressed to or moved through within physical focus, many times the individual focus shall choose to create this in-between state temporarily, for the action of transition is slightly different in the engagement of a final focus than would it be in the engagement of not a final focus.

This particular individual was/is a final focus. Therefore, the action of transition shall be different from an individual focus that is not a final focus. The intensity is slightly greater and the action in your physical terms may be termed to be slightly longer, for there is no choice for a remanifestation.

Now; I am quite understanding that these terms are confusing to you all, for the terms are inadequate in the area of words such as remanifestation. For as I have expressed to you, you are not used parts and you do not remanifest, although an aspect of you may, and this may also be confusing to you, as in reality there is no RE—manifestation, for all of your manifestations are simultaneous. Therefore, you may not repeat or re-enter, for that is a designation of linear time which is merely relative to physical focus and not to non — physical focus.

In this, the individual of Tom, the focus of Tom, has entered into an area of consciousness, as I have stated, of in-between, that he may be releasing this energy; which in this particular situation, the most strongly held energy which was chosen not to be addressed to and not moved through is that of the emotion of guilt, which is a very strong lack of acceptance of self. To be facilitating more of an ease in entering into the action of transition non- physically, he has chosen initially to be addressing to these issues, to this emotion of guilt and the lack of acceptance of self within that particular focus, and in this action, the occurrence and the creation of this is that the individual presently creates a scenario in full imagery, in very like manner to your physically focused imagery, that shall be addressing to these particular issues solely. (#296)

The design of this physical dimension incorporates beliefs. In disengaging this physical dimension, you create an action which we have termed to be transition to be shedding those beliefs, but this is a process also and those issues that you create within this physical dimension … you shall follow you regardless of where you move. Therefore, those beliefs that you associate to be ensnaring you shall not necessarily disappear merely as you move…

Q: Oh no! Our beliefs follow us? Do our beliefs follow us?

ELIAS: They do not follow you, you bring them where you move — temporarily — to the point that you allow yourself the genuine recognition and acceptance of them.

Q: Acceptance of them.

ELIAS: Correct.

Q: So it's not just a task of getting rid of them. It's a task of embracing them.

ELIAS: Acceptance. You need not hold affection for your beliefs, but you need not curse them, either. They are neutral in themselves. Therefore, the acceptance of them is the key. For in the acceptance, you allow yourself the freedom of choice. When you are not accepting, you limit tremendously your choice, and therefore you limit your movement, and therefore you create the snare.

I may express to you, you may choose within any moment to be continuing or to be discontinuing your exploration in this physical dimension. I may also express to you, do not delude yourself. For where you move, there you are. (#850)

Q: I would like to ask you about NDE; near death experience; when people clinically die, but are revived for whatever reason or manner. There have been thousands of cases, but one of the most extraordinary is Dannion Brinkley, who was hit by lightning in 1975, died for eighteen minutes, then came back only to die again several years later from heart surgery and come back a second time. You might say he was almost indecisive about maintaining physical focus! He describes it as a great pain, then as a release followed by a great feeling of peace, and then an out-of-body experience where he looks down on his physical body and those that attended it, followed by a rushing up into a black tunnel, followed by meeting beings of light, as he called them, feeling an overwhelming sense of well-being, and then being presented with a life review in which everything that happened to him is reviewed, and also to the person he interacted with. He could see it from their point of view. He killed people in Vietnam, and was able to experience their deaths. Is this what happens to us when we leave physical focus?

ELIAS: It is dependent upon your belief systems. For this individual, this is reality, for this individual's belief systems dictate this; that you must be approached with a life review and experience what others have experienced that you have inflicted. This is a belief system connected with karma. There is no karma. There are MANY belief systems.

Now; I may express to you that some of these experiences are common to very, very, very many individuals in disengagement of physical focus; that of hovering momentarily and viewing your physical body is quite common. Many individual focuses choose this experience. They are disengaging from the physical body consciousness and evaluating momentarily the choice of their disengagement and how they have disengaged from the physical body consciousness. Therefore, they momentarily view the body consciousness, also allowing a last interaction with this body consciousness; a last communication.

Subsequent to this action, which is quite momentarily, many individuals of focuses enter a temporary state of peacefulness prior to engaging transition. This also may be viewed as momentarily, within your terms. It is what you may term to be a brief, temporary state of respite, so to speak; of peacefulness before entering into the area of transition. Once entering into the area of transition, how you transition is dictated by your belief systems. Some individuals hold belief systems that they shall be moving into the light; the tunnel that shall lead them to the heavenly areas and what they think of within their belief systems as their eternal bliss. Some individuals hold belief systems that they shall immediately move to the area of hell, which also does not exist, but they shall create this temporarily and experience its full force, for the full force and intensity of their belief systems shall come to bear.

What you experience once you disengage is absolutely dictated by your belief systems, and which belief systems you have moved through and which belief systems you have accepted and which belief systems you hold very strongly, and also whether you have chosen to engage transition while you are still within your physical focus. This may also be quite affecting of what you may be experiencing once moving into the area of transition non-physically. (Pause) And how very interesting that you now approach what you term to be very closeness to your cure, so to speak, of your senility!

(*In Elias' terms, we have created senility/Alzheimer's as an action of engaging transition physically, and because we are presently changing this mass belief system, a "cure" will be found in the near future*) (#232)

Q: My mother passed away about two years ago, and in the three or four or five months preceding her disengagement, her death, she was aware of … she called them beings. She had visitors. She had little boys and little girls and people and horses. She was very aware of a great deal of activity that was taking place around her and she spoke about it a little bit, but she did not speak about it a lot.

At our last dinner together, actually one of the main dinners, which was the last Thanksgiving, my sister was laughing at the fact that while she was feeding my mother, who was ninety-seven at the time, my mother was trying to feed a cookie to a little girl who was there and who was an image that she knew was there.

I'm telling you this because I want to ask you if these were not also her projections of images, her holograms, so to speak, that she was creating in response to activities that were taking place in nonphysical consciousness around her disengaging from this reality.

ELIAS: Not entirely. Now; let me express to you the difference, for there are differences that are created by different individuals. This is entirely a choice of the individual.

We have spoken previously of the engagement of transition within physical focus. An individual may choose to be engaging transition while they are continuing within physical focus, and in this, they may be creating certain aspects of the transitional action while they continue to be engaging physical focus. This many times — but not always — creates a situation with that particular individual in which they do not engage much of this initial activity that we have spoken of this day subsequent to disengagement.

Therefore, what I am expressing to you is that generally speaking, if an individual is engaging transition within physical focus, they eliminate much of the need, so to speak — once again, figuratively speaking — to be creating of these initial holographic images before engaging the viewing of all of their focuses, for they have already begun engaging other focuses.

Q: Are you saying that my mother was engaging in transition before her disengagement?

ELIAS: Correct, and in this, what she has allowed herself to be interacting with is other focuses of herself.

Q: Really!

ELIAS: … therefore allowing herself the opportunity to move into the action of transition with very little activity of this holographic projection of imagery.

Q: I see. Okay. Yeah, she seemed to be quite okay with the whole affair.

ELIAS: Quite, and I shall express to you that for the most part, individuals within physical focus do not hold fearfulness of these interactions within themselves.

At times, they may be responsive to OTHER individuals that are projecting their belief systems to them, in their expressions that it is unacceptable for them to be engaging invisible individuals, although the individuals are not invisible! They are merely not visible to your awareness, for you choose not to view them, but they are quite visible and quite real, and the individual that is interacting with them is quite aware of their presence and holds no element of fearfulness within themselves, left to themselves and not influenced by other individuals objectively surrounding them.

Now; they may be responsive at times to this type of action in questioning, and based upon THEIR belief systems that they hold individually, they may hold responsiveness in confusion and they may also rebel objectively with this type of interaction, for their belief systems dictate to them that this is unacceptable behavior and that they are experiencing lunacy.

Q: That did not occur with my mother.

ELIAS: Correct. What I am expressing is that if you are…

Q: If anything, she took it with … I hesitate to use the word humorously, but she certainly was okay with it.

ELIAS: Quite, for this is not a threatening action. It is merely an interaction and viewing of other focuses of the individual, which is the direction which occurs within the action of transition. (#436)

Q: I thought it would be pertinent to bring this up in the light of [a dear friend's]sudden departure and how it affected so many people, and if there was something we haven't touched yet regarding the hole, the emptiness — excuse me — (emotionally) that we feel when a friend has passed on. That's it. It's an open plea, if you will, for understanding.

ELIAS: Very well. This may offer you the opportunity to examine in reality the strength of your beliefs, not merely in concept. In these types of situations, my friend, you present yourself with actual experience in relation to the intensity of the influence of your beliefs in association with your perceptions and the opportunity to notice the reality of your perception and how this perception actually does create your physical reality. For in this, as you allow yourselves to be paying attention to what you generate in such intensity in what you identify as feelings, you also present to yourself now the opportunity to examine the information that I have offered to you not merely in concept but to explore this information and these concepts, and turn to allow yourself to generate them in reality rather than merely intellectual concept.

I have expressed to you that emotion is a communication. I have also expressed to you that within this physical dimension you generate a tremendous expression of separation, which prior to this shift in consciousness has been quite purposeful and has served you quite well in generating an allowance in the purity of your experiences. But I have also expressed that within the action of this shift you are thinning, and even in some aspects dropping, these veils of separation. You hold an awareness of this intellectually and in concept, but you also generate confusion in how you shall be creating that expression of dropping these veils.

From the onset of this forum, my friend, I have been expressing, one of the veils of separation that you are piercing in the action of this shift is that between physical focus and nonphysical expressions, and the concept of death. I have also expressed to you all to turn your attentions to self and allow yourselves to view your actual abilities.

This shift is now progressing into the objective insertion into your reality. Recently I have offered information to you all concerning paying attention to HOW you create your reality, not merely WHAT you create within your reality. And now, my friend, energy surges are occurring in strength to be almost FORCING yourselves to move your attentions to yourselves in association with all of these concepts to generate an actual reality. These are all aspects of this shift, and I have also expressed to you that these movements do generate trauma. In this, as you begin to allow yourself to pay attention to all of these concepts that I have offered to you in information and piece them together as an immense puzzle, you may begin to generate an understanding of HOW you create your movement.

Allow yourself the recognition of what I am expressing to you of the power of perception and how it actually generates all — ALL — of your physical reality, and in this, I am not speaking figuratively to you in the moments in which I express to you that although you do interact with other individuals' energies, you individually actually generate through your perception the actual physical manifestation of other individuals.

Recently I have offered information concerning what you engage in exchange of energy or interaction of energy with other individuals. I have explained that many times you are actually allowing yourselves to receive an energy expression, a projection, from another individual which is expressed with the other individual's attention, but there are also other time frameworks, moments, in which you interact with energy of another individual but not necessarily energy which contains the individual's attention. These may be energy deposits of the other individual, which are just as real and are aspects of the other individual's projected energy but may not necessarily incorporate the individual's attention. I have offered explanation in how you may recognize this difference, for you all engage these actions throughout your focuses.

The point of offering that information was to allow for an explanation concerning the individual's attention, YOUR attention, and what you create through your perception concerning individuals that have disengaged. For even as an individual may continue to be physically manifest within your physical dimension, what you interact with in actual physical manifestation is a creation of your own. It is a projection of YOUR perception.

Therefore, I have offered information to allow you to recognize, in your terms, what it means to be interactive with the energy expression of another individual and that that action is no different within physical focus or within nonphysical focus. The energy that you choose to be interactive with is the same, and you incorporate the ability to generate the configuration of that energy in physical expressions in the same manner as you do with an individual that is participating in physical focus as one that has chosen to disengage through what you term to be death and may be nonphysically focused. This also may be generated in association with other focuses of your own essence within this dimension and other dimensions.

I have offered explanation from the onset of this forum that this is an aspect of this shift in consciousness, but now, as you are inserting this shift into your objective reality, you are moving your awareness to a point of actually recognizing your abilities in these expressions. It may be initially confusing, but now you are actually allowing yourselves to begin creating these actions, not merely assimilating them subjectively.

In this, the reason that you generate such an intensity of sorrow in association with another individual that has chosen to be incorporating death is that this type of choice emphasizes to you the strength of your association with beliefs concerning separation. What is actually being communicated in that emotion is the clear identification of that influence of beliefs expressing to yourself, "Within this moment you are extremely denying your choices and discounting your ability." As I have expressed recently to other individuals, figuratively speaking in a manner that you may understand objectively, denial of your choices and extreme discounting of your abilities is so contrary to the natural expression of essence, for choice is so intrinsic to essence, that this is an expression that may almost move the essence to weep.

I may express to you, my friend, this type of extreme denial of choice within self is not expressed often, but in the moments in which it is, you shall incorporate a tremendous objective awareness for your communication to yourself shall almost be a scream. It shall be generated in tremendous intensity, and this is what you experience in the signal, in the feeling of tremendous sorrow and that which you have expressed as this immense hole. It is not an expression that has been generated by the choice of the other individual or that you are missing the other individual, although this is your automatic response and how you define what you are feeling. In actuality, what you are feeling is a tremendous inability to allow yourself to generate the same action of interacting with the other individual's energy that you allowed yourself prior to the other individual's disengagement.

Let me express to you, quite realistically there are individuals that do allow themselves to continue interaction with other individuals' energy expressions even subsequent to the individual's disengagement. Some allow themselves to open enough to merely allow an audible interaction in which they hear the other individual. Some allow merely for impressions of the other individual. Some allow dream interaction with the other individual. But there are some individuals that allow themselves to actually engage the same type of interaction with energy with an individual that has disengaged physical focus and generate an actual physical manifestation of the other individual in the same manner that they allowed themselves prior to the individual's disengagement.

Now; your societies view this type of expression as lunacy and express tremendous disbelief that an individual is engaging this type of interaction, but I may express to you quite literally, there are individuals that do allow themselves to continue to generate through their perception an actual physical manifestation of the other individual in the same manner that they generated it prior to the disengagement, for it is YOUR creation.

The only veil that stands between your energy and another individual's energy is that which you generate in association with your beliefs — PERIOD. For in actuality there IS no separation. Therefore, the energy continues to be expressed by yourself and by the other individual. (#1018)

Q: When you do disengage ... you've talked about going to an area where people experience peacefulness and tranquility, and you called it an area of just a moment of respite prior to going into transition. Who is it or what is it or how does it happen? What says, "Okay, you've got to go into transition now?"

ELIAS: YOU create this action. There is no other essence or element of consciousness that designates this for you or instructs you to be creating that movement. You shall choose the moment.

Q: So if you're in a place of tranquility and peacefulness, who would want to move out of that?

ELIAS: (With a crooked smile) This is your idea within your belief systems — within your religious belief systems — of the association of heaven, so to speak.

But your manifestation within this physical dimension is not so very far removed from what you create throughout consciousness. This is a physical manifestation — you are creating physical imagery — but you are exploring. You are experiencing. You are challenging yourselves continuously, for you are becoming, and the action of becoming is the action of exploration.

This is your natural movement. This is the natural movement of consciousness. Therefore, why shall you continue in a lack of movement and a lack of exploration or a continuation in redundancy? You shall also create boredom! For you naturally move in energy in the expression of exploration and investigation.

Q: So eventually then, you just get bored with peacefulness and tranquility, and carry on?

ELIAS: Your idea of peacefulness and tranquility appears appealing presently, but I shall express to you presently, you may be creating that action presently within the now. You may be creating that within your physical dimension.

I shall also express to you that most probably, in the most probable probability, you would not continue within that action throughout an entire focus, and the entirety of one focus is but a blink! (#539)

Chapter 13

REGIONAL AREAS OF CONSCIOUSNESS

"There are different areas of consciousness. These are related
to attention. All of consciousness is all of consciousness.
It is all the same. There are no planes. There are no levels.
There are no better or higher places within consciousness.
All is the same. There are different focuses of attention.
In this, there are created what we term as areas of consciousness."

(#157)

Chapter 13

REGIONAL AREAS OF CONSCIOUSNESS

ELIAS: Consciousness and essences within consciousness are in what you may term to be a continuous state of becoming, a continuous state of exploration. Therefore, within consciousness, there is a continuous movement to be creating areas to be exploring. All of these areas are within itself, for consciousness is all.

In this, Regional Area 1 is merely the designation of a physical reality and the objective awareness within that reality. There are many Regional Area 1's. All physical realities hold a Regional Area 1. This is the area in which you hold objective familiarity. It is all that you know objectively. This is your waking state.

In this, you have created manifestations of yourself as essence in this Regional Area 1 to be exploring different areas of reality. In a manner of speaking, it is an experimentation. You are playing and exploring all that you may create within a physical dimension of this type.

Now; as I have stated previously, the base elements of this particular physical dimension are emotion and sexuality. Therefore, all that you create within this particular Regional Area 1 is influenced by these two base elements, and in this, you create many, many different expressions and avenues of exploration to be experiencing different elements of these two base elements of your reality.

Regional Area 1 is not a creation of a dimension or a plane to be learning, so to speak. This is another expression of belief systems that individuals hold within this physical dimension. In actuality, you are merely creating a physical reality to be experiencing. This is the point, to be experiencing, for consciousness is continuously creating exploration and seeking out experience, and experiencing of itself and all of the different aspects of itself.

In this particular reality, you have chosen to be creating a type of separation between the focuses of attention and the known elements of essence. You have created this type of reality quite purposefully, that you may be experiencing the purity of each creation and each experience that is held within this particular dimension.

Were you to be offering yourself the entire remembrance of essence, it would be creating quite a different type of reality within this particular dimension. Therefore, you have created a veil, in a manner of speaking, between each of the focuses and all of essence.

Now; what you are creating presently is a shift in consciousness which is affecting of the entirety of this particular dimension. It is not necessarily directly affecting of other dimensions within consciousness, but it is quite affecting of this particular dimension.

Therefore, the entirety of your globe presently is experiencing this shift in consciousness, and what this shift is expressing is a movement into a remembrance of essence, a dropping of the veil that creates the objective separation of your awareness from essence.

As you move in this direction, you also create a tremendous opening to more of your expressed abilities to be creating within this physical dimension. You drop your limitations within this physical dimension.

But what shall be facilitating of this freedom and this movement within the action of this shift in consciousness is the acceptance of belief systems, for the belief systems that you hold within Regional Area 1 in this particular dimension are those elements that express to you limitations, and in your belief systems, you very strongly influence your perception.

Your perception is how you view yourself, how you view other individuals, and how you view your world and your universe.

Your belief systems directly influence your perception, and your perception is the tool in which your create your reality.

You all each create all of your reality. Every thought, every emotion, every event, every occurrence, every element of your reality you individually create, and all of that reality is created through your perception.

Your perception is not your thought process. Although your thought process and your emotions hold a tremendous involvement in your perception, it is not limited to your thoughts or your emotions. This is the entirety of your view of your reality, and as I have stated, it is the tool that you engage to be creating ALL of your reality within this physical dimension.

In acceptance of the belief systems that are held within this particular Regional Area 1, you also drop, in a manner of speaking, many of the limitations that you place upon yourselves presently in conjunction with your belief systems. There are many, many, many limitations that you place upon yourselves and obstacles that you place before yourselves presently in your reality, and all of these are created in conjunction with your belief systems.

You shall — or shall not — do or create certain elements within your reality as dictated by your beliefs. You may look to

212 THE SHIFT: A TIME OF CHANGE

your religious belief systems, and these clearly define objectively in your language very strong beliefs. You shall do this; you shall not do this. This is acceptable behavior; this is unacceptable behavior. What dictates these elements to you are your belief systems.

In this, as you allow yourselves to be accepting of these belief systems, you also open to your freedoms to be creating much more and exploring much more of your reality within Regional Area 1 OBJECTIVELY.

You already create many wonders and amazements within Regional Area 1, but within your belief systems, you look to these occasional occurrences as miracles, as amazing stories, as gifts, as unbelievable. I express to you, many of the occurrences that you view to be unbelievable are quite natural to you within your abilities. Your belief systems dictate to you that they are unnatural and that you need be holding very special gifts to be expressing of these unbelievable actions. I express to you, these are natural elements of you. These are natural abilities of yourselves.

You express to yourselves tremendous wonderment that an individual may be upon your planet and may materialize an object within their hand before them, within your air. This is a tremendous gift, a tremendous unusual ability. This is quite natural to all of you!

You all hold this ability. You merely do not believe that you hold this ability. This is an example of how your belief systems block your natural abilities and limit what you allow yourselves to create.

Look to your physical reality presently and all of the wonders that you create already — tremendous abilities that you display within your Regional Area 1 objective waking reality — great minds, great abilities, great accomplishments — and now view to yourselves without the limitations of your belief systems how much more wonders may you create and how much more of an exploration of your reality may you be engaged within, and this is what you are creating now.

You are creating a shift in consciousness in your reality to expand and open your awareness within your waking state — within your waking objective awareness — that shall allow you the knowing of what you are creating. You already are creating effortlessly and perfectly within your reality, but you do not allow yourself the understanding objectively of what you are creating.

You may create wondrous elements within your reality, and you express to yourselves amazement and wonderment in how you have created your reality. In your expansion within this shift in consciousness, you are allowing yourselves to be objectively — intentionally objectively — creating your reality in the manner that you choose.

Now; do not be confused, for you are already creating in the manner that you choose. There is no element of your reality that is hidden from you, but as we have discussed earlier within this particular session, you do not pay attention to what you are creating. Much of your creation escapes your attention. Therefore, within your thought process, you think that there are elements of your reality that are being created that you are unaware of and that you do not understand, OR that do not have your permission to be being created. (Pause)

Regional Area 1 is the area of consciousness that allows you the wonder of objective awareness; your waking, sensing, physical awareness; your recognition of all that you create and your participation in it.

Regional Area 2 is that area of consciousness which is closest to and directly in alignment with Regional Area 1. It moves in harmony to your objective awareness. This is the area of consciousness that we term to be subjective awareness. It is another element of you.

Movement through different areas, so to speak, of consciousness is continuously occurring. You as essence occupy all areas of consciousness simultaneously. As we have spoken earlier, once again, it is merely a question of where you are focusing your attention and how you are choosing to be exploring and creating.

As you move through Regional Area 1 and 2 and choose not to be participating in those areas, you choose to move into Regional Area 3, which creates an action of transition. This is what shall be engaged once you create death in this focus.

Upon movement through Regional Area 3, as I have stated, you may be choosing to move into any particular area of consciousness and creating an exploration.

I occupy my attention — of this aspect of this essence, that which you identify as this personality of Elias — within Regional Area 4, for it offers myself the opportunity to be interactive with you within Regional Area 1 without an overwhelming expression of energy translation. There be much more difficulty in expressing objective communication with all of you here within Regional Area 1 if I were to be focusing my attention within a much more far-removed regional area of consciousness.

There are other aspects of my essence which do not occupy Regional Area 4, but this particular aspect is within that area, which affords to myself the exploration and engagement of teaching, and this offers helpfulness to individuals within Regional Area 1.

(Smiling)There is much information in conjunction with other regional areas of consciousness, but I shall express to you that they do not translate well into your understanding within the limitation of physical language. Therefore, I choose not to be offering tremendous expressions of information in conjunction with other areas of consciousness, for this merely offers an element of distortion. (#488)

Chapter 14

REINCARNATION

"Many individuals speak of reincarnational lifetimes.
I find this terminology to be inadequate, as all of your focuses
are simultaneous. They only appear to not be simultaneous
within your identification of linear time frameworks."

(#174)

Chapter 14

REINCARNATION

Q: I'm particularly interested in knowing how long it takes one to reincarnate. I don't think there's a rule of thumb, but for this plane, is it many thousands of years, or can it happen with the next baby, so to speak?

ELIAS: This is a difficult subject matter for individuals within this physical dimension, for you have created very strong belief systems in the area of reincarnation.

Now; I shall initially express to you that reincarnation, in the manner that it is expressed in your philosophy, is a belief system. It does not occur in the manner that you express to yourselves within your ideas.

In actuality, outside of this physical dimension and outside of certain other physical dimensions — for this is not the only physical dimension which is in existence — but outside of physical dimensions, time does not exist in the manner in which you think.

Time is simultaneous. Time is an element which has been created in consciousness, and therefore is, in a manner of speaking, an entity in itself, but it is also relative to each physical dimension in its expression and its movement. In this particular physical dimension, you create the perception and the movement of time in linear fashion.

Now; let me also clarify in this area. The perception is your thought process of how time moves. It is your identification of the element of time and its movement in a fashion of forward. This is what we express as linear time. It moves in a line. You move from past to present to future, and all of your reality is encompassed by this creation of the movement of time. Therefore, even your language moves in conjunction with your creation of time.

Once you move outside of this physical dimension, the element of time is not relative any longer. Therefore, it is not created in the same manner.

This moves in conjunction with your belief system of reincarnation, for you view your reality to be moving through moments of time that you record as history. You also have created a perception of memory, which allows you recall of events and experiences, which also moves in a linear fashion.

In this, your perception of death as not being a final discontinuation of yourself moves into an identification of a return or a remanifestation, for you continue a thought process in a linear fashion.

In actuality, you do hold many focuses, that which you identify as lifetimes. I express the terminology of focuses quite purposefully. The entirety of the summation of all focuses within one particular physical dimension would be designated as a lifetime, so to speak, and all of those focuses — which you identify as lifetimes — are different directions of attention within the lifetime occupied in one physical dimension.

What I am expressing to you is that in actuality, all of your focuses are occurring now. You do not manifest or create being born, and move through a focus and create death, and subsequently remanifest. They are all occurring now, for all of reality is occurring now.

The element of time in linear fashion is a creation that is relative to this particular physical dimension and has been quite purposefully inserted into this physical reality.

You have chosen to be creating a reality in which you shall slow your movement and your actions, that you may experience the fullness of all that you create physically, that you may view and examine and evaluate and experience and assimilate all of the wonders of which you create in this physical dimension.

Now; in this, essences choose different numbers, so to speak, of manifestations that they shall insert into any particular physical dimension.

Each of you, as an essence, chooses how many times you shall focus your attention within this particular dimension, and this is entirely the choice of each essence. As to remanifestation, I shall also express to you that there is an action that occurs in conjunction with your creation of linear time within this dimension. It is not in actuality a remanifestation.

Therefore, as you choose the moment that you shall disengage from this reality — or at that moment that you term to be death — you shall continue the you that you identify. The you that you know shall continue in nonphysical areas of consciousness, for you have already offered yourself the experience of this particular physical dimension, and as essence is focused in many, many different attentions within one physical dimension, it is unnecessary for any one focus to be re—entering into that physical dimension.

As you disengage this physical dimension, you shall move into another area of consciousness which we designate as Regional Area 3, which is the area of transition. In this area of consciousness, the action which occurs is the shedding of belief systems which are held in conjunction with this particular physical dimension, for they are unnecessary in nonphysical areas of consciousness.

You also shall disengage your objective awareness within this action of transition, for objective awareness is also a creation which is relative and useful within physical dimensions, but is unnecessary within nonphysical areas of consciousness.

Your objective awareness is all that you view physically — all that you think, all that you hold in emotion, all that you perceive physically. This is your objective awareness, which is unnecessary outside of a physical dimension. Therefore, this also is shed within the action of transition.

At that point, so to speak, once the belief systems have been shed and the objective awareness has been shed, you hold the choice of movement into any action and any area of consciousness, and you hold the choice to be creating any new action or area of consciousness for your exploration, for essences are continuously within a state of becoming, and in this state of becoming, there is a continuous action of exploration of consciousness and a continuous action of creation of consciousness. This is never-ending.

Now; in this choice to be continuing within any area of consciousness non-physically, at times, that aspect of essence which has been identified as an individual focus may choose to be projecting an aspect of their consciousness into an element of physical focus within any physical dimension.

This is not to say that they are remanifesting. They are merely projecting an aspect of their consciousness into another area of physical reality to be experiencing that element of physical reality.

In this, individuals also create a belief system that they may be reincarnated into a creature. You do not remanifest as a creature. Creatures are not essence. They are a creation of you as essence.

Therefore, you hold the ability to project an aspect of yourself into the consciousness of a creature and to be creating a reality in conjunction with a creature, but you do not manifest as a creature, for this would be quite limiting to you within a physical dimension.

You allow yourselves much more freedoms of exploration in the manifestation of your species than is allowed, so to speak, in the creation of creatures within your physical dimension, for they are a creation of yours, in a manner of speaking.

In this, in agreement, as they are also consciousness, they have chosen to be creating their reality in conjunction with your design.

You have designed this physical dimension, and you orchestrate it, and therefore you also direct it, and in this direction, all that participates within it is consciousness, and is also in agreement with you to be creating itself in the manner that you are directing.

In a manner of speaking, you have created an enormous play within this physical dimension, and you are the directors, and all of your reality are the players — your atmosphere, your planets, your universe, your mountains, your oceans, your weather, your creatures, your plants — everything that is in existence within your physical dimension is a creation of you. You are the directors, and all of it is your players, and you orchestrate, individually and collectively, the movement and the dance of all of it.

Therefore, addressing to your initial questioning as to reincarnation, there are many, many beliefs that are incorporated in this philosophy of reincarnation. You create these belief systems based upon underlying knowings of certain elements of yourselves and of reality.

You hold the knowing that you are much more and much greater than one individual focus of attention, but within your creation of objective reality, you do not understand how this may be possible, for you view one singular body. You identify yourself as one singular individual. You do not view ten thousand clones standing beside you physically!

Therefore, you create a belief — an explanation to yourselves — of how you may be greater than this one individual focus of attention.

In this, as you have created a linear time framework, you express quite logically to yourself that the action which must be occurring is that you must be manifesting and disengaging and remanifesting again. In actuality, you already are all of your lifetimes, so to speak, and you need merely turn your attention ever so slightly sideways — not forward or backward — and you may quite easily view all of the other focuses that you engage within this dimension.

In like manner to how your physical body is affecting of you in any given moment, so to speak — and you may within the moment turn your attention to the affectingness of any element within your physical body and notice that it is affecting — you may also notice that the energy of all of your other focuses is affecting of you, for you are participating within it, and you are also affecting of all of the other focuses within this dimension.

You hold many more focuses of essence than merely in this one particular physical dimension, but within your direction of attention, those focuses which you hold in this particular dimension you may express to yourself are closest to you and the most easily accessed, for you shall understand their reality within this dimension. You do create veils between yourself and other — dimensional focuses, for their realities are quite removed and different from the reality within this particular dimension.

Q: So Elias, sort of on the same subject, are the relationships we have in this physical focus right now the same relationships we have in all the other focuses, or are we just having a relationship with ourselves? Does that make sense?

ELIAS: Yes, I am understanding what you are expressing, (grinning) and I shall express to you in part, both.

You are continuously interactive in a relationship with yourself, for you are continuously exploring and investigating all of the elements of this physical reality. You are exploring your abilities, you are exploring your emotions, you are exploring your thought processes, and all that you may create in any focus. But you also, in the area of relationships, create relationships in interaction with the same essences in many focuses.

Essences quite commonly move in the direction of groups. They group themselves together and create many different focuses in conjunction with each other.

Essences also many times choose to be creating certain types of relationships repeatedly in many different focuses.

Now; in conjunction with relationships, this is also one of the reasons that many times individuals within one particular focus may feel certain familiarities with certain individuals, for they are participating in other focuses with those individuals, with those same essences simultaneously, and they are affecting.

Many times essences may also be creating several focuses that hold the same type of relationship together. This is what you objectively identify to yourselves as "soul mates," for the essences create a specific type of relationship physically focused many times. This may be a romantic relationship or an intimate relationship with another individual that is occurring many times simultaneously, and there is a recognition within the individual focuses that this is occurring, and in like manner to your belief of reincarnation, you hold the belief, in conjunction with linear time framework, that you have experienced many past relationships with another individual, and you hold a recognition of this, and this is what you identify as a soul mate. You also may hold many relationships in conflict with another individual.

Whereas I have stated, generally speaking, essences do manifest in groups, and therefore they focus many different attentions together within those groups. It is quite amusing to us, as we interact with all of you, that you display such surprise in your recognition that you have participated in other focuses with individuals that you meet within this focus. This is very, very common.

All of the individuals that you meet within this focus you have most probably engaged within other focuses, in one capacity or another. You may in one focus hold a relationship with one individual, and within another focus you may merely meet them upon a street, so to speak, but you shall encounter each other in some capacity, for the essences are focused in conjunction to each other.

You also focus yourselves in these groups in like physical locations. Within one time framework, you may focus in this group in the area of Asia within your globe, and within another time framework, all of these essences may focus in the physical location of your Americas, but they shall manifest within groups. This offers you familiarity.

Physical focuses, physical dimensions, are unfamiliar in consciousness. The action of birth and death and a very small time framework of participation — the limitation of that action is very unfamiliar within essence. Therefore, you offer yourselves an element of familiarity in manifesting in groups. This offers you an element of comfort in your physical manifestations. (#488)

Q: I have a granddaughter, an adopted granddaughter, that was born on the exact day at the exact time that my mother had passed. Now she's thirteen years old, and she seems, in almost all of her physical attributes and in all of her normal daily habits, to be my mother!

ELIAS: Now; I shall express to you, in this type of situation, this does occur within your physical reality, and this lends energy to the belief that you hold in what you term to be reincarnation.

I express to you that an individual may disengage physical focus and may project, in choice, an aspect of that focus — or of themselves — which shall choose to be manifest physically. It may exhibit in this new manifestation, figuratively speaking, for all manifestations are simultaneous....

But in this type of action, the aspect of that individual which chooses to become manifest may hold many of the qualities of personality that the other aspect held within physical reality. It is a different aspect, and therefore it is not a repeat, so to speak, or reincarnation of the other individual, but is another manifestation of that focus, another aspect of that same focus, and in this, you objectively may view many similarities in the expression outwardly, emotionally, intellectually, creatively, and even within mannerisms. (Smiling)

These individuals also may allow themselves many times to be recalling, within their individual memory, elements of the other focus, which also lends energy to the belief system of reincarnation, for these individuals may be offering information in conjunction with the other focus that YOU shall all hold in amazement and express, "How shall this individual know this of the other focus? But of course, they are the same individual!" They are NOT the same individual, but they hold many of the same qualities, for they are an element of that focus. (#475)

Chapter 15

KARMA

"There is no karma! You do not hold reincarnational lives! You are a new creation. You, physically manifest, are individual and new and perfect, and shall never be repeated, as you are not repeating another. You are your own individual personality manifest physically, which shall continue and which has always continued previously."

(#131)

Chapter 15

KARMA

Q: So what about karma? There are a lot of people in the world today who believe in karma — that you reap what you sow, " what goes round comes around," cause and effect … that kind of thing.

ELIAS: This is a very common belief system within your reality presently. As you have moved into this century and the beginning throes of your shift in consciousness, you have developed new belief systems which suggest to you alternates for those religious belief systems that you have held for many centuries. You view these to be new enlightened belief systems, although you do not believe that they ARE belief systems.

In actuality, there is no karma. There is no moving from one focus to another focus. There is no repaying of debt. There is no consequence for your action within one focus. The only consequence that occurs within any focus for action incurred is that consequence that you draw to yourself for your own information within one particular focus.

All focuses are simultaneous. Therefore, you are not reborn. You are a new creation in yourself, and shall never be recreated into another creation. You may create an aspect of yourself that shall continue within physical focus, but it shall be its own creation and it shall also be a new creation. You are not used parts! (Laughter) You are continuously creating anew.

YOU are YOU. And you, as a focus of essence, experience within a physical focus, and in completing your experience within a physical focus shall move beyond physical focus and continue within your exploration of self within other areas. You may choose to be exploring another physical focus within another dimension, but you shall not repeat this physical focus within this dimension, for this would be pointless.

You have already experienced, within your countless amounts of counterparts and focuses within this dimension, all that you need be experiencing within this dimension. Therefore, you hold wondrous areas to be exploring within consciousness beyond this one particular dimension and focus.

There is no element that you need be repaying or holding an element of cause and effect within this particular dimension. It is merely one focus of your essence, and in this you manifest to experience, to explore. There is no right and wrong within consciousness. All is an experience. Therefore, what need be repaid? It is merely your own belief systems that dictate to you that you hold karmic debt. (#249)

You think of karma as cause and effect. You think of moving through experiences, and repaying for those experiences that you have created negatively. There is no negative! It is merely your belief system that there is negative. This is not to say that you do not in actuality create negative elements within your reality, for you project energy into the creation of these elements. If you are believing in evil destructive devils, you shall project energy into their creation and they shall be reality! (#193)

You do draw to yourselves experiences in your expressions that what you set forth you shall also draw to yourself, but this is directly dictated and created by your belief in this action of karma. It is not a natural function of essence or of consciousness.

Experiences are experiences. They are not right or wrong or good or bad, and there is no cause and effect. It is all a choice of what YOU choose to be creating.

You shall draw to yourself in conjunction with your belief systems, not that it is dictated by the universe or the cosmos or all of consciousness that this is what you deserve, for there is no measurement of what you deserve. You already are! (#454)

Q: I was understanding that karma was just simply action — good, bad, whatever — just action. If I was to throw this pen, it has to land. It's just action and the effect of that action, not necessarily good, bad, payment, repayment.

ELIAS: This also is cause and effect. If you are to throw your pen, you hold an expectation that it must land.

Q: Exactly.

ELIAS: Therefore, it does; for within mass belief systems, you hold expectations of cause and effect. This is not truth. This is merely belief systems within your particular dimension.

Q: But since it is a belief system, it really makes it part of our reality since we all believe in it.

ELIAS: Yes. It IS your reality, and you shall throw your pen and it shall fall.

Q: So that doesn't mean that karma does not exist totally. It means that we choose to have it exist in our reality. So there is, no matter whatever we do … if say that karma is simply action, then there is action and reaction in our dimension because we choose it to be there, not that it doesn't exist totally.

ELIAS: Because you CHOOSE it to be there.

Q: Yeah, but as a group consciousness, we all choose it to be there.

ELIAS: Quite. I express to you these elements, these truths, that you may expand your awareness, and that you may view that you hold belief systems but you are not bound by your belief systems, and that you may move outside of these belief systems and alter your present reality. I express this to you for the reason that you ARE participating within the action of your shift in consciousness, and within your future time period your reality shall be completely altered and these belief systems shall not hold you as they do presently. Your reality shall be executed differently. You shall throw your pen, and if you are not so choosing, it shall not...

Q: Land.

ELIAS: Correct. (#238)

Q: Can you explain for me what we perceive to be the laws of physics — action, reaction, positive, negative? Are these just something that are created by our belief systems, or do these have some actual permanent significance?

ELIAS: Let me express to you that within this dimension and within your creation of your reality as you hold the understanding of it presently and pastly, they are reality, but they are limited to this particular dimension, for they are entirely influenced by the belief system of cause and effect.

You move into the area of creating mass belief systems as explanations to yourselves of elements that you do not understand. Therefore, you have created the belief system that for each cause of action, there is an effect or reaction. This, as I have stated, is directly influenced by your mass belief systems, which have been hold (held) for many millennium. These have been offered to yourselves by yourselves, in explanation for actions that you create.

Let me offer you an example which may be quite easy for you to be understanding in the area of belief system, and you may apply this also to your sciences that you have created your new religions with, for you hold tremendous belief systems and "faith" in your sciences! (Smiling)

Therefore, they also have become another source of belief systems, another religion which is no different from all of your other religions. It merely expresses belief systems in a different manner that you accept more rationally as opposed to mystically within your present time framework, for now you move into the area of technology, a new exploration.

But in the example that I offer, you hold belief systems in the area of your planet. You look to your solar system, you look to your universe, and you create belief systems in the area of what you term to be astrology.

Obviously this is not scientific, but it serves as a very good example in reality, for in the area of the belief systems of astrology, you believe that your planets move in certain orbs and certain directions and are affecting of you as individuals and en masse according to their movement.

In actuality, YOU are creating of THEIR movement in mirror image to YOUR movement within your focus individually and en masse. Therefore, you have reversed the concept of the action within your belief systems, for you believe that you as individuals, and even within mass, are not capable; do not hold the ability to be creating of all of your reality.

(Humorously) YOU are not manipulating of all of the elements of your reality! THEY are independently creating themselves, or some supreme being within consciousness is creating of them, which is out of your sphere! But you, within this meager small "learning planet" upon this " plane" of existence in this very "low level" that you aspire to move outside of in your quest to become more "enlightened," could not possibly be creating of all of your reality! Therefore, you create belief systems that shall offer you explanations of what you are creating, for obviously YOU are not creating it!

In this, your sciences do not acknowledge the reality of the energy of consciousness and its preceding, so to speak, within linear time frame, of physical manifestations or actions. In this, they create explanations with limited information, for they do not allow themselves to be accessing the information that shall offer them the actual actions that are occurring.

You may step before a carriage and it may be physically engaging you and running you over, and as it runs over the top of you, this is an action, and your belief system dictates to you individually and en masse — which mass belief systems hold great strength and energy — that you shall be injured; you shall bear physical evidence that you have been run over by the carriage. But you may arise and you may choose not to be creating of this, and shall bear no markings of the action at all. Within your sciences, it is dictated that for every action there is a reaction; there is a cause and effect. But there is not necessarily an effect for all cause. (Smiling)

They view behaviors of certain elements of physical creations that you have created to be interactive within this dimension for specific purposes. In this, they view them to be consistent, although they are not always consistent. Your physicists move into the direction of attempting to create a block, a box that they may place physical elements in and express, "These physical elements always exhibit the same behavior." But they do not! At times they deviate from the behavior, for although they may many times move in the direction of displaying the same behavior for the reason that you have created this action purposefully for certain workings of your manifestations within this particular physical dimension, and links of consciousness are in agreement with this and choose to be compliant, each link of consciousness IS consciousness and holds free will and holds it own ability for choice. Therefore, at times, links of consciousness, which are comprising of choice and are the make-up of elements that you view to be as atoms or other physical elements … which to this time framework, you continue to not view these mysterious atoms! But these links of consciousness that make up these atoms may be choosing not to be compliant, and therefore creating of a different behavior and not being consistent.

You may also view in amazement individuals that you consider to hold strange powers or tremendous abilities within enlightenment within your own physical environment, within your own physical time framework; "masters" or mystics that defy the laws, so to speak, of your physical reality. If you drop an apple, gravity shall pull it to the ground; cause and effect. But one of your masters may drop an apple, and it may float and defy your laws of gravity! YOU may float, if you are so choosing to create! Levitation is NOT a fantasy. It is a reality!

And how may you explain this within your laws of your sciences, that you hold these fields that are absolute? THERE ARE NO ABSOLUTES within your physical dimension. ALL may be challenged. It is merely a choice within consciousness.

Therefore, to your question, yes. It is directly influenced by your belief systems, and in altering your belief systems, you also alter your reality. This be the reason that you MAY alter your reality, for as it is presented presently, it is directly filtered through your belief systems.

This is not to say that your belief systems are bad. That perception moves you into the area of duplicity. Your belief systems are not bad. They are not good, either. There merely are, and they are that which is creating of your reality. But in not holding to your belief systems so very strongly, you also allow yourselves the expansiveness of your creativity and the ability to explore more of your reality.

As you hold to these belief systems tightly, you also create your box for yourselves; not for consciousness, not for the manifestation of consciousness or even physical matter, but for yourselves in your explorations, for you limit yourselves in not allowing yourselves to move beyond and view that there is much more to your reality than you allow yourselves to view. If you are allowing yourselves an openness and not boxing yourselves into your scientific belief systems so very strongly, you may view many more elements of your own creations that shall be quite surprising to you! You have already created many objective evidences of this for yourselves, which you term to be "accidents." that you do not understand: your element of your Philadelphia experiment, that even within this present now moment you do not understand. It is not an accident! It is a tapping into more of your reality which does not fit within your scientific belief systems. You hold many examples throughout your history of these types of action that you have "accidentally stumbled upon." And I express to you, there are no accidents!

(Intently) You purposefully create certain actions to offer yourselves evidences that there is more to your reality than you allow yourselves to view, and then you ponder and you question and you retreat to the safety of your sciences and your religions, which offer you familiarity, but offer you also partial explanations for certain aspects of your reality that you may feel comfortable with. (#291)

Chapter 16

BELIEF SYSTEMS

"I may express to you, quite simply, you create your reality.
You create your reality in relation to your beliefs, which influence
your perception, which creates the being of your beliefs.
In this, it also creates the being of your view — your
assessment of yourself, of your worth, of your worthiness,
of your abilities, or the lack of those expressions."

(#732)

Chapter 16

BELIEF SYSTEMS

ELIAS: Belief systems are unique to physical focuses. They are an element of physical focuses. Your individual physical focus here upon this planet, within this time/space and within this dimension, is not the only physical focus and not the only physical manifestation that holds belief systems. There are many dimensions which are physically manifest. All physical manifestations hold belief systems.

In widening your awareness and accepting of belief systems, you nullify their power. You allow yourself more probabilities, for you allow yourself more knowledge and more choices. You do not feel bound to these belief systems. Within a strong belief system, you are held. Any belief system that you hold strongly holds you! It eliminates many of your choices, for you may only see even more selectively and narrowly within that belief system. You allow yourself no information beyond that belief system. Therefore, you are bound. As you accept the belief system, not with the intention of changing or eliminating the belief system, but acknowledging that it is reality and that it is accepted, it loses its power, therefore losing its hold, allowing you more choices (#133)

Let me express to you, a belief system is as a bird cage. I have expressed this analogy previously, but I shall repeat it presently.

The bird cage is the belief system, but the bird cage holds many, many, many birds, and you may include many more birds into the cage, as many as you choose, for the cage expands and is accommodating of however many birds you choose to be placing in it, and it shall continue to expand, for it is quite accommodating.

This is the belief system, as the cage. The birds are all of the elements of the belief system, all of the aspects of the belief system, and I shall express to you that each belief system that you hold holds very many birds and may be quite tricky with you, for many of the birds are hiding behind other birds that you may not even allow yourselves to view. The point of acceptance is to open the door of the bird cage and allow the birds to fly away. Therefore, you continue to hold the cage, but it is empty.

The cage remains before you. You have not eliminated the cage, but the cage serves no purpose, for the birds are not contained, and in this it is merely a cage, an object for you to view and not maintain and not interact with, but merely just view, and in this you may express your opinion of the cage: "I view this cage to be quite lovely. I view this cage to be quite distasteful." But it matters not, for it holds no purpose. It holds no function. There are no birds contained. And as the birds are allowed to fly away, they are transformed within energy and are no longer birds. Therefore, what shall you replace in the cage? There are no birds to put in the cage. It is merely an ornament.

(Intently) This be an action of your shift. This be one of your most affecting aspects of this shift in consciousness which shall be the most liberating of you, for in this action you allow yourselves to divert your attention, which has been held so singularly to your belief systems, away from the cage, which is merely ornamental.

Therefore, in opposition to viewing this one cage within your room, you allow yourself to view the room. You allow yourself to view the vastness of all that is around the cage that you have not allowed yourself the openness in your attention to view, and all the wondrous creative elements that reside in that space, so to speak, that you have not viewed, for your attention has been directed to the cage and all of its birds. (#284)

As you accept self and the belief systems that you hold, acknowledge that these are belief systems — a creation which is an element of this focus, of this dimension, this physical reality — and that there is no existence within this physical reality without belief systems. As you acknowledge this to yourself and you recognize the lack of correctness or incorrectness, of rightness, of wrongness, of ANY belief systems, you become accepting of self; and as you are presented with the belief systems of other individuals which differ from your own, you also become aware that they do not differ from your own. They are merely a construction of creativity, in explanation to yourself of those elements that you have forgotten within essence.

This, be understanding I am quite aware, is sounding quite simplistic! I am also quite understanding of the difficulty within accomplishment of this act, for these belief systems are very strong; but as you accept these belief systems, you also neutralize their hold. You are not subject to them. Within an acceptance of these belief systems, they are neutral. In this, you may also better understand the action of your shift; for those elements that you view as negative, that you disdain — your wars, your disease, your intolerance — those are belief systems also, and they hold power and activity only for the reason that you do not accept them. Once you are accepting of these belief systems and recognizing the lack of rightness or wrongness of them, it is unnecessary to be objectifying them.

Individuals express to this essence questioning of why you are hurtful to each other: "Why must individuals be engaging murderous acts?

Why must individuals be hurtful to small children? Why do we create these elements?" For you hold belief systems that you do not accept. You view right and wrong. You express wrongness for these acts. Therefore they are expressed, for you add energy to the actions within a holding of belief systems. As you believe these acts are wrong, they are a reality which is unacceptable, which you feed much energy, which lends energy to the accomplishment of the enactment. (#185)

As I have stated, your action is not to be eliminating of your belief systems. You shall continue to hold belief systems within this shift in consciousness, for this is an aspect of your reality within this dimension. ALL of your reality is influenced and based upon belief systems within this dimension. You shall merely move into the direction of accepting that you create belief systems, that all of your reality IS based upon belief systems, and that they are not good or bad; they merely are choices. Therefore, they are not warranting of judgments.

Each time you are creating a judgment of "good" you are also creating a judgment — which is NOT acceptance — therefore moving into the direction of viewing all of your belief systems and expressing to yourselves, "These are all very good! I am quite pleased with all of my belief systems, and I hold none that are distasteful to me!" (Laughter) I shall express to you that you have not accepted any of your belief systems moving in this direction, for you are creating a judgment that they are all good. (#307)

Good is a judgment. Pleasing is a judgment. Acceptable is a judgment which is equally as powerful as any negative expression, for accompanying this positive, so to speak, expression is also the recognition that another expression is bad, for what shall good be if you have no comparison of bad? It shall be neutral.

As you continue to create judgments, you perpetuate the actions that you judge. You create by lending energy to the very actions that you disdain.

Q: In the mass consciousness?

ELIAS: Correct, but the mass is affected by each individual, for there is no mass without individuals! And in this, the very elements that you disdain within physical focus, that you deem to be negative, you lend energy to each time you move into the direction of judgment. Therefore, the point is to be accepting, and in this you may offer yourself more of an ability to move into this direction by recognizing that no action occurs between individuals within physical focus that is not agreed upon. You may not be affecting in any manner without being in agreement with another individual, for if another individual is not in agreement with your expression, it shall not be accomplished.

Essences are NOT intrusive. Therefore, it is required, so to speak, that there be agreement for ANY action to be accomplished, and in this, even that which you deem to be the most violent or distasteful, they are all beneficial in some manner, for you draw yourselves to the experience to be offering yourselves information in some manner, and they engage the action to be fulfilling their value fulfillment in some manner, and at times also to be lending energy to you for the accomplishment of your value fulfillment in areas that you have drawn information to yourselves. It may not always be very objectively clear to you why you are drawing yourselves to certain situations, but as you allow yourselves to be more aware of self and listening to your own language — your own impulses, your own impressions, your language of essence to self — and as you are moving in the direction of acceptance of self and addressing to your own belief systems, you also offer yourself more of an understanding of these aspects of which I speak.

(Intently) This is what you move into now within the action of this shift. You move away from your judgments of good and bad and you move into the acceptance of belief systems and the recognition that they ARE belief systems, and in this you neutralize their affectingness. IT MATTERS NOT. (Brief pause)

(Very intently) If I shall express to any of you, within all of my engagements with you within physical interaction, any quote that shall be remembered, it shall become "It matters not," for your expressions are merely those of experience. You are *immensely* vaster than your comprehension of yourselves within this one particular physical focus, and this vastness of self is available to you. You are not limited to the understanding of only this one focus. You hold ALL of essence within you. It is NOT a being outside of you. Your relationship with yourself is not a relationship which is engaged with some elusive entity that floats about outside of you. Information that you allow yourselves to connect to is NOT outside of you. ALL of the information is held within you.

I have expressed many times that the only difference between yourselves and myself is that you do not remember and I do. You have chosen to be forgetful, that you may create within physical focus a purity of experience and a fullness of experience in physical aspects. Therefore, you have CHOSEN to be forgetting of all of essence and the vastness of yourselves. I no longer occupy physical focus. Therefore, I hold the remembrance, but you now move into this action of this shift in consciousness and you now offer yourselves the remembrance also. You each are building your bridges from your individual oubliettes across to the recognition and realization of essence.

You do not occupy a planet of lowly accord. You are not within this physical focus as a learning dimension, so to speak, on your way to higher ground. There is no higher ground! You ARE your highest expression! Even within all of your belief systems and within your physical expressions, you ARE your highest expression. You are one focus of an endless essence, and this one focus holds all of the information of consciousness, of essence, of you, and of all other essences. For although you camouflage within physical focus, and you within your thought processes hold to the belief that you may move in the direction of being secretive, for you are so very separate within physical focus, you are not separate at all. You are all intertwined. Your consciousness is all intermingled, and within essence there are no secrets, for all is known to all others.

You amaze yourselves with your own abilities. You present to yourselves different moments where you shall physically express to each other simultaneously the same thought. You shall verbally express the same words within your language simultaneously with another individual, and you shall call this accident! This is a very simple example of the interconnectedness of you all and that you all are participating within a mergence of consciousness collectively, continuously. Your telepathic abilities would be astounding to you, were you merely to open yourselves SLIGHTLY to your own abilities.

Your inner senses are more fine-tuned, so to speak, than your outer senses. You engage your outer senses continuously. You are quite familiar with touch and the sensation of this. You are quite familiar with your sight and the engagement of your sense of hearing. You do not allow yourselves to recognize your inner senses, which move far beyond these outer senses. Your outer senses are outward mirror images of your inner senses, which hold immense power, and you now offer yourselves the opportunity to not only experiment with these inner senses, but in actuality to open to these inner senses and to be moving into the exploration of consciousness within your physical objective awareness, your waking state within this dimension, offering yourselves much more of your own expressions of creativity.

Let me express to you once again: the one prerequisite, so to speak, for this action is that you are accepting and trusting of yourselves in every area of your expressions, in every area of your creations and experiences. This applies to all of the experiences in their mundane expressions within every moment of your waking day. Each time you move into the direction of chastising yourself, even in the area of humor — of expressing, "Oh, I have created a mistake! I am wishing I was creating of this situation differently! I could have been creating this situation more efficiently!" You have created each situation in the direction that you have created them as the opportunity for you to view your own interaction with your own belief systems and your own responsiveness to the affectingness of them.

Therefore, each expression that you create is purposeful and beneficial, and my expression to you this day, in helpfulness in moving through your focus more efficiently, so to speak, and more effortlessly and with much less conflict — which would be the point — is that I shall suggest to you that you allow yourselves to move in the area of pleasure, for this is the expression that holds the least amount of thickness in energy within physical focus and offers you the most ease in all of your accomplishments.

As you move into areas that are NOT pleasurable, you may also offer yourselves information as to the thickness in energy. Areas that are not pleasurable in your experiences are more difficult! You move more slowly through them and you move into areas of conflict, or you may be experiencing a neutral effect, but you shall not be experiencing the freedom of effortlessness. And as you move into the area of pleasure, you also shall experience effortlessness, for this is your natural expression.

Essence naturally, automatically magnates in the direction of pleasure. It is merely your belief systems that move you away from the expression of pleasure, and in your moving away from any expression of pleasure, you may offer yourself the opportunity to examine the belief systems that are influencing you to be moving away from the expression of pleasure.

These are all opportunities for you to examine and notice those belief systems which are affecting of you and also limiting you and blocking your energy and your expressions and your acceptance of yourselves, for if you are not accepting of this focus, you shall also not be accepting of all of your other focuses, and if you are not accepting of all of your other focuses, you shall not be accepting of essence, and this shall create thickness in energy and this shall also create trauma.

You have already established an agreement within consciousness to be moving into the accomplishment of this shift in consciousness. IT IS ALREADY ACCOMPLISHED.

Therefore, you automatically shall be addressing to belief systems and to acceptance, and in this, if you are not accepting of self, you shall be engaging trauma. And this be the reason that I speak with you, to be helpful in lessening the trauma that is associated with this shift in consciousness, for it is unnecessary. And if you are holding information, you shall be offering yourselves the opportunity to be eliminating this trauma within your individual focuses, and as each individual eliminates elements of trauma within their focus, they also lend energy to all other focuses within this planet to be lessening the trauma collectively en masse in relation to this shift in consciousness. (#302)

The acceptance of belief systems is not the detachment from them. As I have expressed, you are not eliminating your belief systems. You are also not detaching from them. You shall continue to hold opinions, but these opinions shall not be challenged within yourself or by others within the action of this shift, for you shall have accepted the belief systems. In this, you hold no judgment of your own belief systems or of other individuals' beliefs systems, for you recognize that they ARE belief systems, and therefore you do not respond to these belief systems in the manner that you respond presently.

This would be likened to holding differences of opinions between different individuals, but the differences of opinions concern matters of no consequence. Therefore, if you are discussing or sharing your different opinions of this matter of no consequence, it matters not to you that you be right or wrong, for the subject matter in itself is of no consequence and holds no matter to you.

Therefore, you feel no need within you to be expressing in a manner to influence another individual holding a different opinion. As the subject matter itself is of no consequence to you, it also is of no matter to you that another individual holds a difference in opinion. It strikes no emotional chord within you.

The reason that individuals hold conflict within belief systems is that they trigger emotional responses. You respond to these emotions, and this is creating of conflict.

Now; be understanding, you shall not be eliminating emotion either, but you shall hold the understanding and the acceptance of the belief systems, therefore neutralizing their effect which is triggering of emotional qualities within you and therefore sparking of judgment in reaction to the emotional response. (#278)

Judgment in any area is the lack of acceptance, and this is a very major movement of this shift in consciousness. ALL individuals upon your planet are and shall be addressing to these issues of acceptance, not only of belief systems but of themselves and of each other, and this is why this shift in consciousness is expressed in such a long period of your physical time framework, for it moves slowly in the direction of acceptance. In another respect it is moving quite rapidly, for within the presentment of nearly two hundred years — less than two hundred years — the accomplishment of this shift shall be realized, but within that time framework of less than two hundred of your years, there is great struggle for all individuals in the area of acceptance.

(Intently) I stress very strongly that individuals concern themselves with the acceptance of self first and the recognition of their own held belief systems, for in this shall be their movement into the acceptance of other individuals, for a natural byproduct of recognition of self is to be non — judgmental of other individuals, for as you are judging of other individuals, you are judging of yourself, for if you are not judging of yourself, you also do not place judgment upon other individuals. If you hold the recognition and acceptance of self, it is unnecessary to be placing judgment upon other individuals, for there is an automatic recognition that you shall be judging self in judging others. Each time you move into the area of placing a judgment upon any other individual, you also are placing judgment upon yourself. You are mirroring outwardly your expression to self. What is unacceptable in another individual is unacceptable in yourself, and if it is unacceptable within yourself, of course it shall be unacceptable for another individual to be expressing in this action.

This be the reason that I express to you so very many times and so very often to be looking to self first, and all else that you seek shall automatically be expressed. You shall automatically move in the direction of acceptance of other individuals if you are accepting of self, for what you create within you, you also create outwardly, and as you are placing judgments upon yourself, you create this expression outwardly and create judgments upon other individuals.

When you are expressing that you are right, you are also expressing that other individuals are wrong. When you are expressing to other individuals that they do not see, you are expressing a mirror image that YOU do not see. All of your expressions that you project forth to other individuals are direct mirror images of what you are creating within yourselves.

Therefore, I present this to you, that you and all other individuals may attend their attention to themselves and to their own issues of duplicity and their own belief systems, and afford themselves the acceptance of themselves and the trust of themselves, for all other expressions shall naturally follow, so to speak, as natural byproducts of this action of acceptance of self. (#304)

The acceptance of a belief system is NOT the CHANGING of a belief system and is NOT the ELIMINATION of a belief system. It is the acknowledgment of the belief system, the acceptance with the lack of judgment within yourself and within others, therefore rendering the belief system neutralized within its power and allowing you a new freedom within your expression of creativity and an allowance within yourself to be widening your awareness, which allows you the free flow within your creative expression. It allows you a liberation. (#271)

You have designed your belief systems. You have designed your limitations. I express to you that you hold no limitations, but do not be discounting of belief systems because they *are* reality! They create your reality. You create your reality through your belief systems. They are very real! They are very strong! They are not to be discounted! They are physical reality, within all dimensions and within all physical manifestations in all dimensions.

Each physical manifestation in each dimension holds their own set of belief systems. These are their guidelines within physical manifestation. These guidelines are your perimeters that you function within for your experience, for the purity and intensity of the experience. (#166)

Q: Is there a difference between aspects of belief systems and maybe the one, big belief system? I think I look at individual issues as separate belief systems, and perhaps they're aspects of another one.

ELIAS: Correct.

Q: So in letting go of those aspects... I guess I'm concentrating on accepting those aspects, thinking they're belief systems, but in actuality, I would be letting go of those, hopefully working back to...

ELIAS: This be the reason that I have offered the analogy of the bird cage, for the cage itself is the representation of the belief system, an element that is neutral within itself, merely what you may term to be an object which holds no quality within itself but is a thing within itself. But the birds that are contained within the cage are the aspects of the belief system, and THESE are quite alive and moving and fluttering and demanding, and they ARE requiring of your attention! You shall not pay very close attention to the cage, but you shall pay very much attention to the birds within the cage!

Q: Do we have more than one cage?

ELIAS: Yes.

Q: There's not very many though, huh.

ELIAS: Not as very many as you think, but there are many more birds within these cages than you think!

Q: So in acceptance, that's accepting the bird cage, not the birds that are aspects? Is that correct?

ELIAS: No. The cage you are already within acceptance of. The birds you are NOT accepting of! Within your acceptance of these birds, you are opening the door to the cage and you are allowing the birds to fly free and empty the cage, and as the cage is empty, it holds no power, for it holds no more motion, and you may place the cage wherever you choose. You may manipulate the cage in whichever area you choose, but you need not tend to the cage, for it in itself does not demand of you. The birds demand of you!

Q: What if we enjoy the birds? You said something about losing the power. What if we accept that as part of our artistic creation?

ELIAS: And you DO, and you place a judgment upon this and you express that it is good, and where you place a judgment that these birds are good, you automatically — within this physical dimension — also place a judgment upon other expressions and other birds that are bad, and you lend energy to the very elements that you wish not to lend energy.

Q: Going back more to the thing where you said, "If we didn't have beliefs, we wouldn't be manifesting in this dimension." So we need beliefs, right?

ELIAS: Quite, but you need not hold judgments upon the beliefs. You shall continue to hold the cages, and you may manipulate the cages and you may reform the cages. You may melt the metal of the cages and you may reform these cages into new cages if you are so choosing, or you may divide these cages and be creating of many more cages, but the cages themselves are neutral. They are merely tools in your creating within your reality.

Q: Where do emotions come into this? Where are they in relation to the birds and the cages? Which comes first, the birds or the emotions?

ELIAS: (Chuckling) The birds or the eggs? (Laughter)

Emotions are not belief systems. Emotions are an element of your expression that you have chosen to be the method, so to speak, of your expression within this particular physical dimension.

This is not to say that other physical dimensions do not incorporate emotion, for some do, but within this particular dimension, it is one of the base elements of your creation of expression.

In this, the emotion exists regardless of the belief system. The experience of emotion is created and exists and is expressed with or without the belief systems, but you are incorporating belief systems into this particular dimension. Therefore, it is not necessarily a question of which you have created first, for you create them together, but they are functioning differently. The belief systems are influencing of your emotions, but emotion is a translation of a tone quality of essence. It is a translation into a physical dimension for the reason of physical experience. Belief systems are not an aspect of essence. They are a creation, a tool to be manipulating perceptions within physical dimensions that influence and create your reality. (#331)

Q: Okay. The whole thing with the acceptance of the belief or the aspects of the belief – just by acknowledging that you hold the belief and that it's neither good or bad, right or wrong, better or worse, it allows the bird to fly away and it neutralizes it?

ELIAS: Not necessarily.

Q: Okay, now I'm confused, because there's always something new about the belief systems and stuff that I read in the transcripts, and I just continually confuse myself with it. Please explain to me how you're to be accepting of a belief other than what I just asked.

ELIAS: At times, this may be all that you require within yourself. You may be in actuality – at times – accepting aspects of belief systems merely by recognizing, identifying, and acknowledging them to yourself, but this action occurs merely at times, for I express to you that many of these aspects you hold very strongly.

Now; this is not to say that you may not be accomplishing this very action with a very strongly held aspect of belief systems, but you also hold other aspects of beliefs that express to you that you must be engaging a process and a method to be accomplishing accepting belief systems.

Therefore, although you may be spontaneously, instantaneously accepting an aspect of a belief system, you also may not necessarily allow yourself to be accomplishing in this manner, for it is not expressing of a method or a process, and within physical focus, you have created quite strong aspects of beliefs that express to you that all that you accomplish within your physical focus is requiring of a method. Therefore, as you are moving into the area of neutralizing these aspects, accepting these aspects of beliefs, I express to you that within your process, within your method, you move in what you term to be steps.

Initially, you notice. Once you have allowed yourself to be noticing, you begin your process of identification. You begin to recognize the aspect of the belief system. You are not merely noticing that it exists any longer, but you begin presenting yourself with imagery and situations that shall demonstrate the aspect of the belief system that you are viewing at that particular time frame, and you shall begin to recognize the different forms that that particular aspect may present itself within.

In this, as I have stated, you may be continuing to view the same bird, but its presentment may be offered to you in different angles. You may be viewing different elements, different sides, different positions, different angles of the same bird.

This is expressed objectively in different situations. You are con-tinuing to be viewing and presenting to yourself the same aspect of a belief system, but you are offering it to yourself in many different situations.

This offers you the opportunity to view the aspect fully, that you may not necessarily delude yourself into a thought process that you have accepted this particular bird, and subsequently it may present itself once again with a different face.

Therefore, you create a process or a method of presenting yourself many different situations and behaviors and actions and events that shall present imagery to you, viewing all of the different angles of each particular aspect.

Now; once you have allowed yourself to be viewing different angles of the aspect of the belief – not merely noticing its existence, but viewing and recognizing the aspect in different situations – you move subsequently into your next step, which is to be addressing to the aspect.

Now; this is the area that you become confused, for YOU identify in physical focus that your addressing to the aspect is the action of recognizing. Let me explain.

In recognizing and in the presentment to yourself of any aspect of the belief system, as you offer yourselves these types of situations, you also offer yourselves the expression of conflict, confusion, and difficulties. You may at times express emotional expressions in conjunction with these recognitions of the aspect.

In these situations, you THINK to yourselves that you are addressing to the aspect, for you are involving yourself in what YOU identify as motion or movement concerning the aspect, for you are responding to it. You are creating conflict, confusion; you are creating emotional responses. In this, you think to yourselves that this is the action of addressing to the aspect.

I express to you, this is merely you presenting yourselves with the opportunity of recognizing the aspect, and as you are continuing to be expressing RESPONSES to the aspect in conflict, you are not addressing to the aspect. You are recognizing it, and you are offering yourself many different situations to be recognizing it.

Once you begin your next step of actually addressing to the belief, to the aspects of the belief, you begin to notice a lessening of your conflict.

Addressing to the belief is not the objective action, in a manner of speaking. It is not the DOING – in your terms – [of] some action concerning the aspect of the belief. It is the ALLOWANCE for the aspect to be recognized, and figuratively speaking, in your terms, it is your allowance of yourself to be giving up with the battling of that aspect. Therefore, what you are in actuality moving into is the letting go of holding to the energy with respect to that aspect.

Let me offer this to you in another manner that may offer you a clearer understanding.

First you are noticing. "There is a belief that exists. This is not an absolute. It is not some element of my reality which is unchanging or unchangeable. It is an aspect of a belief."

The next step is the recognition in situations; the presentment of the aspect. In this, each time you are presenting yourself with the particular aspect of the belief, you shall notice and you shall recognize. You shall not merely notice a belief system is in place, but you shall move a little further and you shall allow yourself the ability to recognize, "This is a specific aspect of a belief, and this is the identification of this aspect."

Once you have identified the aspect of the belief system, you begin to present yourself with many different situations and circumstances that shall be offering you reoccurrences of the presentment of that same aspect, that you may view it over and over, for this is your choice of method.

As you are viewing, as you are identifying the aspect, as you are recognizing the aspect and you are presenting it to yourself over and over in many different situations and behaviors, you are experiencing responses in conjunction with it.

Now; in your idea of addressing to the aspect, you think to yourself that you ARE addressing to the aspect of the belief, for you are responding to it. You have already noticed, you have already identified, and now you are responding. This is your logic and your rational thought process in your identification of your method.

Now; I express to you that you are not yet addressing to the aspect in this stage of your method. You are continuing in the recognition stage, for you are continuing to be responding. You are continuing to allow the affectingness of the aspect.

As you move subsequently into the next step of addressing to the aspect of the belief, you begin to notice that you are not responding and reacting to the aspect within each of the situations that it is presented to you. It becomes less and less affecting of you. NOW you are beginning to be addressing to the aspect of the belief.

Addressing to it is the action, the implementation of letting go of your hold upon its energy.

This be the reason that I have offered the analogy of the bird and the cage, for within physical visual terms, it is quite easy for you to identify in these terms. You may view that you have set your sights upon one particular bird. In this, let us express, you have chosen a bright red bird.

You notice the belief system by noticing the cage and that it exists. Now, you are not addressing to this cage, and you are not creating any movement in the direction of acceptance of all of the aspects within this cage. You are merely noticing that the cage exists.

Once you have acknowledged to yourself that the cage exists, you view more closely, and you recognize that the cage holds many birds. Now you have recognized that the cage is quite full, and you choose to set your sights upon a particular bird that you wish to be allowing to fly free. Therefore, you begin to open the cage.

In this, you are recognizing this red bird. You are viewing this red bird. You are reaching within the cage to be engaging this red bird, that you may be removing the red bird from the cage. But in the process of removing the red bird, the red bird is flying all about the cage and you are attempting to be catching the red bird, fumbling with yourself to be grabbing at this red bird, and occasionally you are capturing this red bird. But the red bird is also pecking at your hands and it is squirming within your grasp. Therefore, your grip upon this red bird slips, and it may be escaping your grasp.

Therefore, once again, you are presenting yourself with situations to be recognizing, "Ah, yes! The red bird has now moved from this location to this location, and I shall move now to be capturing the red bird here." And once you have moved here to capture the red bird, it flies to another location of the cage, and you present yourself with a new situation to be capturing the red bird.

Once you have moved through your maneuvers with this red bird, you express to yourself exhaustion in attempting to be pursuing and capturing this red bird. Therefore, in your physical terms, you give up, and as you give up and are not in pursuit any longer, the red bird flies to you and lights upon your hand, and there you hold the red bird.

Now; once the bird has flown and has been allowed to light upon your hand, it is no longer bothersome to you, for you are no longer in pursuit. NOW you have moved into your next step of addressing to the aspect. You are now holding the red bird, and in this, you now offer yourself the ability. As it becomes calm and you are not reacting and responding to it any longer, you offer yourself the ability to be moving outside of the cage with the red bird, holding this bird, and once outside of the cage, allowing your hands to open and for the bird to fly free.

The addressing to the aspect of the belief system is not the engagement and the pursuit of it. That is the recognition of it. This is the stage, so to speak, that you move through in your process of conflict, confusion, (coughing) irritation, much pursuit, repeated presentments of different behaviors, of different movements, of different angles, of different locations of the aspect.

Once you have fatigued yourself sufficiently in your pursuit, you shall then allow yourself to be addressing to the aspect, in which you expel much less energy, for it is unnecessary to be creating the vast expelling of energy with respect to the aspect of the belief system, for you are now addressing to it, and in that, you begin to let go, and as you let go, you allow the bird to fly free and you neutralize the effect of the aspect of the belief. If the bird is no longer within the cage, it shall not be affecting of you, and you shall not be responding to it, for you shall not be engaging it.

Q: Okay. So what you're saying is that I'm fatiguing myself by going after them, or I'm supposed to allow myself to become fatigued so I expel this energy when I actually get to the addressing of them?

ELIAS: I am expressing to you that this is the method, the process that you have chosen; not merely you yourself, but many, many, many individuals within physical focus. Generally speaking, this is the method that is commonly accepted within physical focus by individuals to be moving into the acceptance of a belief system. Therefore, you, merely yourself, are not singularly the individual that is creating of this type of action alone.

But as to you yourself, you also are engaging this type of movement. You align with this type of creation in methods and processes, and in this, this is not a bad creation! It is merely a choice of movement that you understand. It is merely a familiar choice of movement, and there is no thing that is wrong or bad with this type of choice.

Therefore, in this, I express to you that it is not a question of what you SHOULD be creating, but what you ARE creating, and what you ARE creating is the situation of the recognition of aspects.

You are within your second step. You have noticed within your first step certain beliefs, and you have moved into your second step of the identification and recognition of aspects of the belief, but you are also continuing to be chasing the bird throughout the cage.

Therefore, you have not quite moved into the position of the addressing to the aspects of the belief systems, which is your third step, but you are moving closer, for you are fatiguing yourself in your pursuit.

Therefore, you are beginning to express to yourself that you are tired of chasing this bird, and you are allowing yourself to become ready to merely STOP, and to sit and to wait for the bird to light within your hands, and in that step, you shall allow yourself to move easily outside of the cage and to let go of the bird. (#415)

Q: I've been incorporating the "it matters not" energy and trying to see things from a larger perspective, and it's made me kind of wishy-washy and ambiguous about things, and not really.

ELIAS: (Strongly) I am understanding, and let me clarify. This is a misunderstanding and a distortion of what I have expressed throughout the entire time framework of this forum. I express to you, in the acceptance of a belief your expression shall be that it matters not, for you have removed the judgment. I have NOT expressed to you that nothing matters, which is quite different. There is purpose. There is experience. There is exploration. There is interaction and cooperation. The expression that it matters not is merely the identification of the removal of judgment, not that there is no matter. (#1368)

Chapter 17

DUPLICITY

"Duplicity is the curse of your present age. Your globe is plagued with this belief system of duplicity, which is so very unnecessary!"

(#180)

Chapter 17

DUPLICITY

ELIAS: Individuals within recent time framework have expressed inquiries of myself concerning interactions that they engage with other individuals or with situations that they wish to be creating or want to be creating within their reality, and feel or perceive that they do not hold the ability to be creating of these actions or that they are stifled or that they are "stuck" in interactions with other individuals, in creations within their reality, in movement. Some individuals may even be expressing that they feel themselves to be moving backward rather than forward, and this creates confusion, or if they are creating movement at all, in their perception, they are moving in circles, and they are frustrated that they are not accomplishing in the manner that they wish to be accomplishing.

And these expressions have been offered in the cries of consciousness recently by very many individuals in many, many, many different types of expressions, from individual exploration of self or what you deem to be spirituality, to interactions in relationships, to curiosities and wonderings of your employment, your jobs, your physical health, your weather — ANY element that you may choose as subject matter has been risen in consciousness recently, in the chaos of confusion of individuals within this dimension expressing within consciousness,

"What are we creating? What am I creating? Why am I NOT creating?"

I express to you, first of all, you are participating within a wave in consciousness presently, which addresses to the belief system of duplicity, which is quite influencing, for our affection for this particular belief system is boundless!

This particular belief system, which expresses the identification of right and wrong and good and bad and better and worse, is coupled with every other belief system that you have created and enters into every movement, every action, every thought, every motion that you create within this reality. You deem them to be either good or bad, acceptable or unacceptable, comfortable or uncomfortable.

There is a tremendous struggle which is occurring in the recognition of this belief system, for this belief system holds great strength. What you identify to be wrong, you identify in absolutes as wrong, and what you identify as right, you identify as absolutely right.

But let us return to perception. Each individual's perception is unique. Therefore, their definition of right and wrong and good and bad and better and worse is different.

You may think to yourselves that there are absolutes. You may delude yourselves in the definitions of absolutes, as to the rights and wrongs and betters and worse, and you may reinforce these delusions of absolutes by interacting with other individuals that hold similar perceptions to yourselves or similar definitions to yourselves, but they are not exact and they are not entirely the same. They are different, for YOU are different.

This belief system is important in its presentment that you allow yourself to view, for a very base expression of this shift in consciousness, in allowing you to widen your awareness and to engage your periphery, is to be neutralizing your belief systems and accepting those belief systems — not eliminating them, but accepting them, viewing them as they are and accepting their existence — and to be accepting your beliefs, you need be creating the prerequisite of acceptance of YOU, acceptance of self, and this presents an enormous challenge within this physical reality, for the expression of duplicity is immense.

But all hope is not lost, for YOU are immense, and you hold tremendous power! You have merely forgotten how to be empowering yourselves by recognizing, through an acceptance of yourselves, who and what you ARE.

And this is the point of this shift in consciousness, to be incorporating the remembrance, and I shall express once again, the remembrance is not memory. I am not speaking of incorporating a memory of past events, but of a remembrance, a state of being of self, an acceptance of self — the knowing and the acknowledgment of the gloriousness of yourselves, and the incredible exhibition of wonderment and energy expression that you hold.

There is no action that you may not be creating! It is merely the obstacle of your beliefs that prevent you from creating ANY element within your reality. But before you may be realizing that you hold the ability to be creating any expression and offering yourself this wondrous freedom of your reality, you must be acknowledging to yourself that you ARE creating your reality, and that no other expression within consciousness is creating it FOR you. For each time you express to yourselves that any other aspect of reality is creating for you, you diminish your power. You deny and discount your abilities and you narrow your expression of your own freedom, and in this shift, you are creating an EXPLOSION in freedom! And how very wondrous is this as a direction to be choosing within a physical expression, that you may be limitless in what you create and what you explore! And THIS is what you present to yourselves now, in widening your awareness and engaging your periphery. (#646)

The belief system of duplicity is slightly different from all of your other belief systems, for this belief system is intimately involved with ALL of the aspects of ALL of your belief systems. There is no belief system or aspect of a belief system that this one belief of duplicity does not affect. It is influencing and affecting of EVERY movement that you accomplish. This is the belief system of good and bad and right and wrong, and this belief system attaches itself to EVERY aspect of EVERY other belief system. There is no action that you create within physical focus that this particular belief system does not enter into. Even within the smallest directions of creations that you may engage within physical focus, you involve the belief system of duplicity.

As you choose to awake within your day, how you choose to awake, is influenced by duplicity. Every movement that you create within physical focus is influenced by this belief system — whether you shall adorn yourselves with certain types of clothing, with certain types of shoes, how you shall place them upon your physical form, in what order shall you place them upon your physical form! How you shall brush your hair, how you shall eat your breakfast, whether you shall eat your breakfast! Every movement — how you engage your physical walking across your room. Are your feet pointed within the correct direction? Is this good or is this bad? Do your feet point to each other and meet each other? This shall be bad! Do your feet point away from each other? This shall be bad! Do your feet point straightly ahead? This shall be good! These are all judgments. This is all duplicity.

These are very small examples of the intricacies of this belief system of duplicity, but this belief system is much more affecting than how your feet shall point, for this belief system is quite affecting of YOU and how you view yourselves and how you interact with yourselves, and how you interact with other individuals.

This is the belief system that is the most greatly creating of judgments, and positive and good is also a judgment. It is opposing bad or negative. It is no less a judgment than what you perceive to be unacceptable. It also is a very insidious judgment, and this is the camouflage of duplicity, for it is quite changeable. It is quite acclimating to all of your camouflages, to all of your belief systems, to all of your thoughts and feelings, and may mold itself in many different manners that may be quite deceiving.

In this, you create judgments of good and right and acceptable, and you justify all of your own judgments, and you justify your lack of acceptance of yourselves and of other individuals, and this is also quite influenced by fear. You are fearful of the unfamiliar, and the unfamiliar is piercing the veil of you, recognizing you as YOU.

But you have created within this dimension the veil of separation, and you have forgotten what you are as essence. You have forgotten the whole of you, all of your abilities, and the gloriousness of yourselves, and in this it becomes unfamiliar, and you do not easily move in the area of unfamiliarity.

Duplicity holds you in the familiar, in the uncomfortable, and it is quite reinforcing of itself! This belief system has been fed so very much that there is no bird that may match the size of this particular bird! No creature upon your planet may match the size of this particular well—fed bird, and this bird is quite efficient at changing colors. It also may change its size, that it may "appear to disappear " to you, and you may express to yourself, "I have viewed this bird, I have set this bird free, and I no longer must be dealing with this particular monstrous bird!" But you merely do not see that this monstrous bird has changed itself quite efficiently [and is] invisible temporarily, merely to elude you and move you into the thought process of deluding yourself in your thinking that it is gone, and as you are thinking that it is gone, you may be perpetuating all of the aspects of all of your other belief systems, and you shall move directly into your own justifications.

(Humorously) Justification is quite a friendly bird to duplicity! They have established quite a relationship, and may be seen with each other quite often! Therefore, be aware, where one lurks, the other is not far behind! (Laughter)

Defensiveness is another aspect of justification. You have created so very many birds in this area that you may look to other individuals and their interactions, and you may express to yourselves YOUR worthiness, YOUR goodness, YOUR great acceptance of all other elements and other individuals, and you may be acknowledging greatly of yourselves in your justifications, but these stem from the lack of acceptance of self.

As you hold a lack of acceptance of self, you automatically project this outwardly to other individuals. It is, as I have stated previously, as a ball rolling down a hill, continuing to roll and roll and gain momentum, for all you need be accomplishing is offering this ball one little push, and it shall create its own speed and its own energy and its own momentum, carrying you along with it, but this is not an element outside of yourselves. This is an aspect of you, for it is your belief systems, and your belief systems create your perception, and your perception creates your reality.

Your perception is, there is a cup upon your table. You each view this cup differently. It may be very slight differences within your visuals, but each of you shall perceive the cup slightly different, and in this, the cup is, in reality, how you perceive it. It is not independent of you. It is an element that you have created. Therefore, how you perceive it IS its reality.

Now; in this, each of you holds different perceptions within your reality. They are no less real than any other perception of reality. They are different, but within your belief systems — and the bird of duplicity creeping around the corner once again! — you automatically move in the direction of your own perception, that this is absolute and truth, and all other individuals shall perceive the same as you perceive, for you perceive reality, and if they not perceiving what you are perceiving, they are not perceiving reality! Absolutely!

Very incorrect, for their perception is reality also! And in this, your duplicity enters once again and offers you an explanation and expresses to you, "Very well. I may be accepting of this concept. Their reality is their reality for themselves, but it is not reality! It is merely their reality for themselves. It is their perception, and therefore it is their reality. It is not my reality and is not THE reality, but it is their reality."

(Humorously) For you all are very aware that there is a "THE reality" which is independent of your reality or your reality or your reality (looking at different people), for all of your realities are merely your realities, and there is an independent reality which is THE official reality. Of course, none of you perceive the official reality, for it escapes you all, for you are very busy perceiving your own reality (laughter) and holding your attention in this area!

But you have quite efficiently moved into the direction of offering yourselves this explanation, which then moves you into the comfortability of expressing to yourselves, "It matters not that another individual perceives differently, for their reality is their reality." No. There is no official "THE reality."

There is a combined collective of a created concept of reality which you all participate within, and therefore you each view an object that you term to be a cup, although each cup is different. There is not one cup set upon your table. There are many cups set upon your table which occupy the same space arrangement, all of which are equally reality, and each of you creates each cup. I have expressed this example previously, but in conjunction with this subject of duplicity, it serves to be reiterating of this particular example with the cup, for this you may view clearly within your own thought process, how you camouflage your own duplicities.

You place judgments upon other individuals' perceptions, for they are not the same as yours. You may offer an excuse for other individuals which you term to be an "allowance for their perception," but in actuality, what you are creating is a judgment, and the judgment is not acceptance, and acceptance is the point.

Each of you within this forum encounters other individuals that you may be experiencing conflict with, within one degree or another. Even within the degrees of conflict, you enter your duplicity by expressing that certain conflicts are more important or bigger or stronger or worse than other conflicts. They are all conflicts. It matters not. You merely choose within responsiveness to your duplicity to be creating of degrees of drama attached to your conflicts. If they are very, very bad conflicts, you shall be creating very strong drama! If they are mild conflicts, you may be creating of mild expressions with regard to them. At certain time periods, you may be engaging intense drama with your conflicts and creating what you term to be your temper tantrums! (Laughter) For this is quite expressive and creative and also quite affecting of the situation, as we are all aware! If you are creating a temper tantrum, it shall immediately alter the reality of the conflict. I think not! (Chuckling, followed by silence)

This has been quite interesting! I truly DO think not! (Laughing) For I hold no thought process! (Laughing harder — Elias is cracking himself up!)

This belief system of duplicity holds great importance within the action of this shift, that you be addressing to this particular belief system and recognizing its affectingness in every aspect of your focus and within all of your actions. Many individuals inquire, "How may we move in the direction of peacefulness, of lovingness, of altering our reality?" Acceptance of self and the acceptance of the belief system of duplicity and rendering this particular belief system neutral shall be affecting of ALL of your other belief systems, and shall be automatically creating of the byproduct of allowing you to more easily move into the area of acceptance of all of your other belief systems. Each time you are creating of any type of judgment, you are engaging duplicity. I challenge you each to hold an awareness, within merely one day within your focus, of how many times you engage duplicity, and you may be surprising yourselves, for you engage this belief system continuously! (#328)

Q: I'd like to know about my own duplicity. Why do I sometimes feel I can move forward, but part of me says, "No, I can't do that."

ELIAS: This is quite common within physical focus and is also much more emphasized presently within this shift in consciousness, for your belief systems move more surfacely. Therefore, they are also more obvious to you within your recognition of your own self and your own behaviors.

Let me express to you that duplicity is the strongest of your belief systems within physical focus. This particular belief system permeates all other belief systems that you hold within physical focus and influences all of your belief systems. It intermingles with all of your focus in its entirety. This has been established for millennium within your creation of this particular reality.

Let me express that in what you would term to be your beginnings within this dimension, an aspect of this duplicity was created through your own wonderings of self and your abilities. This would be what you would term to be the beginnings of this particular belief system. As you chose to be fully objectively physically focused within this dimension, you also chose to be not recalling all of essence, and therefore separating the focus from essence in an objective awareness. In this, you became aware of limitations, so to speak, or what you viewed to be limitations, for you did not allow yourselves the remembrance of all of your abilities.

This particular aspect of your creation within this dimension has followed you, so to speak, throughout all of your creating of linear time framework in this dimension. Therefore, it is underlying in all that you create within this particular physical focus, for you do not hold the remembrance objectively of all of your abilities and all that you know, and in this, as your attention is so very singularly focused, you also view yourselves to be limited. You are only limited in what you do not remember, but this is a continuing state that you create with yourselves, and this has been perpetuated very strongly with the addition of your religious and scientific belief systems, for both of these areas move in directions of perpetuating the belief system of duplicity.

Within the area of religious belief systems, it is expressed that there are elements outside of you that are greater than you, and that you are "less than."

Within your new religion of metaphysics, it is stated that you occupy a state in consciousness in this dimension upon this planet, which is your working class planet, your learning planet, (humorously) which is of the lowly third dimension, and that you shall aspire to the fifth or seventh dimension if you are creating quite " good," which is another perpetuation of your belief system of duplicity.

Your sciences also perpetuate this belief system of duplicity and reinforce your own alignment with it, for you look to your sciences for your answers, so to speak, of your existence. Your sciences express to you that you do not hold abilities to be creating, that you are an accident, and that your planet is an accident which has occurred within explosions of creation and of that which you term to be life, which you differentiate between life and that which you term to be non-life or non - living. A rock is non -living. You are living. A plant is living. In actuality, they are all consciousness. They are merely formed differently and function differently, but within energy, they are all consciousness and are all comprised of the same links of consciousness that you are comprised of. But your sciences express that there ARE differences and that you, although being the most intelligent of life upon your planet, you hold inadequacies and you are not all-creating. You have accidentally evolved from that which you term to be "lower" species upon your planet, and although you have aspired to some greatness, in your assessments, you are not great. You are capable of temporary greatness, but you are not wondrous, for all has been created accidentally.

In the area of your science of psychology, your issues and belief system of duplicity is MUCH reinforced, for this science is continuously, creatively inventing new areas to be expressing to you how very inadequate you are and how very uncreative you are, and narrowing and narrowing and narrowing the avenue of acceptable behavior. Therefore, there are many, many, many areas that reinforce this belief system of duplicity, which creates in the individual the energy of questioning continuously, "Am I creating adequately? Am I moving in a correct direction? Am I right?" In this questioning, you are reinforcing yourself and you are spinning upon your wheel continuously, for you are not stopping long enough to be expressing to yourselves, "Stop! I AM great. I need not question or look to other individuals or those that I view to be authorities, for I am my own authority."

This be one of the reasons that I speak to you; not that you be looking to me and following me, for I do not advocate that any individual be a follower or disciple of Elias, but that you be the followers and disciples of yourselves, for you hold the knowings within you. You merely are presently requiring of a little encouragement, that you look to yourselves and that you be accepting of yourselves and not so very questioning of yourselves.

You have been taught for very much time framework to be questioning of everything, and this is good. "You shall be skeptical. You shall be analyzing. It is good to be expressing this behavior. It is good to be questioning and moving into the direction of rationality. It is good to be logical. Intuition is fantasy. Fantasy is delusional. Delusional is bad!"

I express to you that there is a purpose for your rationality, for you have created it purposely. There is also a purpose for your intuition and you have created this purposely, and these two elements of your objective expression have been at odds for much of your time framework, for your belief systems have set them at odds.

And now you move into the direction of bringing into balance these aspects of your reality and accepting both, knowing that your rationality is a creation to serve your understanding and also knowing that your intuition is your language to yourself, and in this, one may not function properly without the other.

There is an imbalance, and this perpetuates also your duplicity and your questioning of yourself, that you move in the direction of your thought process and your rationality and your logic and your questioning and your analyzation. And in all of this thought activity, you are ignoring this small voice which motivates you, and you question that motivation, for you have learned well not to be trusting of self, for yourself shall betray you, for it is untrustworthy. And you may verify this through all of your authorities: your sciences, your physicians, your clergymen, your psychologists. They shall all be expressing to you not to be trusting of self, for in trusting of self, you shall move into the direction of trusting your impressions and your impulses.

(Humorously) Oh, no! We must not be trusting impulses, for these are quite animalistic and very base! And the element of self that you need be discarding and "rising above". I am so very fond of this terminology! Rising above! And what shall be above? I shall be wondrous to discover what is above, as I have never experienced above! (Laughter) Sideways, but no above! Beyond, but no above ... and no below! And how shall we have above if we have no below? (Chuckling)

Therefore, let me express to you that each time you are battling with yourself, allow yourself the moment of quietness to focus upon your language to yourself, your inner voice which motivates you, and in this afford yourself the opportunity to question, that in how shall it be harmful to you? For you shall not be harmful to you if you are listening to you. You shall be harmful to yourself if you are moving in the direction of your influences of your belief systems which stem from outside of yourself.

Example: Many, many, many individuals approach us and express inquiry to the situation of physical form. It is posed to this essence:

"Elias, I am discontented with the physical form that I have created. I am experiencing overweightness." This is quite amusing to us! (Laughter) "And this is unacceptable, for it is unacceptable to other individuals and it is unacceptable to myself, for it is causing me great conflict and anguish." And I shall express, "Why are you experiencing great anguish in what you have created within your form? And what is unacceptable in what you have created in your form?"

And I shall express to you, what is unacceptable is outside of you, for within you, you shall create what you choose to create, but you shall also align with other individuals' judgments and you shall subsequently place judgments upon yourself, in the same manner as the dis-ease — or the belief system of the dis-ease — of senility, which is not a dis-ease. It is a choice, but the individuals creating of this choice also align with the belief system that their behavior is unacceptable, for they look to outside of themselves and they accept the judgment of others. And within this small example of physical form, individuals accept the judgment outside of themselves and are not listening to their own small voice.

This is not to say that many individuals do not create this overweightness ... which is not overweightness at all, but this would be your term for this creation. This is not to say that many individuals experiencing this situation are not creating this situation in alignment with the officially accepted belief systems and their own issues of duplicity and holding energy in this area, for they are not accepting of themselves. Therefore, they are creating an outward image, a camouflage which mirrors their own lack of acceptance of self, that they may project to other individuals and reinforce their own lack of acceptance.

(Intently) They are not accepting themselves and therefore they shall willingly accept the non-acceptance of other individuals also, for they are deserving of this, for they are unworthy of any else, and this is an example of duplicity.

But many individuals merely are creating of this physical display of what you term to be overweightness for they choose to be creating of this, and they are not holding an issue. But they allow themselves to be affected in what you term to be negativity, for they accept the judgment of outside and are not listening to their own little voice, which is expressing, "You are choosing to be creating of this form, for you choose to be expressing yourself in this manner, and it is pleasing to you. And you are enjoying of consuming substances and therefore you are experiencing pleasure, moving through your focus with less thickness, and this is acceptable to you." (Laughter)

No, YOU shall move in the direction of placing many, many judgments upon yourself and expressing, "Some element is quite wrong with myself, for I am not creating in the manner of the officially accepted reality." And who is creating of the officially accepted reality? The "they." And who are the they? The you! YOU are the they! YOU are the ones that are creating of the officially accepted reality! Therefore, you are merely expressing outwardly your own battles with duplicity.

And what be so very wrong with what you may term to be plumpness? (Laughter) This may be quite attractive, and may be quite enjoyable to many individuals! It is merely a choice for experience. It is an indulgence of physical senses, and be this not one of your reasons for your creation within physical focus, to be experiencing physically? Why shall you not experience physically if you are physically focused? If you are not choosing to be physically experiencing, you need not enter physical focus. You may be experiencing non —physically.

This offers you a small example of the battles that rage within each of you in the silliest areas (laughter) that you create such trauma in regard to, for you hold such deep influence of these belief systems.

THIS be your reason why you choose to be neutralizing — not eliminating but neutralizing — these belief systems, to be quelling these raging inner conflicts and confusions that you create continuously, not only within yourselves, but with each other.

And let me inquire of you, how many of you have moved through — let us focus — this time framework of one month with absolutely no conflicts with any other individual? (Much laughter) And absolutely no conflicts with yourselves? There be your reason. One month — a very small amount of your time framework, and you are not accomplishing one month of no conflict ... but you may!

And beyond this statement, you may also offer yourselves the new freedom of experience, that you may be engaged within a particular conflict and it shall not appear to you within your perception any longer as negative. It shall be within your perception as a purposeful experience that YOU have created and participated within willingly and purposefully, which creates a very large difference. Not that you may eliminate all of your experiences — what be the point in this? — but that your perception of your experiences shall be dramatically altered, that even within a creation of conflict it shall not hold the same meaning to you, for it shall not be conflict within the definition that you assign to it presently. It shall be a purposeful experience for your gaining of information.

And you shall not be responding and reacting to this conflict in automatic manners as you do now, for you shall understand what and how you are creating of it all. And your necessity for creating of your conflicts shall become less and less and less, for you shall offer yourselves the information that it is unnecessary to be creating of conflict.

And this is NOT moving into the area of your psychology, which expresses to you that you shall pound your fists upon your ground or upon a cushion when you are experiencing great anger! I am NOT offering you an alternate route to be "channeling your energy into more productive areas!" This would be quite common of your psychology!

I am expressing to you responses to your own questions, to your own concerns, to your own thoughts that you view to plague your own selves: "How do I create my reality? What am I creating? How shall I create my reality more effortlessly, with less thickness and less conflict?" For this is the direction that you are moving into.

You have created much conflict throughout your history, and you have bored yourselves with it. You have created it and created it and created it, and you have batted this dead mouse enough, and you move into a new direction of chasing a flying bird, which moves much more freely and much more excitedly than the dead mouse! And this be what you offer yourselves now, and I participate in helpfulness for your accomplishment of this choice.

You look to the label of "happiness." It is merely the elimination of your own inner conflicts, and as you trust yourselves more, you eliminate these inner conflicts.

And I shall be repeating of this " trust of self " ten-thousand — and—one times, until the point that you each are accepting of the reality of the acceptance of self and trust of self and the discontinuation of looking to authorities and outside of self for your truths, for they are within you! And you need no Elias and you need no government and you need no churches and you need no sciences and you need no authorities to offer them to you, for you hold them already within yourselves.

And shall it be that one discarnate essence shall continue to be repeating of this, to the point that you view the gloriousness of yourselves? And I shall offer it willingly to you, for you ARE worthy and you ARE creative. You need merely be listening to your own small voice! (Chuckling) (#307)

Q: In regards to what you have already said about people who have conflict about 'overweight ness.' I've had an issue with my weight for most of my life, and I'm really tired of thinking about it, and so instead of thinking about dieting and all that stuff again, I would just prefer to be accepting of self and accepting what I've created here, but that's not been particularly easy either. I know there's imagery presented in the body type that I've created, but I would like to know what exactly the issue is in my case. I've identified many of the beliefs I hold about it, but in accepting it and understanding it better, I'd like to understand what exactly it is I'm accepting!

ELIAS: What you are offering yourself the opportunity to view is an expression in objective terms of the acceptance of self, and in this, you present yourself with an issue that you have held for much time framework. The issue of physical form – and aligning with the mass belief systems as to aesthetic beauty concerning physical form – is that which is creating of the belief system, as you are aware. But within this time framework, you are moving in the direction of the realization that in addressing to this issue, it is not necessarily the presentment to yourself to be altering your physical form, but rather to be accepting what you have created and moving yourself outside of the mass belief systems.

This is an element of what you may term to be the process of accepting aspects of belief systems, allowing yourself to move outside of the influence of these mass belief systems and the officially accepted reality, for in moving outside of this, you no longer allow the influence of energy for yourself in these areas, and this allows you to be liberating of yourself in allowing yourself to be accepting of your own creations regardless of your choice in how you are creating them.

Let me express to you that I have recently offered information to other individuals in very similar manner in this same subject matter.

In this, the base line of the acceptance is to be recognizing all of the aspects of the belief system which you are involving yourself with, and in this, as you recognize the aspects of the belief systems, not to be placing judgment on any of the expressions, but rather to be moving in the direction of acknowledging your own movement, your own alignment with certain aspects of the belief systems, and recognizing that you are much more affecting as you allow yourself to be accepting rather than forcing energy in what you term to be 'against' certain aspects of the belief system.

Let me offer you an example that I have offered to other individuals also. If you are holding an aspect of the belief that certain elements that may be consumed shall be creating of weightiness within your physical form, my suggestion to you is not to be moving yourself into a thought process of denial of that alignment with that aspect.

Such as: If you view that sausage shall be creating weight within your physical form if you are consuming this element, addressing to this efficiently would not be to view this aspect and express to yourself, 'This is merely an aspect of the belief system and it matters not,' for underlyingly, you are aligning with that aspect.

Therefore, as you fight with that aspect, you merely lend energy to its perpetuation. Therefore, if you are consuming of this sausage, it shall be producing of weight, for this is your expectation, regardless of what you are expressing to yourself objectively within your thought process or within your language.

You may express to yourself and to other individuals, 'I do not believe that this holds truth, and I shall view myself in the mirror, and I shall will myself to be holding a thin physical form,' and you shall continue to create the physical form that you hold presently, for your underlying expectation is not in alignment with your thought process. In this, as you allow yourself an acceptance and not the judgment of your alignment with certain aspects of these belief systems, they become less and less affecting and less and less important, for you are lending less and less energy to them.

What I am expressing to you is that each time you are concentrating upon the issue of the weight – each time that you are moving in the direction of attempting to be altering this situation objectively without acceptance of self in this area – what you are accomplishing in actuality is perpetuating the creation that you have already chosen. You are reinforcing the aspects of the belief systems and lending energy to them. You are also reinforcing your own expectations.

But as you allow yourself to relax your focus and your hold upon your energy in this area, and therefore allow yourself to be accepting of your creation without judgment – for in actuality, it matters not – subsequently you may be altering of your physical form, or you may not be, but it shall in reality matter not to you, for you shall be accepting of your own choices and creations…and you shall not be placing judgment upon yourself, and in that, also reinforcing your own duplicity. Are you understanding?

Q: Yes. So, I would guess or I would imagine then, as I am accepting of this and issues come up, then I would just deal with those one at a time, those beliefs, and move through it that way?

I was wondering if there was one particular belief that was ... I guess I'm looking for the key to the whole thing. I don't know that there is one particular issue that I have with this that's sort of the basis of the whole thing. I guess that's what I was wondering.

ELIAS: The key is what I have expressed to you. The basis of the situation and the key to this creation is the expression of lack of acceptance of self, in whatever you are choosing to be creating.

You are placing judgments upon your creations, and this is creating conflict. If you are accepting of your creation, then it shall matter not the physical appearance, for you shall be accepting of that also, in recognition that however you choose to be physically manifesting yourself is worthy, adequate, and glorious!

It matters not that it does not fit into the officially accepted reality and the confines or the narrow parameters of your societal beliefs. These are merely the perceptions en masse that are lent a tremendous amount of energy, but I express to you that although perception may be projected en masse and this IS creating of mass realities, they are all influenced by individual perceptions. Let me express to you that perception itself is highly individualized, and each of you is creating of your reality as through your perception. In this, it is greatly influenced in how you view yourself and if you are accepting of yourself and if you are not accepting of yourself.

I have expressed this many times, and individuals – and yourself – continue to not quite understand that this is the base line to all of your creations and all of your conflicts in every area, involving every aspect of every belief system. The key is to look to self and to allow yourself to begin the acceptance of self in every area of your expression. In doing this, it shall matter not, and you shall eliminate your conflict.

Q: Well … I do understand that. It's just difficult putting that to work sometimes.

ELIAS: Quite! This be your most difficult task, so to speak, is to be accepting of self. Individuals are inquiring and questioning of me continuously to be offering them a method of what you term to be easy routes, so to speak, in accepting belief systems, but the key is to be accepting of self FIRST, and subsequently you shall allow yourself to also be accepting of belief systems. But this is the area of the most conflict and the most difficulty, for this is quite unfamiliar to you all in acceptance of self. Although you objectively offer yourselves information and express to yourselves and to each other that you are quite accepting of yourselves, in actuality, you are not! (#358)

Q: I know that you were discussing a lot about our belief systems, and that it is really important for us to look at the belief systems, and I know that we created these belief systems to begin with, and I'm wondering why it's necessary for us to change them. I guess they're not really serving us any more, but how is this going to help us, to change them?

ELIAS: First of all, let me express to you that you are not changing the belief systems. You are merely moving in the direction of accepting the belief systems. There IS a difference.

In your thought processes, you think to yourselves that if you are changing your belief systems, this shall be affecting of your reality and be creating of more efficiency within your reality.

In actuality, what you are accomplishing in the action of changing a belief system is not changing a belief system! The belief system remains. What you ARE moving into is changing your perception or your viewpoint, so to speak. You have moved your viewing from one aspect of the belief system to a different aspect of the belief system, but the first aspect that you have been viewing continues to remain within the cage. You merely are not focusing your attention upon that particular bird any longer. You are focusing your attention upon a different bird. At times, you may even move in the direction of viewing the same bird, but viewing different angles of the same bird.

Initially you view the head of the bird, and then, in attempting to "change your belief system," you move your attention to the tail of the bird, or you occupy your attention with the colors of the bird or the size of the bird.

The bird continues to remain within the cage. The belief system remains the same. You are merely moving your attention in different directions. This is altering of your perception, but it is not accepting a belief system.

The point of accepting a belief system is to be not eliminating the belief system, but to be eliminating the judgment, and if you are eliminating the judgment, you are also greatly affecting of your conflict that you create within yourselves and within each other. And this would be the point, for within this shift in consciousness, you move in the direction of creating a new type of reality.

In this, I am not expressing that within the accomplishment of this shift you shall be altering your physical form, and you shall be moving about your planet as strange, unusual-looking little creatures and that you shall be consuming of strange vegetation, and that the entirety of your planet and your existence within this physical focus shall be altered radically within these types of manners, but the entirety of your reality SHALL be altered in different respects, and these alterations ARE quite radical, in a manner of speaking.

How you perceive your reality as it is established presently shall be altered. Your structure of your reality shall be different. I have offered information in this once, and I have expressed to individuals that I shall not move in the direction of often repeating that information, for that moves in the direction of what you perceive to be predictions, and I choose not to be lending energy in this direction, for this is another belief system.

I have offered information previously as to the action of this shift and how it shall be definitively altering of your reality in very radical manners, but I also am not moving in the direction of perpetuating your own belief systems in the areas of prophecies and crystal balls and predictions, for all ACTIONS are, as you are aware, probabilities, and therefore they are not concrete. They are very changeable within every moment, and although some probabilities are more probable than other probabilities in their actualization into this particular physical dimension, they are probabilities. Therefore, they are not absolutes.

There are no absolutes! You WANT absolutes, but there are no absolutes! In this, your acceptance of your belief systems allows you to hold an opinion concerning your belief systems, that you may choose to move within them or you may choose not to move within them, but you create no judgment that you attach to them. There is no right or wrong or good or bad that concerns your choices. They are recognized as merely choices, and in this you offer yourselves tremendous freedom, and this be the point.

For within the alignment of these belief systems and the movement of all of the aspects of these belief systems and all of your judgments which are attached to these aspects of belief systems, you limit your own expressions, your own acceptance, and your own creativity. You create limits upon yourselves, and in this, as you allow yourselves to be accepting of belief systems, you not only open the door for the birds to fly free, but you also open the door for the freedom of your own creativity and your own expressions.

You guard yourselves. You do not allow the freedom of your expression, for you fear how this shall be perceived by another individual. You shall guard how you speak, what energy you project, how you think, for you hold an awareness that thought is energy, and although other individuals do not engage their inner sense of telepathy and actively engage in mind — reading with you, you DO hold an awareness that in some subjective manner THEY hold an awareness of your energy, which you project through your thought processes, which is translated as energy projected outward from your physical form in the direction of other individuals.

And do not delude yourselves into the thought process that other individuals are unaware of your projections of energy! It is unnecessary to physically view, to see or hear or touch energy, to KNOW that it is present and to KNOW that it is being manipulated.

You all have encountered experiences with other individuals in which you KNOW what another individual is thinking, and they may say nothing. You may not allow yourselves to engage this continuously, but you ALL have created this experience within your focus. Not one individual has not experienced this particular action! It is natural to you. It is a movement of your inner senses, which ARE natural to you. You merely do not open yourselves to actively engaging these inner senses continuously, but regardless that you notice the workings of these inner senses, they ARE working and you DO allow yourselves to be connecting to their workings occasionally.

Therefore, you hold an awareness that it matters not that another individually, physically, audibly expresses to you. You hold an awareness of their energy and of their thought processes.

(Firmly) There are no secrets within essence!

You may move in the direction within physical focus of fooling yourselves and deceiving yourselves that you hold the ability to be creating secrets from other individuals, but within essence there are no secrets, for there are no judgments. And in this, it matters not what you choose to be creating! You create your secrets, for you hold duplicity and you engage this belief system. You do not move in the direction of secretiveness if you are not creating a judgment that you have engaged something bad or unacceptable or that you fear other individuals shall place a judgment upon, but you have already placed a judgment upon your very creation! This be the reason that you are creating of this shift and that you are addressing to these belief systems, for your own freedoms.

How very often do you each engage the thought of how very liberating it may be that you may express yourselves without limitation? And if you are accepting belief systems you discontinue judgment, and therefore you MAY express yourselves in all of your creations, in all of your thought process, in all of your emotions, in all of your directions of all of your expressions, for it shall matter not. It shall not be hurtful to other individuals, for they shall not be engaging judgment, and it shall not be hurtful to yourself, for YOU shall not be engaging judgment, and THIS is the point.

Q: To view something as being beautiful, is that not a judgment? And if that be a judgment, then where is the duplicity?

ELIAS: Yes, this is a judgment and this would be an expression of duplicity, for in viewing an element as beautiful, you are creating a comparison that another element is not beautiful, and in this you are incorporating your duplicity.

As I have stated, you move in the direction of viewing the action of your duplicity ONLY when you are noticing of negative elements or what you view to be bad, unacceptable, or wrong. THIS shall attain your attention and you shall recognize that you are moving in the direction of duplicity, for this appears obvious to you that it is a judgment. You do not so easily move into this noticing of judgment if you are expressing that an element is good or right or beautiful or positive, and this is the very nature of duplicity.

Q: It almost sounds like it takes a little juice out of life!

ELIAS: No. It APPEARS in this manner to you presently, for you are steeped within this belief system of duplicity, and it is what is familiar to you.

I speak to you of joyfulness — which in your interpretation and in your understanding is translated into great happiness — and beauty. As I express to you of joyfulness, I am not expressing of happiness. This is an emotion. I am not expressing to you of beauty in the terms that you understand within physical focus. I am expressing of liberation and of freedom, which is not necessarily attached to an emotion, but you translate this into an emotion.

Now; I am not expressing to you that your emotions are bad! You have created this particular dimension to be experiencing emotion and sexuality. Therefore, this is not bad. It is what you have created for the experience within physical form. Some elements of your reality are not necessarily elements that attach to emotion or sexuality, but are reality and may be incorporated into your reality.

This also is the point of this shift in consciousness, to expand your awareness and allow you the ability to incorporate more into your physical experience, more of essence and the expression of essence and the remembrance of essence into your physical expression and your physical focuses within your mundane reality. I do not express mundane in the terms that you automatically move into, as boring, but that this is your routine, so to speak, your every day, and in this every day reality, you may incorporate much more freedom and much more of an expansiveness of your own expressions.

Within this shift, you shall not discontinue emotion! This IS a basic unit, so to speak, of this particular dimension. Therefore, you shall continue to be experiencing emotion, but you shall experience emotion by choice. (Emphatic pause)

Within this present now, you ARE choosing the emotions that you experience, but you do not view yourselves to be choosing. You do not see your reality and how you are creating your reality. Therefore, your perception is that you are not always creating your reality and that you are experiencing certain elements of your reality in responsiveness to other individuals' creations, or they are thrust upon you, or you are the victim of other individuals' creations or situations.

In this, as you move in the action of this shift and allow yourselves more of an awareness, as you are widening your awarenesses and expanding your periphery, you allow yourselves to experience the fullness of your emotions and your sexuality which you have created within this dimension, and you shall know why and how you are creating of each direction and event.

You shall not surprise yourself with your creation, for you shall understand why you are creating of it. This is also not to say that you shall hold no surprise within this physical dimension, for you shall continue to incorporate surprise, but not within the areas that you do not wish surprise. (#328)

Q: It seems to me that we have these amazing beliefs in modesty and humility, and so every time we try — I shouldn't say we, I should say me — accepting ourselves … it seems like I'm not sure where the line is drawn between feeling good about yourself, and then these beliefs about arrogance or original sin or the sinful self or whatever. It seems like as soon as I start feeling good, a part of me is always saying,

"Don't feel TOO good!"

ELIAS: Ah, and now we return to our belief system of duplicity! Which, as I have stated previously, couples itself with ALL of your other belief systems. This one belief system of duplicity is quite changeable, and it attaches itself to *ALL* of your other belief systems. It moves quite harmoniously with all of your belief systems. It also is very affecting, for you have lent very much energy en masse to this particular belief system.

I express to you, in actual terms, there is no experience that is right; there is no experience that is wrong. There are merely experiences. There is no choice that is right or wrong. There are merely choices.

Therefore, within this statement, it matters not what you choose as your expression. It matters merely as influenced by the belief systems that you hold, and the coupling of those belief systems with the one belief system of duplicity: of right and wrong, good and bad.

Therefore, arrogance, we may be expressing, may be viewed within your belief systems as the exaggeration of the acceptance of self. Arrogance in actuality IS the acceptance of self, but you also incorporate your duplicity, which expresses to you a false modesty, a false humility.

I express this purposefully, for you may be expressing humility in its true form as a natural byproduct of your own acceptance of self and expression of essence, but this would not be the same expression as YOUR ideas of humility or modesty, for these terms are the terms that you have created — with the definitions that you attach to them — in denying your own expressions, and thusly denying self.

I have offered to individuals previously expressions that your natural inclination within physical focus, as an expression of essence, is to move in the direction of less thickness and [more] pleasure, but within your belief systems, you are QUITE influenced by duplicity. You may be accepting of few pleasures, but not very many! And within these few pleasures, do not be indulging excessively

Q: Don't like it TOO much! (Laughing)

ELIAS: ... for this also shall be viewed as bad and wrong, and you are quite creating of much conflict in these areas, for you battle your own natural inclination. You create many different expressions of pleasure within your physical focus, and you move in the direction of expressing to yourselves, once you have created these expressions, that you may not participate within your creations! And you express rationally and logically to yourselves that this is an acceptable expression, for this is quite logical that you shall create these expressions of pleasure, for they are rising from your base elements, those elements of yourselves that are quite undesirable and very, very bad! Therefore, you are not responsible for these irrational creations of pleasure, but you ARE responsible for not indulging in these pleasures, for you shall know better!

Q: Well, I have kind of a follow-up for that one too. Recently I read a book by Jeff Stern about Taylor Caldwell, and under hypnosis, she said that during the stoning of Mary Magdalene, Jesus said, "Let him who had not lain with this woman throw the first stone." If this is true, there was no implication of man as a sinful self. Is that true? I mean, was that a distortion?

ELIAS: (Chuckling) Ah, you incorporate two different subject matters within this questioning! First of all, in the direction of the truth of the statement as an expression of actual occurrence, I shall express to you that this is a story.

Q: Oh, okay. I get that.

ELIAS: As to the concept in your reference, there is no sinful self. This is a belief. This is a religious belief that stems from the idea of the projection of a mirror image of self, which has created a separate being of God, which resides outside of yourself and holds all of the power that you do not hold, and also holds the judgment that you DO hold. This is a projection concept which mirrors what you know subjectively, but what you do not allow yourself to remember objectively. Therefore, you create this projection.

You project yourself into the image of this god, and you attribute to this god all that you know within your subjective awareness, that this god holds all of these abilities. But you also project what you know objectively, and you attribute your objective qualities to this entity that you have created.

In actuality, this is merely a projection, a concept of yourselves, as you have created this separation of objective and subjective awarenesses. It is, as all other belief systems, another explanation to yourselves of that which you have forgotten.

Q: So that's why it seemed so relevant to me? Actually, I want to make sure that I'm getting this correctly. The reason why this seemed so relevant to me is because I was ... not because. I am projecting subjectively what I know, but also objectifying it in my belief systems too?

ELIAS: Correct.

Q: Okay.

ELIAS: You are correct.

Q: It was very relevant to me!

ELIAS: These are very strong aspects of belief systems that you hold, in expressing to yourselves this element of duplicity: that you hold this aspect of self that is glorious, but you also hold this very distasteful element of self, this base instinct which is quite lowly and an aspect of self that must be attended to, to be eliminated. This be the sinful self, and this...

Q: I'd like to get rid of it!

ELIAS: No!

Q: It's accepting it instead of...

ELIAS: Your   attention   in   this   direction   merely   is perpetuating!

Each time that you are placing a judgment upon yourself in ANY area, you are perpetuating the belief system of duplicity, and you are reinforcing your own strength in energy in holding to this belief system. You are not accepting of this belief system. (Pause)

Q: Isn't even rejecting it giving it power too?

ELIAS: Absolutely, for you are continuing to be creating of a judgment.

Q: So is it more like acknowledging, and then letting go?

ELIAS: Quite, recognizing that this is a belief system, that you hold choices within this belief system, that you are not eliminating this belief system but that you are placing no judgment upon this belief system or its expressions. You may continue to create within the belief system, and you SHALL continue to create within the belief system, for you create your reality within this dimension with belief systems!

I have expressed over and over again, you shall not be eliminating your belief systems! This dimension that you have created within a physical focus is based in your belief systems. It is an intricate element of your physical manifestation within this particular dimension. It has been created purposefully. If you are eliminating of your belief systems, you are also eliminating of this particular physical dimension expression! Therefore, this is not the point.

Your belief systems within themselves are not bad or good. They merely are. They are your own explanations. They are influencing of your perception, and your perception is your tool that you use to be creating of your reality within this dimension. (#331)

This dimension is created based upon what physical manifestations of expressions?

Q: Is that a question?

ELIAS: What physical expressions of manifestation is this particular dimension based upon?

Q: Well, it seems to be based on our belief systems.

ELIAS: Your belief systems are a manifestation. They are explanations to yourselves. They are an intricate element of your creation of this dimension, but they are not the base element of your manifestation. They are not the reason that you have created this particular dimension.

Q: Oh. Physical and emotional experience.

ELIAS: Emotional and sexual.

Q: Oh, sexual. Excuse me.

ELIAS: And what shall be the first expressions of experience in response to your perceptions and your belief systems before you are even creating of a thought? You shall respond emotionally, or you shall respond sexually.

Q: If we're to get to a place where we're able to neutralize our belief systems so that we're aware — just a basic or a higher level of awareness, if you will — does that mean that we will have more experience of emotions and sexuality on a different level? I mean, perceptions and belief systems are clouding that experience?

ELIAS: It shall open to you more elements of your expression of creativity in these expressions and within the exploration of these experiences.

Therefore, in a manner of speaking, there is an element that you DO cloud, so to speak, or block your experiences and your expressions as influenced by your belief systems, for these belief systems shall dictate to you that certain elements of the expressions are bad, and therefore you shall not engage, and in this lack of engagement you limit your own creativity and your own expressions within your experiences, for you deny yourselves your own abilities in the area of your own creativity and your own abilities. (#331)

I offer information generally to groups of individuals, knowing that I am interacting subjectively with each of the individuals that shall draw themselves to the information, and that they shall apply this information to the areas in which their attention holds within each moment.

In this, in general terms, I express repeatedly to you all in literal terms that there is no good or bad or right or wrong. These are influences of your belief systems. I offer this information for the express purpose that you all recognize IN CONCEPT that the reality of essence and consciousness outside of belief systems that you hold within physical focus is that experience is experience. Choice is choice. They are not attached to judgments in the direction of right or wrong.

Now; understand that individually, as I speak to you each, I also hold the awareness that your reality IS real — it is NOT an illusion — and your belief systems are an intricate part of your reality.

Therefore, although I offer you the knowledge of the CONCEPT that you hold a belief system which we term to be duplicity and the CONCEPT that there is in actuality no right or wrong, I also acknowledge simultaneously that within your physical reality, you create a reality which DOES hold right and wrong judgments, and you have moved in the direction of lending very much energy to these judgments for so very long that these actions and behaviors are automatic to you and they are very much a part of your reality.

Therefore, in working within the framework of your belief systems, there is also expressed an understanding and an acceptance of these beliefs and their affectingness within your daily creations of your reality.

In this, I encourage individuals to be allowing more freedom within their expressions, challenging those aspects of their creations and experiences that they deem as bad or wrong and allowing themselves the expression of acceptance in turning that judgment into a right and good judgment temporarily, for as you are aware, within your reality, you all lean in the direction of creating in the manner of the pendulum. You shall swing far in one direction and you shall swing far in the other direction, but eventually you shall swing to the middle and you shall balance.

But prior to your balance, you also are engaged in your method of readjusting your thought process, and in this, you are incorporating new messages and information, swinging now to the other direction with your pendulum, allowing and accepting ALL of your expressions and experiences and deeming them all as good, holding the underlying knowing subjectively that this action shall facilitate the eventual balance and the genuine acceptance which shall swing the pendulum to the middle, and in that expression, you shall let fly free the expression of right and wrong and good and bad, and it shall matter not, for you shall recognize that in actuality, genuinely, your expressions, your choices, your experiences are merely that, and that they are not right or wrong.

I am expressing this to you to be clarifying that within this present now, your pendulum begins to swing to one direction and is not yet in the manner of settling within balance in the middle, for you are addressing to the expressions of duplicity which have gripped you for much of your focus in negativity and judgment, in the direction of bad and wrong and unacceptable behaviors, choices and experiences.

Therefore, you counter that information and those aspects of beliefs with different aspects of beliefs, and lean in the direction of expressing to yourselves the other judgment of good and right and acceptable. This is beneficial temporarily, as you allow yourself to be more accepting of self and more trusting of self. Once you have accomplished the acceptance of self and trust of self, this action shall no longer be necessary. (#397)

Chapter 18

MASS BELIEF SYSTEMS

"All manifestations that you choose to incorporate are influenced by mass events. What you choose to be wearing in your clothing is influenced by mass events. What you choose, individually, to be consuming is influenced by mass events. There is no expression that you incorporate that does not incorporate a basis in mass events and belief systems."

(#90)

Chapter 18

MASS BELIEF SYSTEMS

ELIAS: We shall engage discussion of the individual and mass belief systems, as you presently engage these subjects. Individuals may and can survive without groups. Groups cannot survive without individuals. You ask, "Where do mass belief systems originate? Where do they come from? Who initiates mass belief systems? Who are the "they," that speak for you all?" the "they" are you!

You may not express an alignment with a belief system outwardly, but your non-expression is an alignment. Therefore, I express to you, mass belief systems begin with individuals expressing opinions. In this, they draw to them other individuals who agree with these opinions, creating the beginnings of a belief system. Many, many other individuals may not necessarily be in absolute agreement to these opinions, but their omission of expression lends to the creation of the belief system. The reason individuals do not express is that they do not trust their own voice. Therefore, within the group, which may not survive without the individuals, the individuals choose to express, or not to express. If they are choosing to be not expressing in opposition, the belief system takes hold and is allowed to stand; therefore being accepted and incorporated within your societies.

Many belief systems have originated with one individual expressing an observation, many times connected with elements of nature, as you view it. In this, they form an opinion of the action of a particular element within nature. This is translated into a parallel, within your species, as human behavior. In this, many other individuals view the observation as novel and interesting and new. Therefore, they align with it, believing that the individual who has made the observation, and who has expressed the opinion, is quite enlightened. Therefore, they shall be enlightened also, within agreement with this opinion. Those not in agreement do not always actualize, objectively, their disagreement. In this, they lend their support, within energy, within consciousness, to the formation of the belief system.

You may view your Darwinian opinions, belief systems, as an example. A mainstay within this theory is "the survival of the fittest." One individual makes an observation of nature. This individual translates this into a parallel of human behavior, suggesting to you all that human behavior follows in like kind, in this survival of the fittest. In this, you weed out those which are, or which you believe to be, weaker.

This individual expressed quite confidently. In this, the idea was new. The expression of the idea was new. Many individuals rallied round this expression, and were in agreement. They did not conduct the studies, but trusted the expression of another individual, to which they viewed to be more learned; and also, in this, not trusting their own expression. Many other individuals were not trusting of this opinion, but were not challenging. The opposition was not great enough to suppress the formation of the belief system.

Although this is not a universally or globally held belief system, it is a mass belief system. It exists with other belief systems alongside of it that are quite contrary; but the individuals separate themselves into different groups or "camps," aligning with those belief systems that they individually agree with, or that they agree with "more." They may not entirely agree with a given belief system within mass expression, but they align more with one than another. In this, they do not express opposition, and they lend their energy, within consciousness, to the development and the acceptance of these belief systems. Then you look to yourselves "later," in your view within your time period, and you express, "How do we acquire these belief systems? Why do we align with these mass belief systems? Who has begun them?" Within consciousness, you have begun them; for you have chosen to express favorably, or you have chosen to not express.

An efficient group of individuals allows recognition of each individual, within the group, the expression of their own self; for each individual within the group, within the mass, holds a vital element for contribution to the mass. You do not view yourselves individually as so important. Therefore, you sway to the mass. If you are trusting of your own individual voice, you shall find it is unnecessary to be aligning with mass belief systems. If you are trusting of self, you shall find that it is unimportant. You may align if you are choosing, but it will hold no great importance to you, therefore needing no great expression. (#103)

Q: When it comes to mass realities and global challenges – for instance, things that involve a great many people – how can we understand it in those terms? Instead of reading the newspapers and what the politicians and the media say, are there any ways for us to understand these things in terms of mass beliefs?

ELIAS: Look to your individual belief systems, and you may compare these with the mass belief systems, for mass belief systems are created by individuals collectively. You may not create groups without individuals. Therefore, the mass expressions are collective reflections of the individuals' expressions. In this, they are not quite so very difficult to be understanding. You may also view within the mass expressions

that there may be movements in these societal expressions that
surfacely appear to move in one direction of great judgments
in certain areas, but underlyingly, they may also be affecting
quite strongly in alignment with this shift in consciousness,
bringing to individuals attention the inefficiency of many of
these belief systems and lending energy to the individuals in
moving through these belief systems and moving more in the
direction of acceptance of these belief systems.

You experience within this present now many expressions
within your societies upon your planet, mass expressions of
very strongly held belief systems which are being addressed to
and are affecting of the individuals and how they are beginning
to view these belief systems, not necessarily in alignment with
these officially held belief systems. In this, as you continue to
examine the individual belief systems, you offer yourselves
more information in understanding how you have created
mass belief systems.

You may also look to your religious and scientific belief
systems and view how very strongly they have been accepted en
masse throughout your globe and are very aligned with. Even
individuals that express that they are moving away from the
religious belief systems hold many underlying religious belief
systems, and move themselves into an alignment with your
scientific belief systems very much as strong as they have held
religious belief systems previously. In actuality, your scientific
belief systems are merely a different type of expression,
different language of the same types of belief systems as your
religious belief systems.

All of this information shall circle 'round to the base point in
every area, in looking to self, addressing to your own acceptance
and trust of self, which within your language and within this
objective expression may APPEAR to be sounding very

elementary. But this, in its basic element, is your most difficult challenge, for you have created your officially accepted reality for millennium in the direction of not looking to self and in the expression of projecting outward to all other elements and looking to other individuals and other sources, so to speak, for your directedness. In this, I express to you within this concept an entirely different direction of your attention, in looking to self for your acceptance and trust and recognizing that YOU are creating of your reality, not looking to any other outside element to be expressing to you how to be creating of your reality, for you already possess the blueprints for creating your reality, and all is within your disposal. You need merely be focusing upon self to be accessing all of this information." (#330)

Chapter 19

NEW HORIZONS

*"The action of your shift in consciousness encompasses the
entirety of your globe. It is not limited to any group, any family,
any selectivity of consciousness within this dimension.
It is all-encompassing. It is agreed, but you have also
previously, in your terms, agreed within your religious
focuses to be creating of prophecies and ideas of future events,
also in your terms, which are probabilities.
They are not actual realities that are unchangeable."*

(#185)

Chapter 19

NEW HORIZONS

ELIAS: This evening we shall be discussing a long-awaited topic, for I am aware that all of you and all of our close friends involved with this forum are quite focused upon events occurring futurely. This shall not be a prediction of future events, but offering you the most probable probabilities within the action of this shift as it so exists within this present now.

Within your present now, you are creating probabilities involved with this shift in consciousness. I have expressed to you that within this shift, it shall be accomplished within the third quarter of your (21st) century. In this, great accomplishments shall be occurring within this new approaching century, as dictated by your present probabilities. In this, I express to you that ALL of your reality shall be altered. What you view to be your reality presently and what you know to be your officially accepted reality shall be no longer, and you shall move into a new era of consciousness and physical reality. In this, many elements of your physical reality shall be altered.

Let me express to you that your – what you view to be in your terms presently – science fiction, as I have expressed previously, is closer to science fact than you realize. Within your approaching century, your scientists shall move into new areas of wondrous accomplishments. Elements that you investigate presently shall be viewed as child's play compared to what you shall be accomplishing, as what is dictated within your present probabilities.

Be remembering that your probabilities are probabilities, and that you may alter these at any moment. Therefore, they are not set in stone; but within the most probable probabilities, this shall be what shall be occurring and what you shall be looking forward to within your future elements.

Within the mid-points of your [21st] century, tremendous new accomplishments shall be endeavored within your sciences. I have expressed to you that within this [20th] century, your sciences have mirrored you and essence and consciousness, developing these elements in physical matter of what you know to be within consciousness. You have created many wondrous inventions and have learned many elements within your physical dimension that mirror elements of consciousness and of essence. This offers you much information, and as you move into this new century you shall continue with this endeavor and you shall further your accomplishments and your inventions.

I have expressed to you many times that the most efficient method of travel is through space, not around space. I have expressed to you your abilities to be projecting, but I shall also express to you that within the areas of your sciences, you shall be moving into areas of exploration of your physical atmospheric space within your universe. I have expressed to you that it is futile to be looking to your immediate solar system, for within this dimension no life, as you term it to be, exists within this dimension upon the planets that are within your immediate solar system. But within your galaxy and beyond, within this dimension, there are other forms of beings that are other aspects of yourselves, as you well know, for these are all aspects of the same essences merely focused within different areas and different realities.

Within your coming [21st] century you shall be, within your most probable reality and probabilities, developing technology that shall be enabling you to accomplish feats that to this point in your time framework seem impossible. It is possible for you to access technology to mirror what you do within consciousness. Within consciousness, you exceed light speed. Your thought processes, your ability to project yourselves within consciousness, far exceeds light speed. This is child's play to essence. It is merely the limitations of physical focus.

In this, you may view what I express to you this evening as being your science fiction, but in reality you hold the ability to accomplish these feats and shall be accomplishing these feats by the mid- points of your [21st] century. Therefore, I express to you: You have little time framework to be looking to before the accomplishment of tremendous elements within altering of your reality.

I have expressed to you that your monetary system shall not exist any longer within what you view as your present time framework. Within the end throes of your [21st] century, this shall be accomplished. It shall be unnecessary. You already view the devaluation of your monetary system. I expressed to you previously the devaluation of your exchange, and you view recently a tremendous example within mass consciousness of the lack of value of your exchange system.

You hold world markets. You hold exchanges. You view these to be stock exchanges. They mean very little. Individuals trade what you view to be tremendous quantities of what you value as monetary exchange systems. They hold very little value already. Within your coming [21st] century, which you may view presently to be much time but is very little time, this shall be eliminated, for it shall hold no value, for what shall hold value is what you are moving into the direction of now; the value of the individual, the value of consciousness, the value of your abilities and your exploration of consciousness and of your universe, of what you view to be your universe and beyond. This shall be more important than personal gain. You have moved in the direction of this area for much time period, and it holds little attraction any longer.

Therefore, developments shall be occurring within your coming [21st] century – as I have stated, within your lifetimes, so to speak, within your focuses. If you are so choosing to be extending your focuses to [the] mid-point of your coming [21st] century, which is entirely possible and probable, you yourselves may witness these events which shall be occurring.

You have witnessed many amazing events that mirror what you know in consciousness. One hundred of your years ago, individuals would not dream of placing foot upon another element within your solar system; a moon, a planet. To this present now, you accomplish this. Within seventy of your next years, you shall accomplish more. You shall move into areas of viewing not other dimensional elements, but other life forces; not like yourselves, but existing within your galaxy. This may sound quite, as I have stated, like science fiction to you, but so was it science fiction one hundred of your years ago to be walking upon your very close moon, and you have accomplished, and you accomplish probes upon other planets within your solar system. It shall not be requiring much of your time framework before you are expanding and accessing the ability physically to be moving into areas of mirroring what you already accomplish within consciousness, and exceeding your barrier of your light speed.

I have expressed to you that you are most wondrous creatures and you hold abilities far beyond what you view that you are capable of, but you are capable of many more wondrous actions than you believe yourselves to be capable of. Within this action, what shall enable you to be accomplishing is the action of accepting, partially, some of your existing belief systems, and therefore not being bound to the limitations of your belief systems. I will express to you that even within the action of this shift, you shall not be accepting all of your belief systems, for within this physical focus, as I have stated to you, you shall always hold belief systems. It is the core of your reality. But you shall be accepting many of your belief systems, which shall be eliminating many of your barriers.

This is not to say that I am expressing to you that you may not be also creating conflict before you are accomplishing of these feats, for this exists continuously as a very present and real probability. You hold the ability to deflect this probability, but within the energy projected, it is entirely dependent upon you what you choose to be creating and lending energy to. You may be creating of some destruction futurely, or you may be deflecting of this and inserting different probabilities into your reality. Either direction, it matters not. You continue, as you have continued throughout the entirety of this century, to be creating of the probability that within mid-point of your coming [21st] century, you shall be mirroring your own knowing of consciousness and projection, and developing of technology to be exceeding what you possibly may be imagining of presently.

This shall be one of very few – very few – sessions that I shall move into this direction of expressing to you the most probable probabilities that you hold futurely; but in encouragement of your movement and acknowledgment of your movement, which you presently doubt, I have chosen to be encouraging of you this evening and expressing to you a slight glimpse into what your most probable future probabilities are, as they exist within this present now.

Q: ... It seems like science is going to be in the forefront here. Where is religion going to come into this?

ELIAS: Individuals shall continue to hold their religious belief systems, but this shall also deplete itself as individuals begin to be accepting of belief systems and recognizing that they hold belief systems. Your sciences also hold great belief systems, but they move into, as you express, the forefront now, in mirroring physically what you know to be within essence.

Q: So the social and political systems are going to be replaced by a great deal of cooperation between all focuses?

ELIAS: But shall also continue to hold political influences; but your political influences shall be more directly involved and compatible with all of your societies.

Q: You commented earlier that … we're going to be limited in the [21st] century to the present dimension that we are aware of?

ELIAS: Not so.

Q: Probable dimensions close by, we will be able to look into?

ELIAS: Correct. You shall hold the ability, as you do now, to step sideways and move into other realities and other dimensions. I am merely speaking of the accomplishments that you may physically view within this dimension, of your physical accomplishments that shall be offering you evidence of your movement.

Q: We shall know of the openness of our universe.

ELIAS: Correct.

Q: And the openness of all universes.

ELIAS: Correct.

Q: So this change will also change our way of fighting in wars? There will be no necessity for that either?

ELIAS: It will be unnecessary.

Q: So that won't exist either?

ELIAS: Not within your reality. This is not to say, as I have expressed previously, that these elements do not exist within other dimensions or other areas. This shift is limited merely to this dimension and your physical focus. Therefore, the alteration is great within this dimension and your physical focus, but it does not extend beyond this. It is affecting of all other dimensions and focuses, for you are affecting of all other dimensions and focuses, but this is not to say that the entirety of their reality shall be altered. They shall continue in the direction that they are creating their realities.

Q: All probabilities will be expressed as they always have been?

ELIAS: Correct.

Q: So there will be probabilities that will have wars?

ELIAS: But not within this dimension.

Q: Don't a lot of these changes you're talking about – the changes in our monetary system, all the changes you've been talking about – isn't that pretty intimately tied in with an awareness of how we create our reality?

ELIAS: Yes.

Q: So I imagine science will be conducting experiments that will be indicative of the fact that we do create our reality …

ELIAS: Correct.

Q: ... and that things happen that are outside of the way we believe about them presently.

ELIAS: Correct.

Q: Those kinds of things are going to be, you know, leading people into a way different direction of thinking ...

ELIAS: Absolutely. Your greatest discovery, so to speak, will be your space and time travel – objectively, physically – that you shall discover the methods, the means, to exceeding your light speed. You accomplish this every day within your focus, but translating that into physical movement is a new discovery.

This be what your age-old quest has been – for time travel and your time machines and your machines for travel through space. These machines that you hold presently, that you fire to your small little moon which orbits your own little planet, shall seem to be child's toys, for you shall develop technology that may project you around your space within amazing precision. But these also shall be mirrors of what you already know within essence and what you already accomplish within yourselves; just as your telecommunications are mirror images within physical form of how you already communicate within essence and consciousness. Your televisions are mirror images of what you already view within essence, in connecting to other focuses and other dimensions at the flick of a channel!

Q: So this form of communicating with [someone like you] will be obsolete?

ELIAS: It shall be unnecessary.

Q: Cause we can all do it.

ELIAS: Correct.

Q: The educational systems will be drastically changed?

ELIAS: Quite altered.

Q: I'm looking forward to it!

ELIAS: I have expressed to you many times, this shift that you enter is a wondrous age, and is an age that you have developed and created for the expression of your individual and collective creativity and your abilities, which you hold endless amounts of! (#233)

Q: I have a question. I recently bought a personal computer, 266 megahertz, but maybe six months later, I see 450 megahertz. It appears to me that the speed of these external machines ... something is speeding up rapidly, so it must be reflecting something going on with the larger transition. I was wondering, it must be taking us somewhere. The speed is speeding up somewhere. I was wondering if you could enlighten me as to where this might be going.

ELIAS: You are quite correct! Within physical focus you create objective imagery to mirror your own movements, and within the area of your technology you mirror quite efficiently with your inventions, your own abilities, and your own knowings. All of your creations of your inventions that you move into are all expressions of known information that you hold.

Think you not that it is quite interesting within physical focus that within this time period of this particular century, you have created within your technology more inventions within one time period than within all of your history? And within this [20th] century is the movement of your shift in consciousness, and as this shift in consciousness accelerates and moves into your next [21st] century, you shall be creating of more objective imagery that mirrors what you know within you. Your technology advances at great speed, for you are advancing at great speed within the action of this shift. Consciousness is moving within an intensity and continues to build within this intensity, and in this you shall view more and more evidences of this. I have expressed many times that your science fiction is more true than you think and may be viewed more in the direction of science fact than science fiction, for all that you may imagine, you may also create. You hold the ability! It is merely a question of your own accessing of your own abilities within your own trust of yourselves, and as you move in these directions, you continue to be creating of more and more objective imagery that moves you farther and farther into your science fact.

Q: But where is the long-term for us, or the short-term? Where is this taking us? Obviously, as a mass consciousness, that example is showing us that we're moving in frequency or speed somewhere. Something is either happening to the planet or the systems of worlds and we're being taken along for the ride, or we're...

ELIAS: Or you are creating of the ride! You are not being "pulled along!" You are creating of this collectively together. You have chosen to be in agreement in creating this shift in consciousness, and this is where you are moving to. You are moving to the creation of a new expression of your reality, a complete alteration of your physical reality as you know it. In this, not only your technology shall advance and be created differently, but all of your reality shall be altered and shall be different.

This is a global shift in consciousness. It is not limited to merely this small location. It is an agreement within all of the essences which have chosen to be physically manifest within this dimension. This shift in consciousness is limited to this dimension, for it is a choice of this particular dimension, but it shall move you into much more open frontiers of creating, and this is where you are "going," so to speak! (#328)

Q: Will we be able to develop instruments that reflect our consciousness that have, indeed, conscious intent?

ELIAS: You shall continue to create instruments and technology that monitor your physical reality, although you shall also incorporate more information about consciousness and acknowledge this more freely; but within your sciences you shall continue in the direction that you are moving in presently, in monitoring and developing within physical aspects.

Q: We in this form have a limited awareness of a change, in our view of the world. Will that become quite commonplace by the year 2050?

ELIAS: Yes; much more expanded than you are now.

Q: Will inner senses be used more commonly than they are now?

ELIAS: Yes.

Q: The basic physical needs of entities or focuses here are food and clothing and some shelter. That will be handled by other than monetary means?

ELIAS: Yes. Not necessarily by your specific date of 2050…

Q: Plus or minus twenty-five years?

ELIAS: Correct.

You shall realize that monetary gain is unnecessary and meaningless. You shall move into a new area of consciousness, this being part of the action of this shift in consciousness. In shifting your consciousness, you shall move into the area of realization that the exploration of your existence within physical focus is more important than your monetary gain, and more satisfying.

Q: Experiences that we desire to have, we will be tending toward those experiences rather than making sure that we have a house?

ELIAS: You shall be provided for. It shall not be an issue any longer.

Q: Our creativity will be able to provide that for us?

ELIAS: All individuals shall work together within the area of value fulfillment, and in this you shall be providing for each other in all areas.

Q: In these change-overs that we're going to experience, will they be all gradual change-overs that won't create sudden conflict or panic, or will there be much of that?

ELIAS: Not necessarily. This be your choice, and this be the element of probabilities. You may be choosing of great trauma and tremendous elements of destruction for your own attention. This be your choice. It is a probability. You may be deflecting of this choice and not creating of this, which is what you are moving into now by allowing yourself information concerning this shift in consciousness; to be eliminating those probabilities and inserting other probabilities into your reality, but they are a continuing probability. (#233)

Q: Your statement in regard to the possibility or probability that money would no longer be needed is certainly intriguing from several different aspects. I'm trying to visualize a society that doesn't need money, and it would certainly be an idealistic society. Are we truly going for an idealistic society?

ELIAS: This would be an interpretation of a belief system, that you believe this to be idealistic. It is merely more creative, expansive, a knowing of more of your reality, less limiting.

Q: The total potentiality is going to be much more enormous than it is today.

ELIAS: Your awareness shall be wider. Therefore, you shall allow yourself more of your abilities. You hold the abilities now, but you do not allow yourself the awareness within your attention.

Q: And it's a cooperative effort, too.

ELIAS: Yes.

Q: And that cooperation was really necessary for all of us to arrive at those capabilities, not singularly, but...

ELIAS: You may singularly, but you have chosen in agreement to be accomplishing this globally.

Q: Our creativity ... will we be able to create our own basic needs? If I wanted to create a turkey dinner, I could do that? I could just create a turkey dinner?

ELIAS: (Grinning) You are not becoming magicians! (Laughter)

Q: Shucks! Well, I'm trying to figure out how I would get a dinner!

Q1: Are you hungry?? (We're all cracking up)

Q: No! You know, fifty years from now, I want to get a dinner! If I don't have any money in my pocket...

(Somebody says, " barter.")

Q: Yeah, right.

ELIAS: No.

Q: No?

ELIAS: It shall not be necessary. Trade shall not be necessary.

Q: That's an exchange too.

ELIAS: All that you require shall be, for you shall each choose to be accomplishing, within what you now term to be jobs, what you choose, what you wish to do, what you wish to be accomplishing. Therefore, it shall be unnecessary for trade, for all shall be available. Within your present now all is available, but you hold belief systems that you must trade for different objects.

Q: We don't really have to eat. Isn't that right, Elias?

ELIAS: (Grinning) I have not expressed to you that you do not require some type of sustenance. I merely expressed to you that it matters not what you are consuming.

Q: You said we could eat rocks.

ELIAS: If you are so choosing.

Q: And survive on that.

ELIAS: If you are so choosing, and if your belief systems allow.

Q: There's plenty of rocks!

ELIAS: There are also plenty of turkeys! (Much laughter) (#257)

Q: The question I have, as I'm sure many others do, is how will industry operate without a medium of exchange? What value will be used to cause the creation of concrete and steel to build a building, to create fuel in order that we have transportation, electricity? Will all workers work, from the company president to the guy who sweeps the floor, just for the hell of it? Suppose I want to buy a yacht for my pleasure? What will I need to have to exchange for it and maintain it once I get it, if we do not have this medium of money?

ELIAS: The expression of EXCHANGE shall be eliminated, for you shall be allowing yourselves to direct yourselves, and create and generate all of your resources or all that you desire simply as you desire it.

Individuals that express their value fulfillment in creating steel shall do so, for this is their desire. Individuals that express pleasure in creating fuel shall do so, for this is their preference.

The concept of exchange shall no longer be necessary, for as you continue in the movement of this shift in consciousness and become familiar with what you are as essence and become familiar with your abilities and what you may generate and what you HAVE generated in the creation of this physical dimension and your physical planet, you shall realize that there is not limited supply.

Q: I think I understand what you're saying. Everybody is going to be doing their own thing, and we'll just fit in with that.

ELIAS: Correct — in cooperation. (#857)

Q: I know you said that there … isn't anything bad or negative. But violent behavior, hurting one another, will that exist [after the shift]?

ELIAS: Once this shift occurs, and is experienced globally by your species, this will no longer be necessary. As you each will know in acknowledgment of your essence, if you are focused with your essence and not separating this part from it, your essence possesses nothing harmful or negative. That is purely a physical focus. Therefore, in incorporating your essence and its new focus physically, it will not be necessary for negative expressions. This will take much time to completely accomplish, in your terms, on your planet. But, it will be accomplished.

You will notice, even now on this planet, as many things as you can focus on that seem to you to be so negative, you can also acknowledge many positive movements. You are presently, as a species, more aware than you have ever in your history been of your relation to nature, and to the universe, and to each other. You are even politically becoming aware of the unnecessary aspects of conflict, violently, in wars. They do still exist, but you are much more aware of peaceful coexistence than you have ever been in your history. This is all a part of this shift that you have already agreed on, and begun creating.

In creating a religious shift of consciousness in the focus of your Christian beliefs, this was not accomplished in one day, but it was accomplished extremely imaginatively and artfully, and inhabited an age. This focus and age no longer serves your imagination. Therefore, you have chosen to move beyond it and incorporate yourselves, instead of only your ideas. (#13)

Q: Within the shift, can those people that are aware of the shift and are working with the shift … There is the other part of our populations all over the world that seem to be working in the opposite direction. I'm talking about those people that are so involved in gang warfare and that kind of thing. I understand about accepting belief systems. My question has more to do with, where will these people and their awareness of their consciousness go at the end of the shift time? What is their point, their place?

ELIAS: As you hold these belief systems of right and wrong and good and evil, which are elements of your religious era, you view actions and experiences within this framework. Each action contributes in a fashion to the whole. You may not understand completely the benefit that occurs, but let us view within a different angle of perception.

You view much violence and negative behavior within your planet presently. I have stated previously that this is not an escalation from your past history. It is manifest differently. Therefore, it is attaining your attention differently. In this, the manifestation of the violence that you view is a rebellion against established, accepted, societal systems. Within your viewpoints you view this as wrong, but they also are making their statement in alignment with the movement of consciousness away from your established belief systems and your established accepted reality, within this what you may term to be past era.

You may symbolize this in many ways, as do religious individuals and psychological individuals, and within one layer of consciousness it may hold validity in its symbolism; in that within the emergence of any new creation there is a birth, and within the throes of the birth there is also what you term to be painfulness or pushing. It is not necessarily always painful to be emerging, but it is necessary for a push. In this, you choose collectively to be pushing in many directions. Young individuals choose to be pushing in non-compliance with established belief systems. Other individuals move into other areas and push also.

All of these individuals drawn to this forum are pushing within consciousness. This all lends to the movement of the shift.

This is not to say that hurtfulness is acceptable, but although hurtfulness is not acceptable it may be beneficial within your physical reality, and beneficial is not necessarily positive in your estimation. You may benefit from many elements that you create, that you view to be destructive and negative and violent and hurtful. Within essence and expression of essence this is not acceptable, but you are within your dimension of physical focus which you have created in this manner. Therefore, you also allow for these experiences.

Within the action of your shift, as I have stated previously, these actions and events shall become unnecessary, for the belief systems shall not motivate this type of action. You witness these types of occurrences in response to established belief systems presently. If these belief systems were accepted, they would hold no power. Therefore, there would be no motivation for these actions. (#178)

In regards to negative cultures or expressions in this physical focus, as I have stated in this session, when this shift of your planet is accomplished, these expressions in this physical focus will be eliminated, for they will no longer be necessary. They are merely expressions of experiences through misunderstandings. Once you understand and are connected with your essence, it is not necessary to create conflict within yourselves or with other essences. Even presently, if you are in connection with your own essence, it will be so tolerently expressed, and incorporating so much more understanding and acceptance of other essences and of itself, that its natural expression will be of acceptance, and there will be no negative expression. In this same manner, with the occurrence of this global shift, this will not be the physical experience anymore. You will occupy yourselves with much greater things to do than fight with each other, or occupy your time with negative superstitions. It will not be necessary.

You have much experiencing in this physical focus to do yet, in very grand ways. Your expressions in your imaginations of your motion pictures of fantasy of your science fiction is more real than you believe.

In this respect, you have much more to experience in this physical focus. The experiences that you will encounter in your future, in your terms, have no place for your current smallness and negative expressions.

I cannot express to you enough what wonderfully divine creatures you are, and your tremendous creative expression, and your ability to create such beauty. You would do well to focus more in this area, for you possess a tremendous ability of expression. I have expressed to you the concept that you are energy. I have also stated that energy cannot be separated. Just as you may not cut your air, you may not separate energy. Therefore, you are connected. In the essence state, as you would call it, you are very aware of this.

Q: Is the shift that we are currently experiencing, is this similar to the shift that occurred in the time of Atlantis and Lemuria?

ELIAS: No. This shift has never actually been experienced on this planet of yours. This will be the first experience of this ... excuse me ... other than when you initially created this focus, but since that time, your species in this dimension has not experienced this type of a shift.

It has been building to this shift in consciousness. You have all been practicing in creativity of imagination for thousands of your years. You have created tremendous belief systems to experience your ability in creating. Now, you have chosen to expand your focus. You have experienced all things possible for this physical focus in its present state. It is not necessary to continue repeating. Therefore, you choose a new experience.

The new experience is to incorporate your essence and your consciousness into your physical focus. Even a child will become bored with playing the game too many times. You have been playing this game for thousands and thousands of your years. You are presently and globally bored with it. It is time to express yourselves in a new manner. You can only experience the same experience so many times! It is not necessary anymore.

Q: Are we going to see this shift happen in our lifetime, in our terms?

ELIAS: You will see parts of it. This [shift is being rapidly created], in your terms. This new [21st] century you are approaching will be of tremendous creativity in this shift. The beginning of it will be most dramatic. Depending on how long, in human years, you chose to continue in this developmental focus, you may see tremendous shifts. It will be very much accomplished within this coming [21st] century, which you have at least half to experience!

Q: So this global shift that's happening, is this what people have been referring to as the Armageddon, the end of the world, the second coming of Christ, etcetera, etcetera, etcetera? (Laughter)

ELIAS: Some etceteras! (Smiling) This would not be classified as this Armageddon, although your Christians will believe this to be true. There is, in reality, no Armageddon. There is ... this is difficult to explain. In your expression of your religious imagination and story, your Christian beliefs express a time coming when souls, so to speak, would be reunited with physical form. The story is continued by saying that then you will be gathered up to heaven in this physical form. The concept is a crude preliminary sketch leading to the expression of the final painting. The concept of going to the heaven is incorrect, but the expression of incorporating the physical form, and the essence or soul, is closer to truth.

In this respect, they are almost correct in their interpretation. As I have said, the initial sketch of a picture may be changed many times before the finished product of the entire painting has been completed. In this, your painting is nearing its final stages. It does not look like its original sketch.

This shift has been anticipated by your essences from what you term the beginning of this physical focus. It was part of the plan. It has taken many different religious expressions. Eastern religions are partially correct also, in their expression of becoming one universally. Where they deviate is that they do not incorporate the individuality at the same time.

Individuals who believe in this Armageddon and Rapture will be quite surprised when it does not happen, and it will not! They may also experience a relief! (Laughter) They should more focus their attention to their creating power, and their connected creating ability to manipulate conditions presently with their own planet, more so than so-called heavenly events that will not materialize. There are conditions in their own physical focus that they help to create and manifest through their own energy. They would be more advised to not create earthquakes, than to wait for a rapture! (Smiling) (#13)

Q: So within your consciousness, are you interacting and communicating equally with others right now, as you are with us?

ELIAS: Correct. Within your perception presently, our engagement through this phenomenon seems singular. Elias arrives, Elias interacts, Elias departs. In actuality, Elias does not arrive, for Elias is already present! Elias is also present within many other areas of consciousness simultaneously to what you would view to be equal, within perception.

Q: And that's what we're shootin' for! (Laughter)

ELIAS: (Humorously) Eventually, within your time phrasing! Within your shift, you will not incorporate becoming demigods! (Chuckling)

You shall hold an awareness of elements of essence and focuses within physical, to which you discount presently. You shall hold an understanding of belief systems, accepting these, allowing yourselves to be not responding and reacting to these belief systems. You shall experience interaction, with individuals within transition areas of consciousness, without effort; as you would view to be commonplace. You shall view elements of yourselves; other focuses of your essence, other aspects of yourselves; your counterparts, your facets, your fragments ... effortlessly. You shall hold the awareness, allowing yourselves an undistorted interpretation of your experiences; therefore not detracting from your experiences, but enhancing these experiences with a clear understanding of the experiences. In your terms presently, you shall know quite a lot! (Grinning)

You shall be very aware. You shall also enhance and expand your creativity immensely; for presently, as tremendous as your creativity is expressed, it is quite limited. You shall eliminate these limitations, and hold the ability to express your creativity multidimensionally. (#106)

You have been offered the opportunity to recognize the existence of belief systems and how they integrate themselves within the creating of your reality. Now you offer yourselves more information to be accepting belief systems – not eliminating, not changing, but accepting – and in this recognizing that your creations are all filtered through your belief systems. This is your creation. This is a magnificent invention of creativity within your dimension, but your creativity now becomes limited. Therefore, in a recognition of this limitation, you offer yourselves new horizons in objective awareness. (#185)

You seek now within the action of this shift a new consciousness, to widen your awareness and to hold an objective understanding of HOW you create your reality. You DO create your reality, but much of that doing is veiled from you. You do not allow yourselves, within your singularity of attention, the viewing of how you are creating your reality within the creation of your line of probabilities in every action that you choose. This is the action of this shift, to be objectively aware of your creation of your reality, and therefore allowing you a fuller expression of your creativity and more of free movement through consciousness. (#275)

You shall objectively hold the awareness of HOW you create your reality, and you shall hold the ability to consciously, objectively, intentionally manipulate your reality and the energy that is within your reality. You shall not be inquiring of yourself, "Why am I creating of this?" You shall know. You shall understand. You shall not be expressing to yourselves, "I do not understand or know how to be altering my reality." You may alter your reality automatically. You shall not be expressing that you are making mistakes, for you shall realize that all is your experience. You do not make mistakes! You BELIEVE you make mistakes. (#188)

Q: I was talking to someone yesterday who expressed something about a K-Y-C, something to do with what's happening on the planet, and there's apparently someone channeling information, an entity, about that at a certain point, some people are going to be going to another dimension. He was curious what you thought about it. I don't have a whole lot of information on it, but I said if the opportunity came up, I would ask.

ELIAS: I have addressed to this previously, and I may express to you that there are, as you are aware, many alterations occurring within your dimension, within your reality, as this shift in consciousness comes to fruition.

In this, as you move more fully, individually and collectively, into the action of this shift in consciousness, you shall not be transporting yourselves into other dimensions, so to speak. But as I have expressed to you previously, you shall hold the ability to access other dimensions objectively as you begin in your action of out-of-body experiences, your transportation of yourselves through consciousness.

I have spoken much in this area, that you shall be moving THROUGH space — not around space — THROUGH consciousness, accessing other dimensions and accessing many more realities, for you shall allow yourselves more of your own fullness of your own abilities and not be limiting of yourselves within this particular dimension.

I have also expressed to you that other dimensions are not participating in this shift in consciousness. Therefore, you shall not be transporting yourselves to other dimensions to be taking up residency, for you are already focused within other dimensions!

You may visit other dimensions to be accessing information of those other dimensions if you are so choosing, and you may also be accessing areas of consciousness that you view to be veiled presently. One area is that between yourselves and individuals that you view to be disengaged. You view a veil between yourself and those individuals. There shall be no longer this veil, and you shall allow yourselves interaction and communication, with the recognition of all of the aspects of the action of transition.

In this, certain elements of this information are correct, and certain elements are quite influenced by belief systems.

Q: That's what I told him you'd say!

ELIAS: The aspect that you shall hold the ability or you shall allow yourself the awareness of the ability that you already hold, that you may access other dimensions and other areas of consciousness, is correct; not that you shall be transformed to another dimension, for you are not moving, as I have stated previously, from what you perceive to be your third dimension to your fourth or fifth dimension! You are merely within this particular dimension within your focused attention, but you also occupy all other dimensions simultaneously. So in this, where shall you go that you do not already occupy? (Chuckling)

As to the element of information which is presented presently in the fashion that it is being offered within elements of energy exchanges, you shall not be requiring of this action, for you shall hold the remembrance and the information yourselves, and you shall allow yourself the abilities. Therefore, what be the point of interaction such as this energy exchange, as you may access this information yourselves.

Q: Thank you.

ELIAS: You are very welcome.

And this IS the point that I have been expressing to you many times. YOU shall offer YOURSELVES the remembrance, and you may access this information yourselves. You each are glorious beings and hold the same abilities as I, and as I have expressed to you many times, the difference is merely the remembrance, that I remember and you do not, but you shall! And in your remembrance, you also shall allow yourselves the freedom of great expressions and the ability for great explorations, within this and other dimensions. (#339)

Appendix 1

THE SAPLING STORY

ELIAS: I will give you a small story which you may contemplate through this week. In this, be thinking of belief systems and of connections.

My story incorporates two saplings, both exactly identical, both newly growing; one growing naturally and reaching towards the sun and basking within its rays and drinking naturally of the rain and resting to the moon.

The other is looking around and is viewing the sky and is seeing the sun and is saying to itself, "Maybe I should be growing at night. The sun is very hot. It may burn me or it may sap my energy, and the rain is very wet and it gets all over me and I am not sure I am liking of this rain and I am not sure that it is making me grow properly, and maybe I should be investigating where this rain is coming from and I should be analyzing the sunrays to be sure that I am incorporating the proper vitamins, or maybe the moon is more friendly to my growth and I would grow taller if I am growing at nighttime, while this idiot sapling next to me is being stunted by the sun."

And in the morning, the one sapling is stretching its newly formed branches and uncurling its soft leaves and growing within complete trust, and the other sapling in the morning is viewing the same sun and is looking at the beautifully formed other sapling and is looking like this: (Here, Elias twists his body and face into a grotesque contortion)

Now; this story is about belief systems and the noticing of these belief systems. It is also about trust and connection. It also incorporates proper personal responsibility. The one trusting sapling incorporates a genuine personal responsibility in not trying to change or help the analyzing sapling, but as it grows true and strong and trusting, it radiates an example. It shines in its essence as an example to the other sapling, and as the other sapling unconvolutes itself throughout the day, it notices the straight sapling and it chooses the focus of effortlessness and trust as being easier, for it has been shown an example. Therefore, be all the trusting straight saplings, radiating your example.

Appendix 2

GLOSSARY OF TERMS

ACCEPTANCE: "Acceptance is the lack of judgment." #257

"The action and the expression of acceptance is the LACK of expectations and the LACK of judgments, upon self or upon other individuals or upon situations. This is the expression of acceptance." #519

ALTERNATE SELVES: (see also probable selves)

ANGER: "The expression of anger is yourself communicating to you that in that moment you are not viewing your choices. You are expressing to yourself in that moment that you do not hold choices; you do not see them. This is the expression of anger."

"Anger, as I have expressed, is the extreme of frustration. For as you move into an expression of anger, you are not viewing ANY choices any longer, which is also an expression of being a victim within self." #918

"Anger is an extreme of frustration. Frustration is a communication that you recognize that you incorporate choices, but you are confused in viewing those choices. This may escalate into an extreme in which you view that you incorporate no choices any longer. This is an expression of anger." #937

ASPECTS: " Aspects are all of the you's of you within THIS focus." #346

"As to aspects, you are essence. I do not appreciate the term of parts. therefore, I am eliminating parts, for this encourages sections. You do not possess sections. You possess aspects. All of your focuses that you view are aspects of essence, all incorporated within essence, but all separate and individual." #51

BELIEF SYSTEMS: "Belief systems are those inventions that you create to explain what you do not understand. Truths are unchanging. Reality is a truth, but your viewing of reality is a belief system." #45

BLEED-THROUGHS: "Bleed-throughs may occur in many different ways. This is subjective consciousness, that which you think of in your terminology as unconscious, which is not unconscious for there is no unconscious! All is conscious! But subjective activity and consciousness is that which you are not objectively or wakingly always aware of.

These are elements of yourself. They are elements of your essence; activity, action, events, movement that occurs continuously within the movement of this shift in consciousness. As you have all agreed upon this shift, you allow yourselves now to experience what we term to be bleed-throughs of subjective activity or consciousness into your objective waking awareness. You do this as you would be traumatizing yourselves if you were to be opening entirely at once objectively to all of your subjective knowledge. Therefore, you have chosen to be bleeding through in increments this information. It may be occurring within visions. It may be occurring within events, identifications of other focuses, increased dream imagery activity. You may visually experience differences within your waking state of physical objects and also individuals; this seeming to you at times, without information, to be a distortion of your vision. In actuality, it is a bleed-through of subjective knowledge." #178

COMPASSION: "Compassion is the act of understanding" #902

...and the definition of compassion as you redefine your reality is simply understanding." #871

CONFLICT: "It is a manifestation of the limitations that you place upon yourself in alignment with your own belief systems." #352

DIS-EASE: "Dis-ease is merely an action of altering energy into a manner of disrupting the natural flow of your physical function." #325

DUALITY: DUPLICITY

"Duality is suggestive of two, or a double of elements.

Duplicity, although it incorporates what you term to be opposites, it is not necessarily merely two. It is an incorporation of very different conflicting elements within you simultaneously, in opposition to each other. Duality does not always suggest conflict or opposing elements. You may hold duality in certain areas that may complement each other. Within duplicity, these elements of the belief system that you hold do not complement each other. They are opposing of each other and creating of conflict." #328

ESSENCE: "Essence is a term that is used for your benefit; for your understanding of identification of a tone of consciousness which holds a certain direction, a certain intent for its creation of manifestation. All consciousness holds intent within its own value fulfillment.

Essence is that tone which chooses manifestation within personality for certain experiences. This is you." #147

ESSENCE NAMES: "An essence name is a tone. What I have offered to you is a translation of this tone in part, which translates into your language that you may identifie components of your own tone if you are allowing yourself to be tuning to your essence." #275

ESSENCE TONE: "Even within essence you hold your own tone, which is unique to you and not the same as other essences. The qualities may be the same, but the tone is different. You each hold your own individual tone in essence, which is the whole of you, the sum of all of your focuses, not merely within this particular physical dimension but all other dimensions and all areas of consciousness." #177

EXPECTATION: "Expectations many times move you into areas of disappointment. An expectation is an expression of a judgment, for regardless of the outcome, you shall move yourself into what you view as a positive accomplishment or a disappointment. Both are judgments upon your movement. The goal is the expectation." #519

FEARFULNESS: "Each time you experience fearfulness, you are creating an objective expression of a lack of trust within self." #302

FOCUS: FOCUSES: "I define what you term to be a lifetime as a focus, for lifetime is encompassing. In this, your lifetime is the sum of all of your focuses within this particular physical dimension.

Each segment is a focus. They do not occur linearly. You do not move into birth, move through a focus, die, and remanifest into another focus. This is your perception of your linear time framework, but it is relative only to physical focus. It is how you have designed this particular reality, but be remembering that all of your focuses are simultaneous." #270

FREEDOM: "Freedom is simply choice and the knowing of it. You define freedom in many different ways. You define freedom in financial expressions, in activities, in the lack of activities. In actuality, freedom is merely the knowing of the expression of choice in any and every situation. " #1368

GUILT: "Worry is the perpetuation of a lack of trust of self. Guilt is the perpetuation of a lack of acceptance of self." #510

IMPATHIC SENSE: "The empathic sense is your inner sense which allows you the ability to merge with another individual or thing, so to speak, and to be experiencing their experience." #376

INTENT: "An intent is the potential that an individual holds to be fulfilling of their individual value fulfillment within their pool of probabilities that they have chosen for the individual focus." #264

"Intent is your overall direction, so to speak, within the lines of probabilities that you create within any given physical focus, or within ANY focus of essence, physical or non-physical.

The intent is the direction of probabilities in the potential of its creation. It is the direction of your desire within any particular focus of essence." #321

INTENTION: "Your intention is more immediate. Your intention moves more in the direction of your physically focused wants. Therefore, your intention is the momentary movement in any given situation and your ideas and your feelings in regard to any of these given areas, which are affecting of your creation of your probabilities, but they are different from your intent. Your intent is the overall direction of your desire within a given focus." #321

MEMORY: "Memory is an objective physical expression. It is associated with your recall of events. " #1368

MIRACLE: "A miracle is an action which you perceive to be impossible." #303

NATURAL TIME: "Natural time is your own natural inclination to be moving into areas of pleasure and not obligation. Your essence naturally magnates and moves in the direction of pleasure. This is the least amount of thickness in energy within physical focus and affords the most efficient movement." #304

OBJECTIVE: SUBJECTIVE: "Your objective awareness is that which occupies your attention within your waking state. Your subjective awareness is that awareness which is a part of you, which moves in harmony to your objective awareness and includes your dream state and all other states of consciousness associated with this reality; not your waking state." #270

"All altered states of consciousness, such as your dream state, your state within out-of-body experiences, and all other altered [states of] consciousness, as you view them, including your view of "subconscious", shall be referred to as subjective consciousness or self.

These terms are more efficient and encompassing for your understanding, for all of your conscious state that you view within your waking element deals with information projected out and received from "out". All other information is directed from within and processed within. " #92

OUBLIETTE: "I will express to you that you are stuck within the plastic oubliette of your physical perceptions. In this, I will explain to you what is my meaning. I use the term plastic, as this is a description of something synthetic, something that YOU create, an element that YOU mold into what you wish it to be. An oubliette is a place. It is a place of forgetting and remembering. It is an isolated place. It is an old term, but it holds to your present reality." #65

PAIN: "Let me express to you, pain is the identification of a feeling that is held in negativity. You may experience the identical same feeling and it may be perceived as pleasure. It is your perception that identifies pain, and pain is the physical expression of negativity, negative energy. Therefore it is, in your terms, the counterpart to pleasure. " #484

PATIENCE: "Patience is an allowance. Patience is an objective incorporation of movement; an intentional, objective action of allowance for the natural flow of energy. Patience is a direct implementation of action in conjunction with the selection of probabilities.

Now; returning to the term of patience, you may substitute the word allowance" for the word "patience," for the action of incorporating patience is merely the action of allowing yourself to move naturally and to flow within your energy without complication." #510

"Patience is not the expression of waiting. Patience is the expression of allowance, an allowance of a free flow of energy, as it is recognized — in TRUST — that you have already created certain probabilities and certain directions, and you ALLOW their movement and the materialization, so to speak, of those probabilities in your reality. This is the action of patience." #519

...And be remembering what the definition of patience is: for patience is not waiting, patience is allowance. Therefore, if you are creating impatience, you are creating a lack of allowance; #862

PERIPHERY: "What you view in your physical waking objective reality is one aspect of this dimensional reality. It is one focus of attention objectively, but side—by—side with this one area of attention that you focus upon are many other areas of your reality that you do not allow yourselves to view at all, but they exist. These other areas of consciousness, that are only very slightly removed from your objective attention and are also objective, may offer you more information of the area of consciousness that you focus your attention within, for this is an action of engaging your periphery. If you are opening your periphery within consciousness, you offer yourself more information of your reality. " #231

PROBABLE SELVES /ALTERNATE SELVES: "Probable selves are projections of yourself that you project outwardly from yourself, so to speak, in a manner of speaking, into a probable reality which occupies this same physical dimension, within a dimension of this dimension." #313

"Probable selves are a different type of creation. These are projections of yourself in areas of consciousness that you project elements of yourself that you choose not to be experiencing within this particular focus. Therefore, you project outwardly another image of yourself and are therefore creating of a probable self which moves into a probable dimension and is creating of its reality independent of you and your choices. Once projected into a probable reality, these probable selves hold the ability to be creating of their own choices independent of your choices, and they may be creating of their own reality in whatever direction they may be choosing. " #309

"ALTERNATE SELVES are different. They are YOU. They are all of the you's of you, all of the aspects of you. Just as you may within your imagining create a whole other you from each cell within your physical form, this would be another aspect of you." #313

PROBABILITIES: "You each create a pool of probabilities as you enter into a physical focus. Probabilities are created within the moment. The pool of probabilities is a pool of potentiality. It is not a pool of actual events or choices that lie before you that you may choose from. It is an area of potentiality, and in this potentiality you may move in any direction of which you choose in creating your own probabilities. " #324

"A probability is a possible choice; therefore, there are countless numbers. You incorporate them singularly, one at a time. You choose one action. You choose from myriads of possibilities, which are probable choices. Each of the choices that you do not choose manifests elsewhere. All probabilities are actualized. All are not actualized within your focus. You possess the ability to choose the most efficient probability; efficient being the probability which incorporates no conflict. You do not always find the probability which incorporates no conflict, but it is always available to you." #65

PROCRASTINATION: "Procrastination is the action of waiting, and in this, many times this action serves you well and may be quite beneficial." #561

REGIONAL AREAS: "Regional area One. Physical focus.

Regional area Two. All things that you draw to yourself initially are created within regional area two.

Regional area Three incorporates non—physically focused consciousness interacting with physical focus; not in creation into this focus, but within interaction in consciousness, the connection is made in this area of consciousness. It is a wider awareness; what you would term to be your "next step outward", what I would term to be your "next step inward" within consciousness. " #85

REMEMBRANCE: "Many, many individuals shall be experiencing the beginnings of a remembrance, of which we have spoken previously. In this, you are allowing yourselves to identify with your own language, your own communication with essence, your own identification with self, which is to your way of thinking unimaginably immense; and this is you." #147

"As you move into the action of your shift more intensely and are allowing your awareness to be widening, you shall also allow yourselves more of a remembrance and therefore an identification with information that you do not understand presently." #193

SIMULTANOUS TIME: "As to simultaneous time, the meaning of this is that all things are happening now; within all dimensions, within all focuses, within all consciousness. All occurs now, within the moment. All consciousness is in a state of becoming. There is no past. There is no future. There was no beginning. There will be no end. " #88

SHIFT IN CONSCIOUSNESS: "Within this present now, you are experiencing what I have termed to be a shift in consciousness. You are moving out of your religious era and moving into a new reality which you are creating." And how shall you accomplish this action of this shift? It has already begun. You are already participants." #270

SPIRITUALITY: "The genuine expression of spirituality is to be incorporating ALL of your reality, the physical and the nonphysical; in a manner of speaking, it is a viewing of the big picture." #828

SUBJECTIVE: see also objective.

THOUGHT: …thought is a mechanism that you have incorporated in the blueprint of the design of your physical focus to be an interpreter. It translates and interprets objectively information that you offer to yourself through the avenues of communication that you incorporate. It is a function, a mechanism." #874

TRAUMA: "Trauma incorporates tremendous conflict, but also holds an element of shock. You experience shock when you are confronting yourselves with extreme situations and unfamiliarity. This may be in emotional areas, or mental, or physical. Any area that you present yourself with tremendous unfamiliarity, which may also be triggering of fearfulness, you experience exaggerated conflict in an extreme manner, and this would be designated as trauma." #361

TRUTH: "A truth is that which is common to all areas of consciousness, and may be translated into any particular area of consciousness. Be it physical or non-physical, it shall be an element within all areas of consciousness. Regardless of how it may be translated or interpreted, it IS in itself, and therefore is also a truth. It is a basic element of consciousness." #364

UNOFFICIAL INFORMATION: "Unofficial information is that information that is reality, but does not fit within the guidelines of your framework of reality that you accept." #147

WORRY: "Worry is the perpetuation of a lack of trust of self. Guilt is the perpetuation of a lack of acceptance of self." #10

For further information about the Elias information,
there are two websites you may visit:

www.eliasweb.at

www.eliasforum.org

Both are independently run websites containing
full-length transcripts of individuals who have had
private and public sessions.

Contact Publishing

-.-. --- -. - .- -.-. -

Making a difference

Visit us at

www.contact-publishing.co.uk

for information about:

Readers

Latest book releases

Catalogue

Ordering our books online

Writers

www.contact-publishing.co.uk